Praise for *Moveable Feasts*

'A deep dive into a city you thought you knew, revealing something much more complex. Newens is the perfect companion, curious and knowledgeable. A joy and an education for anyone who loves Paris'
Diana Henry, author of *From the Oven to the Table*

'A delicious journey through Paris. Chris Newens shows us the city from a fresh, modern and diverse perspective. He makes me want to follow his trail'
Sami Tamimi, chef and co-author of *Falastin*

'A gorgeous romp through the city's culinary past and present that made me hungry for Paris. Fun, thoughtful and comprehensive'
Olivia Potts, author of *A Half Baked Idea*

'There is a distinguished list of writers through time talking of their love of Paris and French cooking. Each new generation brings forth the familiar as well as the tucked-away gems, both old and new, that show how a great city evolves constantly. Chris Newens does just that with this charming book on a latter-day Paris'
Jeremy Lee, author of *Cooking*

'Enchanting, hunger-inducing stories beautifully told with wit and intrigue. An absolute must-read for Paris lovers everywhere'
Carolyn Boyd, author of *Amuse Bouche*

'A homage to the vibrant multicultural city of today, Hemingway's Paris, and the City of Light across all the ages, this joyful, delicious book is a feast for all the senses'
Ned Palmer, author of *A Cheesemonger's Tour de France*

'Transporting the reader from the dazzling heights of Parisian fine dining to market stalls and kebab shops, this culinary Odyssey through the City of Light is both fascinating and wonderfully entertaining. *Moveable Feasts* is an utter delight'
Ferdia Lennon, author of *Glorious Exploits*

MOVEABLE FEASTS

Paris in Twenty Meals

CHRIS NEWENS

Profile Books

First published in Great Britain in 2025 by
Profile Books Ltd
29 Cloth Fair
London
ECIA 7JQ

www.profilebooks.com

SRD

Typeset in Sabon by MacGuru Ltd

Printed and bound in India by
Manipal Technologies Limited, Manipal

The moral right of the author has been asserted.

A CIP catalogue record for this book is
available from the British Library.

Our product safety representative in the EU is Authorised
Rep Compliance Ltd., Ground Floor, 71 Lower Baggot Street,
Dublin, D02 P593, Ireland. www.arccompliance.com

ISBN 978 1 80522 420 4
eISBN 978 1 80522 422 8

MIX
Paper | Supporting
responsible forestry
FSC™ C104740

For my parents.

'No matter what bestial tricks history might be playing,
there were always looms at work in Illyria.'

Rebecca West

Contents

LES ARRONDISSEMENTS DE **PARIS**

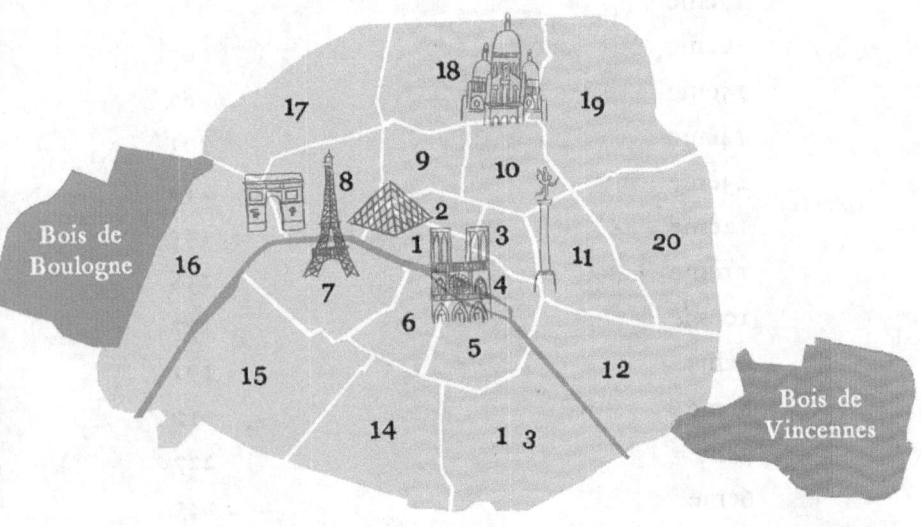

20ème arrondissement

A Paris bistro is the stage of a thousand clichés. Surly waiters in their suits, barflies crowding the zinc, a terrace of small tables and rattan chairs that all face the street; coffee, croissants, *steak frites*.

Le Mistral, at the corner of the rue des Pyrénées in Belleville, fitted this description so perfectly it deserved World Heritage status; it was a place so familiar to the global imagination that, like Paris itself, I felt I knew it before I even came to visit the city, let alone live here. And pulling up a stool at its bar – which in a small but acceptable deviation from the archetype was clad in copper – I experienced a flush of pleasure at playing a supporting role to such a timeless scene. Even the conversation going on between the nicotine-pickled locals was almost cartoon-ishly French.

It was about the definitive cuisine of the 20th arrondissement.

'*Bah, c'est la chinoise, évidemment!*'

'*Ah vraiment?*' – Oh, really? – '*Et quand tu dis la cuisine chinoise, c'est-à-dire la cuisine indochinoise.*' And when you say Chinese cooking, what you mean is Indochinese cooking.

'No. I mean Chinese.'

'Even though most of the Asians who live in Belleville are from Cambodia or Vietnam.'

'*C'est n'importe quoi,*' chimed in a third patron. 'The most typical cuisine of the 20th, of *all* the 20th, is obviously couscous.'

I listened in with growing delight to these three bickering men. Truth be told, I don't usually sit at the bar in Paris bistros, being content to set up at one of the tables and observe rather than get involved with the cast. But I had already decided that today was going to be different, and besides, nothing interests me like food.

'What do *you* think?' One of the barflies had caught me eavesdropping and decided to canvass my opinion.

'I'm sorry,' I stuttered. 'I'm English.'

'But you speak French,' he told me. 'I've seen you here before. You live in Paris, no?'

'I ...' a strange feeling came over me: pleasure at being recognised, unease that I was not as much of the background as I'd thought. 'Yes. For ten years.'

'Yves,' the man held out a moist hand. He had a face like a melting candle to which he had tried to add structure with a fiercely waxed moustache.

'Chris,' I said.

Yves indicated the men beside him. 'Yannick, Ahmed.' Both were ashen and scrawny. Easy to believe they had not moved from this spot for years, kept alive only by the calories in their Kronenbourg *demis*, perpetually half-drunk in their bar-rested hands.

'*Et donc?*' Yves continued 'What do you think it is, the typical cuisine of the 20th?'

'Well, it's a difficult question,' I said, my mind flashing through the streets of this hilly, working-class neighbourhood that I knew so well, lying next door to the one in which I lived. I thought of its crumbling Paris elegance; its vast seventies social housing estates. Its tree-lined boulevard patrolled by Chinese sex workers, its cobbled side streets spangled with retro commerce and silted in grime. The outposts of hipster gentrification, the pho joints, the pizza shops, the shisha bars ...

'I've no idea,' I concluded. 'It's a district of immigrants, no? There are Chinese people here, yes—'

'It's only the second largest Chinatown in Paris,' interjected Yannick, who had been taking the pro-couscous line. 'It's nothing compared to the 13th.'

'Right,' I continued, 'because then there's, I guess, a very big North African population.'

'*Exact.*'

'And a lot of people from the rest of Africa too.'

The men looked confused.

'*L'Afrique noire*,' Yves added helpfully.

There was some general nodding.

'And, I don't know,' I went on, 'wasn't it Jewish historically?'

'Tunisian Jewish,' Yannick said.

'I mean, one cuisine for the whole arrondissement – you might as well try to choose one for all of Paris.'

'This is what you get for asking the English about food!' cried Ahmed, and the other men laughed.

'You would prefer *fish-and-chips*. Ha ha!'

'A *cup-of-tea*.'

'*Marr-ma-lad sandweechis!*' Yves was particularly proud of this one. So much so that he said it twice. Funny to think of this Belleville barfly being familiar with the work of Paddington Bear.

'But *en fait*, perhaps he is not wrong, this English.' This was a fourth voice, Le Mistral's barman, who until that point had been as still and proud as the figurehead of a ship, silently surveying his bar, tea towel cast roguishly over one shoulder. He was a large man, prosperous looking, and his words rang heavy with authority.

'The 20th *is* the arrondissement of immigrants,' he said. 'And therefore, it is the food that we serve here in Le Mistral that is its most representative.'

I wasn't sure if I'd understood. My French is decent, but I am not above mistakes. Surely he couldn't be suggesting that this bistro, which was as Parisian as a, well, as a Parisian bistro, was an import. Yves was also confused.

'So now *steak frites* is immigrant cuisine?' he said.

'*Steak frites* is not cuisine,' the barman snapped. '*Blanquette de veau, that* is cuisine.'

What a tremendously French thing to say.

Except now I was wondering, where *did blanquette de veau* come from? The uncompromisingly white veal ragout enriched with egg and cream had always seemed to me so

4

deliberately aesthetic and bourgeois that it surely had to have an urban origin.

'We are from the Aveyron,' the barman announced. 'Like the original owners of all Paris bistros. We were the first immigrants to bring our food to the city. The first!'

Now, the Aveyron, I knew, was a beautiful *département* in France's south-west, a volcanic region just below the Dordogne. All green valleys and crumbling medieval towns. I searched my memory, trying to remember the food.

'*All* Paris bistros?' Ahmed was saying. '*Mais, c'est pas vrai!*'

'Very nearly all of them,' the barman countered. 'Café de Flore, Les Deux Magots, Le Dôme: all Aveyronnais. I am surprised you don't know this. Those are just the famous ones.'

'But, how? I mean, why?' I blurted.

The barman sighed, as if he had told this story many times before.

'When we came here in the nineteenth century, it was to sell coal. Look ...' He gestured over our heads towards the landscape amateurishly painted on Le Mistral's wall. I'd barely noticed this painting before, its pale blockish houses, corduroy fields and pastel-blue sky.

'The Aveyron,' the barman elucidated, 'is very beautiful, but also very poor. Bad for farming. But we had coal. And they needed coal in the cities back then, so many people left the Aveyron to come here and trade coal. *Les bougnats*, we were called. And the city-dwellers would buy the coal in large quantities. It took time to fill their sacks. So, while they were waiting, we would offer them glasses of the wine we had also brought with us from our vineyards.

5

'We still sell Aveyronnais wine here.' He changed tone. 'My brother has a vineyard. *Ce n'est pas un grand cru* but ... you should have a glass.'

Though it was only three in the afternoon and I had planned on sticking to Perrier water, this was a hard sell. The barman, who I now understood to be Le Mistral's owner, pulled a simply labelled bottle of red from behind the bar and worked out its cork with a flourish. The wine was light and sharp, and, thanks to its backstory, one of most satisfying glasses of anything I'd tasted in a long time.

'It was not long until people started coming to the coal shops just to drink,' he continued. 'And the Aveyronnais began serving food as well. Soon, we had given up on the coal entirely and started growing our restaurant businesses instead. *Et voilà.*'

That '*et voilà*', as '*et voilà*'s tend to, covered a lot of history. Of, I could only imagine, the tenacious drive of people from the Aveyron to capitalise on a new business model. Of families getting each other jobs in the trade, of whole generations learning the new skills of how to be bistro owners, waiters and chefs, of the birth of the look of these cafés that had come to seem typical of the city. But the brute facts of what Le Mistral's owner had said remained, and I had no reason to doubt them: Parisian bistros were not as Parisian as I had, until that moment, believed them to be.

'It's not the same now, of course,' he went on. 'Young people, they don't want to work in hospitality. So all over the city we're selling our family businesses. To the Chinese, mostly.'

'My family used to run a restaurant,' I said. I suppose I was trying to build a connection with him before I realised the implications of what I was saying. 'In England,' I gabbled. 'Well, a bakery and tea rooms.'

'Oh yes,' the owner said, rounding on me fully, a cloud of disdain passing across his heavy brow, 'and what has happened to it?'

'I, well ... They sold it,' I confessed.

'So you were free to move to Paris?' But he was smiling. 'It's fine. I understand. You're smart. It's terrible, restaurant work. Very hard. That's why I am sending my sons to university.'

I wanted to protest. To tell him I had liked restaurant work, how I knew the long hours and the stresses of serving food to others, but how the pleasures always outweighed them. On the other hand, when my dad had decided to sell this business that had been in my family for six generations, I hadn't offered to take it over, I hadn't prevented him. So I remained silent.

'*Alors*, food from the Aveyron is the original cuisine of Paris immigrants,' Yves picked back up. 'And the 20th is an arrondissement of immigrants. So, what are we concluding is the 20th's most representative dish? *Blanquette de veau?*'

The owner laughed, 'I don't know. I don't believe *blanquette de veau* is originally Aveyronnais.'

There was a short silence.

'So it is Chinese food, after a—'

'No!' the owner pounded his copper bar, making the glasses on it clink. '*Aligot*. It would be *aligot*.'

'*Aligot?*' I asked.

He scowled at me as if I'd just spat on the bar.

'It's potato and cheese,' Yannick said helpfully.

'Potato and cheese!' the owner exclaimed. 'Pah! And

7

wine is grape juice? *Aligot*, my friend, is the combination of potato and *Tomme de vache* in nearly equal measure. It is flavoured by garlic, then mashed smooth like velvet. It is an ancient dish. In Aveyron we served it to pilgrims on the Chemin de St-Jacques. It would have been everywhere in Paris once. Now you only have fries.'

As I walked the short distance back to my apartment, over the invisible arrondissement border into the 19th, the Mistral conversation repeated on me like an overly rich meal. I climbed rue de Belleville – pausing to gaze at the expansive view of the city, the Eiffel Tower small and iconic on the misty autumn horizon – then passed along the rue Manin, around the belly of the parc des Buttes-Chaumont, and I thought about what I had just learned of Paris bistros. What that conversation had really done was reveal even more starkly how little I knew this city. As I had already several times that past month, I found myself questioning how much I belonged in this place I had come to call my home.

When I arrived in Paris a decade ago, I had, like many before me, come chasing a fantasy, searching for the city of ex-pat writers and artists: the playground of Gertrude Stein, Pablo Picasso, Ernest Hemingway. I wanted late-night indiscretions, literature-worthy romances, up-till-dawn debates. Against the odds of the twenty-first-century, I had found what I was chasing, or as near an approximation as it was possible to get; and it can be tough extricating yourself from a dream. I had friends here, a decent life, but the Paris I could truly say I knew was embarrassingly small.

This is the most densely populated city in Europe; it is as

complicated and gritty and multifarious as any capital on earth. This was no longer something I could nonchalantly both feel proud of and ignore, but a truth I had started to feel on every corner. When I spoke to waiters and beggars, *boulangères* and flower sellers, binmen and *bouqinistes*; when I crossed on the stairs with my Bangladeshi neighbours, smelled the lamb curry wafting from their apartment which they shared four to a room; or locked eyes with the old woman who was always last to quit the terrace of my own street's corner bar; or drifted by the men who stared into rheumy nothing from city benches, quarter-nibbled baguettes at their side – I stood accused of ignorance by all the Parises of which I was not a part.

More and more, I had been thinking about the quote that opens Hemingway's famous memoir of the city. About how he claims that, if you are lucky enough to have lived in Paris when you are young, 'then wherever you go for the rest of your life, it stays with you, for Paris is a moveable feast.' But a moveable feast, literally, is a religious holiday that, while shifting about the calendar depending on the year, is still parenthesised by certain dates. It's never going to be Easter in January. I wondered, had Hemingway been saying more than he realised? Was it possible that one day I would return to a life in English suburbia and all the spirit and adventures I had experienced here would not come with me?

My decision to sit at Le Mistral's bar that afternoon had been intended as one of the many small gestures I had been making recently to fight against this possibility. I should have been happy that it had worked, up to a point. The story I had learned about the origins of the typical Parisian bistro had peeled back a layer of the city's myth to reveal a hint of the richer stew underneath. But as with any good meal, I wanted more.

By the time I turned onto my own road, I found I was cooking up an idea.

Food and service *were* things I already knew intimately. As a toddler, growing up around my family's café business, I had played with pastry as play-dough and food colouring for paints. Later, I worked there: washed dishes, iced cakes, blitzed soups, bussed tables. The language of cooking and hospitality and shop gossip were how I had communicated with my parents and grandparents; and how they must have communicated with their forebears in turn. Now, I started to wonder if my fluency in the kitchen could become a key to unlock Paris, to step from my one-note fantasy into a more complex reality.

Because wasn't it also the case that Paris's reputation as a global mecca of cuisine is among the first myths about the city that even casual visitors discover is very different to the reality? While Paris may be where modern dining was invented, the home of *Larousse Gastronomique* and Le Cordon Bleu, it is not a town where it is always easy to find a decent meal. In bistro after bistro, corners are cut, pre-made meals are reheated, the cheapest cuts of meat are fried. There is excellent food here, just not always of the kind people expect. Many of the best bouillons these days are Vietnamese pho, the most popular sauce is a spicy ketchup called *algérienne*, and only tourists eat frogs' legs. I knew these things already, but on that misty autumn day, I was seized by a conviction that I needed to dig deeper, and the city's food was the way in.

My path into doing this, meanwhile, had been decided for me by three men propped at a copper bar.

I would seek out representative dishes not just for the 20th, but for all the Paris arrondissements. These may only have been administrative categories, established in the mid-nineteenth century around the same time that Paris was being reconfigured by Napoleon III and his city planner Baron Haussmann, but even administrative categories soon take on a more soulful shape. And while the borders between arrondissements were porous and invisible, didn't each at its core, after almost two hundred years of existence, have a character and culture and food that could be called distinctly its own?

I would find the people – find the Parisians – who could teach me how to cook these dishes. I would learn their recipes and hope at the same time to discover their stories and their worlds. Through food, I would aim to discover and understand the city I had lived in for so long, but did not know. It would be a way of making Paris feel a part of me, of making sure it would stay with me wherever I went for the rest of my life. I would turn the city into not one, but a whole collection of moveable feasts.

Back home, I started to jot down ideas: a list of the arrondissements and their possible corresponding meals, drawing on my own knowledge, books, the suggestions of friends. I would begin in the 20th and spiral my way backwards – the arrondissements of Paris are arranged like the swirl of a snail's shell. My choices were driven in large measure by my experiences – any individual's vision of a city will always be more autobiographical than definitive – and by a search for the city's contrasts, the food of its immigrant populations as much as the food of its traditional tables. I did not want to be iconoclastic. There is a certain kind of person who would have it that the true Paris is nothing like the face it shows to the world, which is rubbish; it is still as much a city of croissants and *coq au vin* as it is of kebabs and couscous. My selection had to show this breadth in order to be representative of how Paris truly ate.

For the 20th, meanwhile, my choice of dish had already been made.

Le Mistral's chef looked more like a bank clerk than a gastronome. Hailing from Sri Lanka, just shy of sixty, he wore wire-rimmed glasses and a striped black and purple shirt under his whites. He had grown long the nail on the little finger of his left hand: a status symbol in some Asian cultures of not doing manual work. It made me reflect on his attitude towards his job, and the artistry with which he must perform it. Keeping a little fingernail long is no easy task when you in fact do work all day with your hands.

His meticulously clean kitchen was a tiny space to the side of Le Mistral's bar, from which it hardly seemed possible he could stay on top of the bistro's forty or so covers a night. A large pot of potatoes was already on the boil.

At first, he seemed suspicious of me. Who was this outsider who'd called Le Mistral earlier that day wanting to learn his recipes? But as the conversation went on, so he became increasingly loquacious, eager to share his art.

He had always cooked, he said, but only began doing so professionally when he came to Paris in the early 2000s. He chose the French capital because he had distant family here but he arrived penniless and without a word of the language. Fortunately, he found himself a job as a dishwasher in the kitchens of Les Deux Magots, the Aveyronnais-run former hangout of Sartre, de Beauvoir and other intellectual luminaries. There, he worked his way up the kitchen ranks, spending nearly two decades learning and perfecting another country's regional cuisine, so that when he had heard Le Mistral was searching for a cook, he was well qualified.

I asked him if he had ever been to the Aveyron.

Once. He went to stay on the vineyard belonging to the brother of Le Mistral's owner.

'And you know, it was strange,' he said, 'it reminded me very much of Sri Lanka. All that green they have in the Aveyron, the small villages, the quality of the air; it seemed just as it was in Sri Lanka. Going there, it was like going home.'

Now, I have never been to Sri Lanka. So perhaps it really is more like the Aveyron than I suspect. But I was moved by this evidence of our ability to layer a landscape or place with our beliefs, to bring a sense of belonging with us. A green hillside and a blue sky can be a porthole from the temperate zone to the tropics, and a dish placed on a table can transport us anywhere in the world. It was partly a similar desire to see my own home in Paris that had brought me to this tiny bistro kitchen.

Eventually, we got on to cooking. The chef confirmed that yes, *aligot* was certainly the most typical of all Aveyron's dishes. It was also, he said to my relief, very simple. Really just potatoes and Tomme.

'That's all?' I asked.

'Ah,' the chef said with a twinkle. 'In cooking, there is never an "all".'

I waited for him to expand on this gnomic utterance.

'For example,' he said, 'you must always choose the best

potatoes you can. Ones that are big and fluffy and expensive. Because they are most of the dish, and even an expensive potato is not expensive.

I nodded, feeling a quiet thrill at this small transfer of knowledge, at how readily these old Paris ways were being given up to me.

'Let your potatoes boil for a long time,' the chef continued. 'Much flavour is brought out by boiling and they must be very soft before you start to mash.'

'How long?' I asked and received a shrug in return.

'I never time. But they must be soft. Half an hour, a little more.' He then explained how I should put the potatoes back on the heat after pouring off the water, to make sure they were as dry as they could be before I added butter.

'But only a very a small amount of butter,' he cautioned, as strict with this instruction as any Aveyron-born Frenchman talking about the dish of his homeland. '*Aligot* is about the cheese. It should be 70 per cent potato, 30 per cent cheese.'

'That's a lot of cheese,' I said.

'Yes,' he agreed, 'a lot of cheese. And you must add it a little at a time, and always, always beating it in. You must be vigorous. With a wooden spoon.'

Aligot
Serves 4 as a side
Ingredients:
700g russet potatoes
Small knob of butter
300g Tomme cheese
½ tbsp garlic paste

I began by washing and peeling the potatoes.

The chef was right about buying expensive, of course. What a pleasure to consider the russet spuds in my kitchen sink, the dirt of their Breton pastures still clinging to their skin. Peeling them was like the unwrapping of so many gifts. One after another, I dropped them whole into my largest saucepan, half-filled with cold water.

My own Paris kitchen, which would be the site of my forthcoming explorations and experiments in recreating the city's cuisine, is small, with no room for people to pass along its two-metre length. The fridge and washing machine serve as additional work surfaces to the cheaply tiled countertop, allowing for space, albeit cramped, to prepare several things at once. My spices, grains and cooking oils are crammed onto a rickety wood shelf balanced precariously at the back of the counter. Plates and pots and pans are stacked tight underneath. I hang fresh produce in mesh baskets from the ceiling. The oven and hob are both, joyously, gas, while the sink, shallow and wide and robust, could almost belong in a modest farmhouse kitchen. This last feature is the only anomaly, except in the sense that unexplained idiosyncrasy is one of the great constants of any Parisian apartment. Everything is wholly typical of most domestic cooking set-ups in this densely populated city.

I set the potatoes on the gas to boil, and before tidying away their skins began to grate the *Tomme de vache*. Mild yet sour, and just on the crumbly side of rubbery: I was gentle with it against my grater, through which it spooled in long strands.

The potatoes were starting to boil. Fidgeting in the pot, steaming ferociously, fogging up the tall, narrow window behind my oven so that I was forced to crack it open despite the cold autumn night.

Waiting, I uncorked a bottle of red wine picked up from Le Mistral, sourced from the owner's family vineyard. It had the same light taste I recalled from the bistro counter and went well with the crumbs of leftover Tomme.

Off came the potatoes, tumbling into my colander in an explosion of steam. Once drained, I returned them, just as I'd been told, still smouldering, to the saucepan in which they'd been cooked.

I added a small amount of butter. A homeopathic amount of butter. I wanted this to taste right. Which is to say I wanted it to taste *different*: to be more than just cheesy mash. I wanted it to be Aveyronnais; to be Parisian. So I set to pulverising those potatoes, and only when they were desiccated to the consistency of a cloud did I add the cheese.

The chef had made a motion for me to follow: a simple stirring mime. But recalling the electric flicker of tendons in his forearm – muscles honed from half a lifetime of beating *aligot* – I knew this would be a task I had to put my back into.

The sprinkled Tomme streaked into the potato as I stirred and then was gone. I sprinkled more, I stirred more, and I returned the mixture to the heat as it began to loosen. My arm Wurlitzered. I beat the ingredients away from their previous forms, transformed them into region, into cuisine. And suddenly, I had *aligot*, or very nearly. It pulled like silk about the pot, a luxuriant scarf against the cold night. Its smell was thick and indulgent, but still with that hint of farmyard sourness: the countryside brought into town, into my tiny kitchen. Finally, to this mixture, as instructed, I poured a swirl of garlic paste and olive oil – its insistent scent heady as a drug.

It was time to eat.

The mixture wrapped about my fork like glue, though at the same time clung to the plate in strings as though reluctant to part from it. The first bite was rich and warm, with a sophistication that belied the dish's simple, hearty ingredients: the tastes of the potato and cheese still distinct as themselves, yet coming together in a unique combined flavour. It was a paradox.

It tasted too rural to be representative of Paris. Here was a dish to be eaten in a hillside shepherd's hut with a gale outside and maybe a goat at your feet. Its presence here, though, spoke of the city's willingness to accept and imbibe flavours from beyond its limits. A willingness that at that moment I believed was most exemplified by the 20th out of all the arrondissements. And, indeed, the *aligot* literally offered comfort. It tasted like an embrace, was a flavour of a particularly French welcome, which, through a chance conversation at a copper-topped bar and the patient instructions of a man from the Sri Lankan interior, I had made for myself.

19ème arrondissement

Paris, like many old cities, is saturated with blood.

Standing on the place de la Concorde, encircled by the indifferent thrum of cars over cobbles and the enlightened spires of civilisation, you'd never believe it was once a field of death, where the guillotine did bloody business during the Terror of the French Revolution. Likewise, in front of the Hôtel de Ville, where the medieval city gathered to see its own 'traitors' dispatched. Then there are the streets – Rohan, Lepic, Saint-Honoré and numberless others – places of massacre and murder, firing squad and last-ditch barricade. All now made almost pure again by the relentless street-cleaning of urban life and time. Ghosts don't hang about in cities like they do elsewhere. Perhaps that's why cities are so popular with the living.

In the most blood-soaked corner of Paris, however, scrape just a little, and traces of the gory past remain. It was a kind of carnage, after all, that still goes on in modern France, albeit beyond a veil of secrecy that most prefer to ignore. For in the 19th arrondissement, from the mid-1800s to the 1960s, were the abattoirs of the entire city. For a century, every *gigot d'agneau*, every *bavette*, every *tête de veau* consumed at Paris tables belonged to a lamb, cow or calf that at one point passed through their gates. Here was a whole phantasmagoria of cutting: a 39-hectare complex dedicated solely and ceaselessly to the production of meat. The sheer tonnage of tendon, cartilage and offal sliced and auctioned here over the years is almost impossible to imagine.

Today, where this industry once stood, is the parc de la Villette. A peaceful public green space constructed to a postmodern design. Yet the park is as evocative as any ruin. Much of the slaughter yard infrastructure is still here. A glass front seals the entrance of the former killing floor, which is now a concert hall, bike paths follow the grooves of old train tracks used to haul livestock, and metal sculptures reshape the pavilions that housed the bureaucracy of slaughter. At the park's edges, beyond the blast radius of municipal spending, living remnants of the lost *quartier* endure in the form of a number of cavernous butcher's shops.

The oldest of these is the appropriately named Abattoirs de la Villette, founded in 1903 by a former abattoir worker. Its current owner, the great-grandson of the founder, is Richard Gordon. In his late fifties, he seems straight from a Happy Families card deck, with a taut-drum belly and rosy-pink jowls.

Villette was a city within a city once, he told me. Nearly everyone who lived in the arrondissement either worked in or had some association with the slaughter yards. Now, the 19th could feel characterless, especially compared to its neighbouring districts formed around the communes of Montmartre and Belleville. 'Its heart has been removed.'

Monsieur Gordon still sold plenty of hearts. Mostly to African customers. They bought most of his offal these days, along with the local Chinese, while restaurant owners from across Paris still came for the finer cuts.

'For quality, we are cheapest in town,' Monsieur Gordon crowed. 'Though now we get our meat from all over Europe.'

He described a life on the move, travelling the Continent to inspect different slaughterhouses, checking that their livestock is good and their practices humane.

'If an animal has been treated poorly, it's there in the taste.'

How much easier it would have been when the entire industry was at his front door, he lamented. But those days were gone.

He guided me along the nearby parade of shops. Many were old cafés and restaurants left over from the boom times. They still had shower blocks in their basements, M. Gordon said, where slaughter-men would wash the day's blood from their skin.

'And look,' he pointed to the columns that framed the entrance of one of the cafés. I had seen this architectural feature in many Paris bistros but never considered its purpose. 'They have gas pipes inside them, and there would have been a hole in each leading to an always-lit flame.'

I was confused.

'For cigarettes,' he explained. 'The workers were always

smoking. But they stayed healthy, because the slaughter yard was such physical work.'

There was melancholy in his voice. Nostalgia for a world he had not quite known, where the folly of smoking could be remedied by swinging a spiked mallet into a cow's head. A simpler time.

I still eat meat. Most of us still eat meat, despite the guilt that growing numbers of us feel about how our meat is produced and slaughtered. It's an ethical inconsistency, but there it is. Here is no place to unpack it, save to say that I try to limit my meat consumption, and when I do eat it, to seek out meat that has been humanely treated and killed. I sometimes slip up. Often when I'm drunk. Often late at night, on my way home to my apartment, which is in the 19th as well, past tower blocks and social housing and a proliferation of fast-food joints. On those occasions, I close my ears to the panicked lowing of the phantom livestock, which can seem to roll with the wind down the canal, and I eat a kebab.

In my personal food odyssey around Paris, then, what could be more apt to represent the 19th arrondissement than those waltzing columns of miscellaneous flesh, which quietly comprise one of France's favourite foods? Also, kebabs are cheap. In addition to being the traditional home of its slaughter yards, the 19th has a long working-class heritage, and still ranks as the poorest arrondissement in Paris. The choice was easily made.

From the front door of my apartment building, there are seven kebab shops within less than five minutes' walk: in ten minutes, that number quadruples. So when I stepped into the October drizzle of the avenue de Flandre, with its chaotic central reservation and unlikely constellation of classic and postmodern architecture, the direction I took was random. I reached a kebab shop in seconds.

You don't know the Restaurant Bodrum. But also, you do. For there are Bodrums in every city of the world. Name spelled out in red plastic above its door, high-contrast photographs of its dishes peeling in the window, and inside, between strip lights and tile floor, a miasma of frying. The two men behind the counter had grey, exhausted faces. The older man, customer facing, forced himself awake with banter and a rictus smile; the other was a hunched back over hot oil.

'*Bonjour, chef*,' said the front-of-house guy. 'What do you want?'

'Actually,' I started, 'I'm just trying to find out more about how kebabs are made in Paris, and I wondered—'

'No, chef.'

'I'm sorry?'

'I cannot tell you about that,' he looked almost frightened. 'We're too busy.'

The shop was empty.

'What do you want?'

To talk to you, I thought. To find out more about kebabs. But his hostility had unnerved me. I panicked.

'Uh, a kebab, thanks.'

The hostility disappeared, replaced by that exhausted smile.

'*Salade, tomate, oignon?*'

In other cultures, salad additions to a kebab sandwich come as standard. It's up to individual customers to speak up if they want something left out. In Paris kebab joints, however, the question is always posed, and always in this exact manner: *salade, tomate, oignon.*

'*S'il vous plaît.*' I played my own role in the ritual, even as I was wondering if I really wanted a kebab before twelve in the afternoon.

'Which sauce?'

'Uh, which sauce is most popular?' I tried to get back to my mission, but the server's defiance resurfaced.

'We have all the sauces,' he said.

'Yes, but ... which sauce is chosen the most?' I tried to elaborate, 'Because sauces are important in France, right? In England we barely have a choice of two. Chilli or garlic. And mayonnaise and ketchup,' I was babbling, 'but here you have ... I mean, how many sauces do you have to choose from?'

'Twelve.'

I almost said how interesting it was in a nation with an *haute cuisine* formed partly around the creation of elaborate sauces that you should see some reflection of that in its fast food. But I was being stared down.

'*Algérienne,*' I buckled.

'Good choice,' the kebab man said. 'Yes, *algérienne* is our most popular sauce. *Algérienne* and ketchup.'

As he spoke, he pulled a great bottle of the stuff from behind the counter and violently piped the grainy, spicy, sweet orange gloop into the sandwich that was taking shape. Meanwhile, the man behind him was shaving from the great column of meat, which had been keeping a steady rotation all the while.

'Do you like *sauce algérienne*?' I dared another question.

'I don't have sauce on my kebabs,' the server said. 'I taste the meat.'

From there, we were off: nattering away like people who'd known each other for years.

I discovered that he was from Turkey, that he'd come to Paris when he was seventeen, that this was the first place he had worked because his family knew the owners. That had been twelve years ago. I asked him if he had any part in making the doner kebabs. He did not, he admitted. The kebabs were ordered in. They got through about seven a week, he said; shaving down 30kg of meat a day, though the Restaurant Bodrum was not even an especially popular kebab store. Then, the kebab was ready, and he thrust it into my hands. Our conversation was over.

I took a seat, hunched over my sandwich and stared into space. I didn't want to eat the kebab. It was too early in the day, it had too much fat and salt, was too processed and morally suspect to happily eat sober. But here I found myself. I took a bite.

What dissonance! The bland cushiony pliancy of the bread (another way in which French kebabs reflect broader French tastes is that they come in thick baps reminiscent of baguettes), giving way to the salt crispness of the grilled-then-fried meat. Cutting through it all, the fresh crunch of the lettuce, the cool sweetness of tomato, the sharpness of onion. All held together by the spiced umami of the *sauce algérienne*.

Christ, kebabs are good, I thought, and this wasn't even a good kebab.

People have been roasting meat on sticks ever since there's been meat and sticks to roast it on. Less than inventing anything, the Turkish simply refined this practice and gave it a name. Shish kebabs, however, were not the food I was pursuing. For while skewered chunks of whole lamb or chicken were available in most, if not all the *kebaberies* I visited, their popularity is nothing compared to their all-conquering Frankenstein cousin: the doner.

The origin of these vertiginous meat carousels dates to the mid-nineteenth century. Almost unbelievably, their invention can be traced to a single individual, a restaurateur named İskender Efendi from the town of Bursa in modern Turkey, who looked at the traditional method of horizontally roasting stacks of seasoned sliced meat and turned it on its head. Or on its side. Roasting meat vertically gave gravity a bigger role in the cooking process, allowed the juices to better ingratiate with one another, and made carving something that could be easily accomplished while the dish was still on the turn. The concept spread rapidly, and was refined in the 1970s by the Turkish diaspora of Berlin, who realised the ultimate application of such easy-to-shear meat was sandwiches. No sooner had Europe blinked than there were kebab shops on street corners from Dublin to Donetsk.

In France, kebabs found a particularly warm welcome. Introduced, as elsewhere, by Turkish immigrants, the dish also gained a loyal clientele among the country's large North African population. As such, kebabs soon came to prove tiresomely political, with certain French nationalists coming out against the dish with the rubbishy claim that it disrupts traditional values. A stall at the 2013 conference for France's far-right party, then known as the *Front National*, even made headlines with the slogan '*Ni kebab ni burger, vive le jambon-beurre*' ('Neither kebab nor burger, long live the ham sandwich'). Frankly, anyone who thinks a ham and butter baguette is better than a kebab deserves the sad, bland life they've made for themselves.

This said, even on a culinary level, kebabs don't have the best reputation. They look like the ultimate in junk food. Reconstituted, of non-distinct origin, sweating grease: there is something of the fatberg to a doner in its pre-sandwich form.

Defiantly, however, French *kebaberies* have made an emblem of this unappetising appearance. The trapezoid silhouette of a full doner is as common a Paris shop sign as the diamond shape indicating a *tabac* or the green cross of a pharmacy. Nevertheless, the hostile response I encountered in the Restaurant Bodrum, which was repeated with only mild variation in all the other kebab houses that I visited in the 19th, did not come as a great surprise.

They thought I was a snoop. Why would someone be curious about kebab recipes if not to expose how awful they were – how pumped full of salt, and preservatives and connective tissue? No one I spoke to was proud of the food; they were proud of the work. Of the Herculean shifts they put in, from 11 a.m. to 2 a.m. every day of the week. The kebabs themselves were for them symbolic of a Sisyphean labour. For no sooner was one carved to its skewer than another would be put in its place.

I was learning that most kebab places in the 19th are still owned and run by people from Turkey, often supported by immigrant workers from Bangladesh or Sri Lanka, rather than being the pan-Muslim concern that many on the political far right assumed. The clientele, meanwhile, hail from a very broad background. Many customers treat kebab houses as a refuge. They are shelters to asylum seekers, drunks and madmen, whom I saw set up at tables over single trays of fries, eating with the pedantic lethargy of the truly hungry and bored.

Most intriguingly, I learned that the majority of kebab stores in the 19th got their doners from a single supplier, a firm called Bay Tat located deep in the Paris suburbs. If you want to learn how to make a kebab, I was repeatedly told, get out of here and go and visit them.

After several unanswered emails to Bay Tat and three phone calls informing me that the factory manager was nowhere to be found, I took a risk. Two trains, two buses and a half-hour walk later, I reached my destination. Beneath grey-white skies, surrounded by unsuspecting two-storey homes, I stood before one of the secret engines of Paris: the factory where its doner kebabs were made.

The gate to the compound was open, and I walked in unannounced, surprised to feel a pinch of fear. Few places are as lonely as a suburban corner where you have no business being. And here I was, approaching a meat-mincing factory to which I had received no official welcome. I'm not saying that I truly thought anything sinister was going to happen to me, but I was very aware that if it did, there would be no trouble hiding the body.

There were eyes on me as I crossed the cracked concrete forecourt. The only sign of what might be going on inside was a chimney on top of the large prefab structure that belched out smoke as black as an undecided conclave. In the reception window, a young woman was watching my approach with the hawkish look of someone about to reach under their desk for an alarm. Or a gun. But soon I was talking to her, and she was polite but firm. No, I would not be allowed to visit the factory floor.

My face fell. It had taken me the best part of two hours to get out here, I protested.

You've wasted your time.

Couldn't I at least talk to the manager?

He will say the same as me, the woman said. But fine.

The manager was summoned. Young, nice looking, reassuringly not covered in blood.

No, there was no way I would be allowed in. I could not even ask questions about the kebabs.

It was the same thing as in kebab shops of the 19th; they seemed to think I was out to get them. I protested I was there for my own benefit. I just wanted to know how their kebabs were made so I could make one for myself.

No, came the answer again.

I considered slipping into a more journalistic idiom, saying that yes, I *was* writing an exposé and if they didn't let me in, I'd be forced to assume the worst, that they were hiding something. Eyeballs, testicles, calf foetuses: if I wasn't allowed to see it, I would be at liberty to write that *anything* could go into the kebabs.

I didn't say any of this, however, because it was certainly untrue; because not letting me in was simply a question of insurance, hygiene, lack of time in an already busy day to show around a nosy stranger. And because, let's be honest, I still felt a little intimidated by this unfamiliar meat-mincing factory in an unfamiliar part of town.

'You will never learn how to make a kebab,' the *kebabiste* said, keeping his smile fixed on my face while with his knife he deboned raw chickens. 'I could tell you every one of my secrets, but still you would not be able to do what I do.'

'Are you going to tell me your secrets?' I asked.

I had cheated.

My visits to the *kebaberies* of the 19th and to Bay Tat had not yielded a single doner merchant willing to talk, so I had dipped into the 11th, to a kebab shop on the rue Saint-Maur called Le RDV. On a previous visit there, I had complimented the proprietor on one of the dishes (a lamb kofta, succulent and aflame with cinnamon seasoning), eliciting a great monologue about technique and pride, about how many other kebab shops around Paris did not care about quality and just ordered from big industrial suppliers.

'But I,' the man talking was middle-aged, very short and bald, and effervescing with recent success, 'I make everything myself. And I make it well.'

If he had been so willing to talk after a mere passing compliment, I figured he would respond at length to a deeper probing into his craft. And I had been right. Mostly.

His name was Adel. Originally from Turkey, he had lived in France for nine years. He greeted my arrival in his shop and my questions with delight.

'Sit down. Have a coffee. On the house, my friend.'

His 'house' was not so different from any of the other kebab stores I had been to. Brightly lit with white tile flooring and cheap aluminium furniture. There were no photographs of dishes, however, only a short, handwritten menu above the counter; and no faded pictures of the Bosporus decorated the walls. It was also meticulously clean. Rather than rancid grease or frying, it smelled, fantastically, of roasting meat.

'I am not surprised people in other kebab stores would not speak to you,' he said. 'Most are not chefs. Many do not have papers. They are like people in factories. They have no passion. With me, it is different.'

He continued carving, working blindly, but with the precision of a surgeon. Not an ounce of flesh was being wasted of the chickens he was filleting.

'I have worked as a chef in many restaurants. In Turkey and in Paris. I have done everything. I *can* do anything. So maybe you want to know why I only make kebabs? There is no need for kebabs to be bad, my friend. And it is an inexpensive way to start a restaurant. Even if you buy the very finest meat, which I do.'

'Do you have any advice for me, then, if I want to make a kebab from scratch?' I asked.

'Impossible. Can you do this?' he nodded down to his carving.

'No.'

'You cannot learn it either. After a year, perhaps two. But to leave here now, there is nothing I could tell you.'

'Oh,' I said.

'Listen,' Adel said, 'you cannot ask a man who makes kebabs for a living how to make a kebab. Those who do not take it seriously will not know, and those who do will not tell you. Understand?'

This was, to put it mildly, deflating. Still, I was not about to walk out. Besides, I wanted to say, isn't it just meat on a stick?

'The marinade is the important thing,' Adel said. 'The technique is unteachable, the marinade is the secret.'

'Ah.'

'And I will not tell you my secret. But if you insist on trying to make a kebab for yourself, go to a butcher. Go to the best butcher. Get him to prepare the meat. At least that will be a start.'

No need to ask him if there was a particular Paris butcher that he would recommend; I already knew where to go.

Doner Kebab
Makes 8–10 sandwiches
Ingredients:
800g lamb belly
800g turkey thigh
Salt
Pepper
Olive oil

Serve in a fresh baguette with chopped romaine lettuce, sliced tomatoes and sliced onion.

There was a severed-head-in-a-box quality to the plastic bag of raw meat I set down in my friends' kitchen.

'We're really doing this?' said Lucie, one of the kitchen's owners, eyeing the package with obvious revulsion.

'We're going to try.'

I had come to the north-eastern suburb of Noisy-le-Sec because I was not about to fork out €200 for even the most basic kebab grill, and so I needed to build a fire. Inadvisable in my third-floor apartment, but thankfully (by no means a given in Paris) I had friends with a garden.

'What meat did you go for?' Lucie dared to peer into the bag.

'Turkey leg and lamb belly,' I said. 'Though technically it was chosen for me.'

I'd arrived at the Abattoirs de la Villette that morning in time for the Saturday rush, a fast-moving queue crowding out the entrance. Inside, I could spy a six-metre-long meat counter was staffed by a team of seven, their white overalls dotted by blood. Reaching the front of the queue, I told the dome-headed giant at the counter that I wanted to make a kebab for eight people, but I needed him to prepare it. He answered with a grunt, and at once began to search his counter for cuts. I watched as he took out the lamb and turkey, weighed them for price, then turned his back to me to work them with speed that was all the more frightening because it involved a razor-sharp blade. The very thing Adel had told me I would not be able to do, he did for me in seconds. The lamb belly, which began as a ribbon of sinew, marbled by rib and fat, was fast sculpted down to a half-dozen swatches of lean and unblemished pink. He trimmed a huge turkey leg to the last millimetre, leaving nothing but naked bone. He arranged the meat into a gelatinous pancake stack and wrapped it all together in white paper.

'*Courage*.' He passed me the bag.

'Wait,' I said. 'Do you have any advice for a marinade?'

'And,' Lucie asked, 'did he?'

'No,' I said. 'Not exactly. Just lots of salt and pepper. He said keep basting it in its own juices. That with the quality they sold, the important thing was to taste the meat.'

The Noisy-le-Sec house came with a basement of old junk from which we requisitioned a curtain pole to act as a skewer, punching it through a cheap baking tray for a base. Then, it was as simple as pulling the seasoned meat over it one swatch at a time, layering turkey then lamb, turkey then lamb into a jowly mound half a foot high. It looked disgusting, like something that could block the plumbing of a whole neighbourhood. It looked like a failure. After all my research into kebabs, I had been left with this. Nevertheless, I had come this far …

The fire, I confess, I had researched on YouTube. The barbecue situation in Noisy was just a pit formed by loose bricks, which could be reconstructed into a wall. In front of this we pinned chicken wire to buttress a half-bag of charcoal which we set aflame. Soon, all that was left was to place the kebab monstrosity in front of the heat, and to rotate it by hand. While drinking beer.

The night was unseasonably warm, and this combined with the heat of the fire meant we were able to tend the meat in relative comfort. Which was lucky, because the kebab cooked slowly. One beer gave way to two, and soon enough, two became five. At least this felt an appropriate appetiser. Meanwhile, something magical was taking place.

The transubstantiation of raw into cooked is a low-grade miracle. You witness in real time something repellent become its opposite. Never, though, had I seen a change as profound as I did then. Raw, the kebab had looked like a prolapse, but now it was starting to resemble, well, a kebab. The layers of turkey and lamb were drawing into one another: sizzling, browning, beads of flavour escaping from within. And the smell: that commingling of proteins which hits somewhere at the top of the nose, combined with a base note of smouldering charcoal. It was actually working! Of course it was working. It was meat on a stick.

At last, the time came to carve, a little unsteadily now because of the beer but with a good knife. The action seemed to be the only small contribution I could offer to all the expert butchery that had got us to this point. The meat fell into the tray like manna from hell. I scooped it up and transferred it to a frying pan set up on an electric hotplate we'd trailed outside. I'd never fully understood this stage, common to all kebab shops. But now I recognised it for what it was: a safety precaution. Just in case something in the roast kebab is not fully cooked, the frying stage kills off any lingering microbes. Whatever added flavour it imparts is almost incidental.

We had lettuce, tomato and onion, and fresh baguettes, ready to go. I muttered the call and response to myself as I assembled the sandwich. '*Salade, tomate, oignon?*' '*Oui.*' '*Quelle sauce?*'

I paused. Though I had gone out of my way to find a bottle of *sauce algérienne* in a supermarket, it no longer seemed appropriate. For the 19th, for the history of the 19th, for all the animals slaughtered there for the benefit of Parisian stomachs, I should taste the meat. So I let the condiment stand. And I took a bite. It was delicious. And wasn't this the paradox I'd discovered about kebabs? That their creation, good or bad, is shrouded in secrecy, and yet they are among the most meritocratic and accessible of foods in the city. Which is another way of saying: it was slow-grilled meat. Of course it was delicious.

18ème arrondissement

I was diagnosed with type-1 diabetes a month before my thirtieth birthday. Checking into the Hôpital Lariboisière, following weeks of stomach cramps and excessive thirst, I was told I had so many ketones in my blood that I should be in a coma. Or dead.

After an initial treatment, I lay in A & E for hours. Gurneyed deeper into increasingly forgotten corners, growing hungrier and weaker, I felt trapped in a tightening vice of anxiety about what my newfound condition would mean for my life, and more specifically, my diet. Diabetes was like being surprised into an arranged marriage; I knew it would be with me the rest of my life, but understood nothing of its demands. Only after I was taken to the hospital's sixth-floor diabetic ward, with its view out across the Gare du Nord train tracks, did a nurse tell me how with the right dose of insulin, I could eat whatever I liked. Seldom had I known a greater appetiser than those words. I fell upon that evening's insipid hospital meal (a kind of beige *bourguignon*) as if it were a Michelin-starred feast.

To begin with, then, Brice and I were two strangers who shared only a hospital room and a diagnosis. He had been a politician in the Democratic Republic of Congo but had fled to Paris after upsetting the wrong people. He lifted his hospital gown to show the mess of scar tissue that was his belly, on which boiling water had been poured long ago as an instruction for him to leave Kinshasa. He was a big, strong-looking man, though the experience had left him with a heightened sensitivity to pain. He flinched when piercing his skin with the insulin pens that we had to get used to injecting ourselves with before every meal.

It was inevitable, given our condition, that many of our conversations ended up revolving around food.

There was a restaurant in Paris, Brice said, where they served dishes just like those from back home. Called Mbuta Lombi, it was in the Goutte d'Or neighbourhood, an African enclave of the 18th arrondissement. Just over there, he said, pointing at the window of our hospital ward.

'What kinds of things do you eat in the Congo?' I asked.

'There is much fish, and wild plants, and every part of the animal is eaten.' Brice's eyes went misty as he reeled off fantasy menus. The words alone felt exotic in my mouth: dongo-dongo, makayabu, madesu. Brice told me about okra stews and salted fish and more – a whole history of taste I had never experienced. Then our dismal hospital food would appear, with its sorrowful nods to the traditions of France: wilting *salades Provençales*, vulcanised Camemberts, and *poulets rôtis* that had only ever rotated in a microwave. I found myself depressed by this evidence of French cooking, and in my desire to escape my hospital bed, longed for flavours from the wider world.

'And when we get out of here, we'll drink Guinness.' Brice raised his glass of water in my direction. 'We'll drink a lot of Guinness.'

Brice and I never had our emancipatory meal. For my part, on being discharged, I found I wanted to leave my hospital experience behind. Apart from Brice, it had consisted of many unpleasant memories I preferred to forget.

Today, however, some six years later, when it came to finding a representative dish for the 18th arrondissement, there was only one food and one restaurant that came to mind. I sent Brice an email. The response came back the same day:

'Hey, brother, I'm back in Kinshasa. But you should still go to Mbuta Lombi. Order the malangwa! I still dream about that malangwa! And have a Guinness. Have a lot of Guinness!'

I did not know what malangwa was, but I said I would do just that.

Paris, more than many other cities, is a place of imagined barriers. From the lobbies of luxury hotels to staunchly local bars, many are the establishments that are technically open to all but simply feel closed to outsiders. 'The wall is also inside each one of us,' John Berger once wrote.

These barriers, made close to tangible by money, are more numerous and are felt more keenly by poor and minority communities. As a middle-class, white European male, I had long been aware that one of the many privileges I held in Paris was my relative freedom of access. I may not be able to afford the Ritz, but should I want to use its toilets, I can swagger past the front desk unseen; I have sat in plenty of old-man *tabacs* for hours, unhassled by sexual advances.

Nevertheless, when I reached Mbuta Lombi, despite its cheerful yellow frontage, I could not immediately bring myself to enter. It had corrugated metal shutters pulled half down like heavy eyelids across its windows, concealing its interior from the street. Peeking beneath these, it was not the uniquely African crowd so much as the unfamiliar atmosphere that made me waver. The scene did not follow the codes of any restaurant with which I was familiar. It seemed more like a social club or a house party. Everyone was talking to everyone else: there were people leaning back on chairs to chatter between tables, crowding the aisles, circulating at the bar. I worried that my presence would be an intrusion. Before I went inside, I needed time and I needed courage: I needed a drink.

Once upon a time, the Goutte d'Or was a hamlet outside of Paris. Situated on the slopes surrounding the city, its vineyards produced some of the finest white wine in the medieval world. (In a contemporary Europe-wide competition – a sort of Sommeliers Choice Awards for the thirteenth century – it came third.) Hence the quarter's name: the Drop of Gold. The vineyards have long gone. The only evidence of the appellation's past is the 0.15 hectares of vines on the northern slope of neighbouring Montmartre, which today is little more than a curio, producing a scant eighty cases of middling plonk a year. Still, wine above all foodstuffs is lifted by its fictions. It took only a small act of imaginative will to think the smudged glass of cheap Chardonnay I had ordered in the Café Titanic on the rue Dejean held a flavour of the past.

The rue Dejean is among Paris's livelier market streets. Cacophonous with barter and movement, it overflows with produce that speaks of a less squeamish age. The outside counters of its butcher shops are stuffed with tripe, sheep knuckle and cured goat heads – buck-toothed and mummified brown. The fishmongers' stalls are stacked with such variety that they resemble illustrations from a marine biology textbook. Even the vegetable stalls display an abundant chaos. And down the middle of the street runs a seam of individual tradespeople flogging cheap electrics, knock-off fashion and bruised fruit from cardboard boxes and upturned crates.

I sipped at my wine, at its mass-produced crispness, which frankly was probably better than anything made in the Middle Ages. A fishmonger walked out in front of his stall and threw sardines to the seagulls perched on its awning. Their red-flecked beaks opened in a ravenous caw.

As Paris grew, so the wine-producing hamlet that was the Goutte d'Or was subsumed. By the 1800s it had become home to a large community of the working poor, and like much of the 18th, absorbed a new influx following Napoleon III's remodelling of the city, when vast swathes of Paris's ordinary population were pushed out to make room for the elegant boulevards we see today. With the construction of the nearby Gares du Nord and de l'Est a few years later, the Goutte d'Or filled further with labourers who had come to work on these infrastructure projects and then stayed. At that stage, the Goutte d'Or's population was still overwhelmingly white.

In fact, no reading I had found had offered much explanation for when or why this had changed – or even a reliable account of the extent to which it had changed, as some official statistics suggest its population is still mainly white. Yes, it was not unusual for new arrivals to gravitate towards certain districts, but the reason why so much of the African diaspora should have made their way to the Goutte d'Or was unclear. The closest I came was a suggestion on a tour company's website that it was connected to the jazz scene of the 1920s, when African American musicians in Montmartre popularised the north of the city for other black migrants. This claim was unsubstantiated, however, and seemed too romantic to be true.

I finished my wine and stepped into the market's flow, determined to weave my way back towards the restaurant through the crowds of women with their shopping carts and close-swaddled babies. Under my feet was the crushed mulch of dropped produce, foot-smoothed cobbles and the watery blood hosed clear of butchers' floors. I gravitated to the vegetable stalls. Much of the produce was unfamiliar; even the things I recognised, I had no idea how to cook. How *did* you prepare manioc? It looked like a carrot made of wood. I longed for guidance, so that when I stepped into Mbuta Lombi I might not feel so catastrophically naive and out of place.

'What are you searching for?' The question broke through my thoughts. I turned to see a man a good foot shorter than myself, with yellowed eyes and a prayer callus on his fore-head. Dressed in a tattered dark jacket, he clutched a sheaf of papers in one hand.

'I am Master Samou,' he continued. 'I can help with your problems.'

He passed me one of his papers. Printed on it was a black and white image of his face like a police mug shot, and a paragraph of text that introduced him as the most powerful sorcerer in Paris, capable of bringing me riches, love, curing all manner of physical ills and safeguarding my driver's licence from penalty points.

Such self-proclaimed magic men are a familiar feature of the Goutte d'Or. Known as marabouts, they hawk their 'powers' to the credulous and claim legitimacy from the ancient Senegalese tradition of the wandering mystic. He was an answer to my prayers.

'I was wondering about these vegetables,' I said. 'Like these,' I pointed to a pile of what appeared to be miniature aubergines.

'You are looking for something to make you healthy?' Master Samou said, on the sell. 'There is something wrong with your health.'

'No, not particularly,' I started. 'Well, I'm diabetic, but—'

'*Vous êtes diabétique!*' he did not even try to hide his excitement. 'But that's bad. Very bad. Of course, something I can help you with.'

'I really just wanted to know about these vegetables.'

Master Samou considered the situation, clearly weighing up whether playing along might lead to a sale. 'They are safou,' he said. 'From Congo.'

'And are they like aubergines?'

'Like avocado,' Master Samou said. 'Very good, though you must boil them first. Jaxatu are like aubergines.' He pointed to a pile of red vegetables, which looked like tomatoes.

'And manioc,' I continued, 'how do you cook manioc?'

'You don't know how to cook manioc? You peel it, put it in stew.'

'How does it taste?'

'It will not help your diabetes.'

He wanted to get me back on to the subject of my ailment to propose a way of taking my money in exchange for a 'cure'. But some months earlier, for a magazine piece, I had interviewed a private eye who specialised in uncovering spiritual scams. I'd learned of the crippling extortion rackets many marabouts ran, often targeting some of the most vulnerable members of society. Which is all to say I did not feel too bad about wasting Master Samou's time.

As the market bustled about us, I shrugged off concern for my chronic illness, and pointed to different products in turn. For the sorcerer's part, he warmed to the questions, confessing to be something of a home chef.

'My wife lives in Senegal,' he explained. 'I must know how to cook for myself.'

'And you cook mainly African food?'

'I cook many things. But perhaps yes, mostly the things of my home.'

So I learned about the ubiquitous starch-rich yams, whose name derives from a word found in several African languages and literally means 'to eat'; about gumbo, which I'd known as okra, and which Master Samou said should be boiled down into a paste; and about the great bushels of unknown herbs: the basil-like igbo, the *corète potagère* for soups, and more.

'What I was really wondering,' I said, 'is: have you heard of malangwa?'

'Malangwa?'

He looked confused. Perhaps my pronunciation was wrong. But before I had time to correct it, Master Samou remembered why he was talking to me.

'Please,' he said, 'none of this will cure you. Only I can cure you.'

He managed to intone this in such a way that it sounded sincere. I felt an involuntary flicker of belief.

'I've never heard of anyone being cured of diabetes.'

Master Samou took my hand.

'Come.'

'Where?' I asked, allowing myself to be led all the same.

'To my office,' he said, 'for a séance.'

I should have said no. For whatever a séance consisted of, it did not sound free. But my curiosity was piqued. 'Is it far?'

'No, no,' Master Samou smiled. 'Not far at all.'

The marabout led me to the door of a dilapidated apartment block next to a large butcher's shop on the rue Poulet. The building's hallway looked much like the one in my own building: a tight stairway with a wrought-iron banister, linoleum steps and peeling, filigreed walls. Everything was happening so fast; I was still thinking I should back out when we reached the first floor and the marabout was opening the door to an apartment. I followed him across the threshold.

The interior was bare and lights-off dim: a long, thin space, practically an extension of the corridor, with no decorations and hardly any personal belongings. We passed three bunk beds squeezed along its length, each recently slept in, top and bottom. The kitchen was a double hotplate stove wedged between the bunks, beside which was a single saucepan, a 50kg bag of rice and several bottles of hot sauce. I wondered if Master Samou's home-cooking claims were as much a fantasy as what he was selling.

He led me to another room at the end of the corridor-apartment. It took me several seconds to realise we were standing in the bathroom – what threw me off was the large desk at a diagonal in the room's centre, a chair either side.

'Sit, sit,' the marabout gestured towards the seat nearest the shower, then sank into the one opposite. This made him seem even smaller: a tiny, bureaucratic man. The strangest thing about all this was how it didn't feel strange at all. The marabout was acting with such brusque professionalism that I might have entered a doctor's office, albeit one with an excess of plumbing.

'OK.' He reached into the top drawer, pulled out a plastic bag and emptied its contents onto the desktop in front of him: a jumble of coins, cowrie shells and a silver ring. Without ceremony, the ceremony had begun. He was jerking his right palm over the pile, pushing the coins, the cowries and the ring this way and that, while he looked straight ahead with amber-coloured, bloodshot eyes. Then he gazed down at the disorder he'd created.

'Yes, yes,' he said. '*Comme prévu*, I can save you from diabetes, but it will take some sacrifices.'

'Sacrifices?'

'Twenty-seven chickens,' he said. 'At four tomorrow morning I will sacrifice twenty-seven chickens on your behalf.'

'That will cure my diabetes?'

'You will live to be a hundred and twenty years old.'

I asked where he was going to get twenty-seven live chickens by four tomorrow morning.

'There is a place,' Master Samou said. 'Here in the Goutte d'Or.'

It was rubbish, surely. Only now, Master Samou was pulling a business card from his desk. He handed it to me. It was for a place called La Ferme Parisienne, 'the last *poulailler* of Paris' – a shop, just a few streets away, that traded in live poultry. I felt an uneasy sensation in the pit of my stomach.

'For most people here, they are food,' Master Samou said. 'There is nothing like eating something that was only just alive. And you get the blood. I will give the chickens I sacrifice to the poor of this neighbourhood, of course.'

'And ... how much will it cost?'

'I can tell you need this,' Master Samou said. 'And you are a good person. So I will not charge for my work.'

For the briefest of moments I forgot myself. What if I had met Brice precisely so that I would have this encounter? Had the path to curing my diabetes been lying in the hospital bed next to mine on the very day I got my diagnosis?

'But you will have to pay for the chickens,' Master Samou continued. 'For twenty-seven ...' he did some fast calculations '... it will be €1,000.'

That, I said, sounded like a lot.

'For the end to your diabetes, to live to a hundred and twenty, it is nothing,' said Master Samou. He looked at me so imploringly then, I wondered if he believed his own lie. 'You do not believe me?'

45

'I'm sorry but ... no.'

I thought the would-be sorcerer might get angry, might put up more of a protest. But he just looked sad, defeated; any faith he might have had in his magic, which was really the magic to conjure money from strangers, was suddenly gone.

'You will pay me €40 for the *séance*,' he resolved.

OK, apparently not gone entirely.

When I emerged back on the streets of the Goutte d'Or, however, I felt that the world had changed: whatever had been holding me back from going to Mbuta Lombi was no longer there. Perhaps this had something to do with the sacrifice of €40. More likely it was the small sliver of knowledge my short conversation with Master Samou had offered me, and there is no question that being invited into a stranger's apartment to talk chicken murder does wonders for collapsing barriers. If Master Samou could accost and demand a thousand euros from a random guy on the street in exchange for a blood rite, then I could walk into a restaurant.

Mbuta Lombi was almost empty now. Two huge TV screens were hung either end of its L-shaped, yellow-walled room, blaring African pop videos at full volume. The air smelled of soap and beer and faintly of spice. Because of the shutters lidding the windows there was no natural light. If it's always five o'clock somewhere, I had just found where that somewhere was.

The single waiter was young, perhaps not yet twenty. He wore a baggy grey tracksuit and had stripes shaved into his hair. He slouched out from behind the bar where he'd been playing on his phone and offered me a suspicious smile.

'Is the kitchen open?' I asked.

'You want something to *eat*?' he said like he'd expected me to ask to check the electric meter.

'I was hoping to try the, um ...' I hoped I'd pronounce this right '... malangwa?'

'Malangwa?' the waiter repeated.

'Malangwa,' I said. 'Do you serve malangwa?'

'Yes,' the waiter said. 'We are known for our malangwa!'

'Excellent,' I said. 'Um, what is it?'

'It would be too big for you alone.'

The Afropop continued to thump, the videos continued to strobe, their colours flashed on a silver balloon banner that spelled out the word 'Happy' strung across the ceiling.

'If you want malangwa you should come back another time. With someone else,' the waiter said.

'Right ...' I was being pushed out.

'Now it is better to have something lighter,' the waiter said. 'Like beans.'

I wasn't being pushed out.

'Beans sound great!' I said, maybe a little too enthusiastically. 'Um, just beans?'

'In a tomato sauce.'

'Excellent!'

After delivering my order to the kitchen, the waiter returned. Bored on a slow afternoon, he introduced himself. His name was Franklin and Mbuta Lombi was his dad's restaurant. The family had arrived from the DRC in the early nineties, before Franklin was born. They'd established the restaurant on this street in 1996.

'It was different then, my dad says. We were the first Congolese restaurant in the area. But you know, the Goutte d'Or is not as African as it seems.'

'Really?'

'There are many African businesses here. But my family doesn't live here. Few of our customers live here. We all travel here from the *banlieue* and many from other countries. The Goutte d'Or is our place to shop, to meet, to eat. Every Saturday is a party,' he said. 'We have people visit from Congolese communities all over the world on Saturday. Come then!'

There came a shout from the kitchen. Franklin hurried to fetch my food, then left me alone to eat.

The dish was massive and magnificently stodgy. If Franklin considered this to be 'light' I dreaded to think how gargantuan a malangwa might be. The beans still had the metallic tang of the tin they'd been kept in, and the tomato sauce was only lightly peppered. Lifting the dish was a jar of home-made peri-peri, which I applied liberally, and the occasional grey ball of chewy, rich meat: tripe. Franklin had not mentioned this ingredient, nor did I see it on the menu, where, with a thrilling disregard for vegetarians, the dish appeared only as 'tomato and beans'. At €6 it surely offered one of the biggest protein bangs for your buck of anything served in the city.

While eating, I chewed over how what Franklin had told me reframed the *quartier* and many of the barriers I had perceived here. Far from being a fiercely local enclave, it was a tourist hub, a kind of alternative centre: a place of passage and mixture rather than barriers. The wall had been inside of me even more than I had realised.

'So, why did so many African businesses set up here, do you think?' I asked when Franklin came to clear my empty plate.

'Because of the Gare du Nord,' Franklin said, as if it was obvious. 'It's easy to get to from the suburbs.'

'Of course.'

'So you'll come back Saturday for malangwa?'

'Absolutely,' I said. 'Wait, I still don't know what malangwa is ...'

On Saturday evening, I arrived outside Mbuta Lombi with Alice, my wife, to find the restaurant packed. Crowds-between-the-tables, spilling-into-the-street packed. So busy it seemed impossible we would find space inside.

Shouldering between the people at the door we entered that same room, but now as it was meant to be. Mbuta Lombi was in full *fête*, bright with wax-print cotton fabric and statement jewellery; heady with the commingling of perfumes and sweat, alcohol and cooking; with shouted conversation and laughter and those music videos that throbbed away unceasingly. Here was Franklin, squeezing his way towards us with a grin on his face like he'd never been happier to see two customers in his life.

'Told you we were busier on Saturdays!' he yelled. 'I'll find you somewhere to sit.'

He proceeded to magic up space from nowhere, pushing us in among a table of strangers who greeted us enthusiastically then slipped back into their own chatter.

'What can I get you to drink?' Franklin asked.

A Guinness, obviously.

'How many?'

'Sorry?'

'You order all your drinks for the evening now,' Franklin explained.

49

Well, hadn't Brice instructed 'a lot'?

'Four,' I said. Alice ordered a mini bottle of wine.

'And to eat, I already know,' Franklin smiled, and rushed off to the kitchen to place the order.

The atmosphere was so electric that in the moment it precluded any conversation that was not simply a grinning acknowledgement of everything that was going on around us. Our drinks arrived and, shortly after, an enormous river fish, served on a platter like an offering to a god. Its silver skin was striped with the carbonised black of a charcoal grill and over it a sauce had been poured that was as rich and shiny as gold.

'Malangwa!' Franklin declared. I'd seldom known greater delight in a mystery solved. The malangwa was accompanied by fried plantains and a mountain of rice, and a jar of the house piri piri.

Unthinkingly, then, I performed the small intimate sequence of gestures that has become close to second nature before any meal, ever since my hospital stay with Brice many years earlier. Remove my insulin pen from my bag, eyeball the carbohydrates in front of me to adjust the dosage, then lift my shirt to plunge the needle into the pinched flab of my flank and hold it there for five seconds, flesh momentarily exposed to the world.

'*Ah*,' a woman seated almost across from me acknowledged, '*le diabète*.'

I offered an apologetic smile and began to eat.

Good does not come close. It was a perfection of flavour. Not of fish, exactly, but rather – and hear me out – of McDonald's. As if someone had taken all the salt and fat and acid and sweetness that is so scientifically balanced by the fast-food chain into singularly moreish dishes and fleshed it out into something wholesome and natural. All the same endorphin-releasing taste receptors were hit in each buttery bite and yet when it was over there was none of the greasy emptiness or regret. Washed down with the bitter velvet of Guinness, it was a meal worth the years' long wait.

'Good, eh?' our tablemate remarked while Alice and I surveyed the carcass of our feast.

'It was,' I agreed. 'That sauce, I mean, do you have any idea how they make it?'

'The sauce?' She rumbled a tectonic laugh. She was big, tall, dressed magnificently in blue and orange. 'C'est simple. It is not how I would normally cook malangwa, but it is good for an occasion.'

I fought to concentrate through my post-gorge haze, because wasn't learning how to make these dishes myself the final goal of why I was here? I'd almost forgotten.

'So, um, what kind of fish is malangwa? Is it from Congo?'

'Oh no. In Congo we use all sorts of fish. We have a very big river. I believe malangwa is from Asia. But you can use any catfish.'

'So how would you cook one? No, wait, how would you cook one *like this*?'

Malangwa
Serves a very hungry 2
Ingredients:
1 whole malangwa (pangasius), around 1kg
    For the marinade:
    ½ cup sunflower oil
    1 tsp salt

1 tsp white pepper
1 tsp chicken stock
1 tsp Dijon mustard
2cm ginger
Juice of ½ lemon
1 tsp Aromat

For the sauce:
½ cup sunflower oil
1 generous knob butter
1 large yellow onion, sliced
2 leeks, sliced

Serve with steamed rice and Guinness.

As instructed, I used a sharp knife to score the fish's skin.

'The marinade,' the woman in Mbuta Lombi had told me, 'the taste of Congo is in the marinade.'

This meant salt, white pepper, chicken stock, mustard, freshly grated ginger, lemon juice and a spice called Aromat. I was excited by this last ingredient. Imagine, a whole new spice I'd never encountered!

It turned out to be a seasoning mix developed by Knorr in the 1950s, consisting largely of MSG, and extremely hard to find in Paris – I had to visit almost a dozen Goutte d'Or supermarkets before I struck lucky.

'Massage this all into the fish with some sunflower oil, then leave it overnight,' she had said.

Usually, I don't have much patience with marinades, but now my cooking instincts – such as they were – were intuiting ahead of time how this would work: there was so much flavour being packed into this marinade that it was sure to make a difference. I slipped the marinating malangwa into my fridge and waited twenty-four hours.

'Then, for the sauce, it's easy,' she'd said. 'Onions and leeks fried in butter and oil. Lots of onions, lots of leeks. Lots of butter. Lots of oil.'

'And I fry the fish in that?' I had asked.

'Did it look like a fried fish?' the woman had tutted. 'No, no. You will have already taken the fish from its marinade. Here they have used a grill but at home you will be baking it in the oven. Once you have started to cook the sauce, sweating the vegetables together, you add what is left of the marinade to it.'

The sauce frothed briefly and steamed, then settled into a mixture of tawny silk. The odours rising in my kitchen took an olfactory step towards the less familiar: umami-rich with that high-in-the-nose manufactured stock flavour, but uplifted too by the fresh ginger. The fish was still baking. I put rice on to boil at the back of my stove, and I opened a bottle of Guinness.

17ème arrondissement

Batignolles on that blue-skied October morning was a Netflix idyll. The old Paris has abandoned this former village district of the 17th, but a scrubbed-up dream of it has taken its place. Here were artisan cheese shops, curated *brocantes*, *caves* selling natural wine. Batignolles today is ground zero for the most modern of Parisian tribes: *les bobos* – bourgeois bohemians with well-paid jobs and 'creative' tastes.

They came in the early 2000s, for the cheap rents, the charmingly shabby property and the cobbled streets, replacing families who'd been here for years. This morning, though, it felt hard to blame them. The sun bounced bright off latticed building facades, fresh water sparkled in the cobbled gutters and angelic kids scootered down pavements, hallooing as they went. If only Americans knew this part of Paris existed. They'd lose their minds. Yet there were no tourists: Batignolles is not on their map. I had come for that exact reason, to observe what *les bobos* do when there is no one to see them: have brunch.

They were spread around the terraces of the place du Docteur Félix Lobligeois in their plain, expensive clothes. Men with good skin and neat beards, women with large sunglasses and straight hair, and all with that particular kind of attractiveness that comes from being monied, healthy and largely untouched by life.

On solid circular tables teemed the ambrosia of this modern pantheon. Scrambled eggs, foamy coffee, orange juice, fruit salads, pastry. Brunch. An Anglo-Saxon import, emblematic of a reward for the week's work in the office or studio, taken on terraces that might look French but were really stamped with a more global brand.

'Just because the world loves Paris, it does not mean we don't want anything from the rest of the world,' one of the diners told me when I insinuated myself into his company. Benoît was a junior architect from Nantes; thin, in a clean white T-shirt, with narrow teeth and close-cropped black hair. Unfazed and polite about my interrupting his meal, he continued in English, 'France is still a formal society. There's an expectation to eat at certain times. For meals to involve certain things. Brunch is like our stand against that.'

'Really?' The relaxed dining around me hardly seemed an act of rebellion, and if it was, it was a rebellion against which I wanted to rebel.

However representative of the modern 17th arrondissement brunch may be, I already knew I wasn't going to waste
my time 'learning' how to make it. Notwithstanding that I
already knew how to make brunch – everyone does – I have
a personal dislike of the meal. Call this inverse snobbery,
a conservative romanticism, the narcissism of small differ-
ences – I am not so far from a *bobo* myself. (It's there in
that 'everyone knows how to make brunch' assumption;
everyone *I* know, knows how to make brunch.) Also, it is
criminally overpriced.

Instead, I had set my sights on just one element of the
meal that adorned those terrace plates. A foodstuff that,
though part of the table, seemed to speak of a more eternal
Batignolles, and a Paris that belonged not only to the *bobos*
but to everyone. A foodstuff that had been here long before
the brunching crowds and would remain long after they'd
moved on to other portmanteaus. The croissant.

Descending into the boulangerie basement was a madeleine
moment. A return to the sensations of my bakery childhood. The dry scent of flour dust on the air, the soft tones
of white, silver and dun, even the grip and slide of my shoes
on the floor – the particular slipperiness of bakery floor
tiles filmed by a microscopic layer of dough, against which
muscle memory in my legs told me how to balance. How
had I never considered that on nearly every Paris street such
biomes of nostalgia had been concealed from me all this
time?

There was more: the dull refrigerator throb, the stacked
shelves of warm rising dough, the multistorey oven whose
cool facade contained a roaring heat. Bakeries are whole

microclimates to facilitate the taming and slaughter of yeast that is their stock-in-trade.

'So have you made croissants before?' Frances, the baker, asked.

'Um, no,' I admitted. 'My dad always said they were too difficult. But it *was* a proper bakery.'

I found myself wanting to impress. Frances was a real rarity: an English *boulangère* in Paris. When I'd spread it about that I wanted to learn how to make croissants, a friend had put us in touch. Already I could not help but see in this woman of a similar age and background to me the skills and lifestyle of a person who I might have been, had I chosen differently. Who on some deep, deluded level, I liked to believe I still was.

'No doubt it was a proper bakery,' Frances said, leading me through the cramped underground space to an ante-room workbench away from the heavier baking equipment. 'Croissants *are* difficult. Getting the honeycomb all the way through, the flaking on the outside: dough and butter don't just *do* that. It's a process.'

Her accent was glazed by a faint French twang.

'So, no shade,' she went on. 'Even in Paris only 20 per cent of boulangeries make their own. That's the statistic that you hear, anyway. Because it takes so much time. It's only profitable if you have a big team and some guys whose job it is to do nothing *but* make croissants. There aren't many boulangeries like that. Most are still run by husband and wife teams.'

Frances started pulling large square sheets of the croissant dough she had made the day before from another fridge; there was no time *not* to talk and work simultaneously.

'Because they'll put in ridiculous overtime for no pay. From 4 a.m. to 6 p.m., that kind of thing.'

She began to feed the croissant dough into the electric table-top rolling machine that I recognised as a pastry sheeter.

'Twenty per cent,' I mused, 'that's a lot of businesses doing something that doesn't turn a profit.'

'Most boulangeries don't make much of a profit,' Frances said. 'The average mark-up on a baguette is only 80 cents.'

'Sounds OK.' I was lingering at her shoulder, trying to follow the process.

'On croissants it's even worse,' she said. 'Imagine how many you have to sell in a day to start making enough money to pay staff, cover rent ...'

'So how come they're so cheap?' Few croissants in Paris cost more than €1.30.

'The market sets the price,' Frances said. The croissant dough was flattening, speeding back and forth through the sheeter. 'Maybe I'm not the right person to ask about this. I got my training in a communist bakery. The guy who taught me used to say that the trouble with boulangeries is that although they're all exploiting their staff, no one's working harder than the boss. So no one's incited to revolution.'

'Even so,' I said, 'why don't you buy croissant dough in?'

I might as well have asked why, after university, Frances had refused an easier corporate career path and come to Paris to be a baker at all.

'Uh, because of passion,' she said. 'Pride in the work, you know?'

'Ah yes ...'

'Also,' Frances continued, 'croissants get people through the door.'

She pulled the flattened dough from the sheeter to the work surface, did some measuring, then started to slice it into neat, long triangular strips.

'Parisians can tell a handmade croissant from a factory one?'

'Can't you? There's so much choice among croissants in Paris, it's like you can't help but become an expert. Anyway, most handmade ones are obviously worse.'

'Sorry?'

'Because they're so difficult to get right. Talking of which, here, we don't have long.'

She picked up one of the newly sliced triangles, let it dangle long-point down, then pinched her thumb and forefinger close to its base and pulled it to almost double its length in a single motion.

'You want to touch the dough as little as possible.' She laid the strip out flat, its wider end nearest to her. 'Every time you touch it, you're heating it up. That makes the layers melt into each other. Then it's not a croissant, it's just brioche.'

'What's wrong with brioche?'

'It's not a croissant.'

With the very tips of her fingers, she rolled the dough-triangle away from her into a tight tube of four tapering layers ready to be baked. Or rather, ready to sit another three hours in a proving cabinet, and *then* be baked. And this was already towards the end of the croissant-making process – the minimum amount of time it takes to make the pastry is ten hours. In most boulangeries the work is split across three days. Such laborious, technical work, combined with the relative similarity to brioche, plus the low market price all begged the question: how did croissants even get invented?

Perhaps this is why the story of their creation is among the most famous in all culinary literature. During the Siege of Vienna in 1683, the legend has it, Ottoman attempts to tunnel under the city walls were thwarted by bakers who heard the burrowing from their own subterranean workspaces. After the siege was lifted, the bakers were invited to create a new pastry to commemorate the victory, and they came up with the croissant: a taunting nod to the Islamic crescent. Quite why they should have insisted that it be so hard to make is not mentioned. Probably because the story isn't true.

In reality, the shaping of pastries into crescents is far older. Listen to food historians rather than myth-makers, and they will tell you that the first bakers to do so were the ancient Greeks, intending their proto-croissants as tributes to the moon goddess. The modern pastry, as best as can be determined, was a Parisian creation, spurred by the new baking techniques of the Boulangerie Viennoise on rue de Richelieu in the early nineteenth century, then refined by various French pastry chefs over the decades, with the current iteration appearing at some point in the 1920s. If the precise inventor of the croissant has been lost, however, so much the better. For I was beginning to feel that the exactitudes of the croissant-making process were really a creation of the mores and desires of Paris itself. The market sets the price; it also demands the quality.

I was put to task shaping. This was not as easy as Frances had made it appear. Despite my wish to show I still had the craft, my results were mixed. With just the few extra seconds of touching that I took to get things right I could feel the dough melting into itself under my fingers. The work of hours dissolving in moments under my palm.

Soon enough, though, we had filled a half-dozen trays. Or rather, Frances had filled five trays; I had filled one. My croissants were one sixth as good and I had taken six times as long to shape them. As with so many recipes, the most important ingredient could only be bought at a great expense – for it lived inside the maker's wrist.

And I wanted to make these things from scratch by myself?

'Making croissants well at home is nearly impossible,' Frances reassured me later, after walking me through the whole process.

'So you don't think there's any point?' I said, looking for a way out. 'Like, maybe I should just try for brioche, instead?'

'No, of course you should try,' she said. 'Just, before you start, you offer up a small prayer: *Thank you for letting me fail.*'

Croissants

Makes 8 croissants

Ingredients:

For the détrempe:

250g bread flour

1 tsp salt

35g sugar

10g fresh yeast

120g warm water

1 tbsp melted butter

125g unsalted butter

1 egg for wash

The dough used to make croissants is called the détrempe. Made of flour, water, sugar, yeast and butter, it was an easy enough first step. I know how to mix a dough.

Soon, on the thin worktop of my apartment kitchen, I had massaged out a bouncy supple ball, which I wrapped in cellophane and pushed to the back of my fridge. The proving of croissant dough is a slow, controlled process, so that it is not only air the yeast imparts to the pastry, but also flavour.

Meanwhile, from outside my windows, the taunting smell of other baking rose. Another reminder of the path not taken. It was nine o'clock in the morning; I had only just got out of bed. In the boulangerie across my street, they were already on their second, or perhaps third batch. In any case, there was no sense in being guilted into working harder; there was nothing to do but wait.

For six hours, the détrempe sat in my fridge's chill, the yeast feeding, breathing, making the dough expand. Then came time to show it who was boss, knock it back: I put the dough in the freezer compartment.

The hard part had begun.

The key to making croissants, Frances had explained, is to fold butter and dough over and over each other, with those two substances squeezing into ever-thinning sheets but never becoming one. The butter must be soft enough to bend, but not melt. The dough should be the same consistency – hence the freezer. In Frances's bakery, the butter came in ready-made, almost flat squares specifically for this reason. At home, I had to bash out my own pad. Using a rolling pin, I beat a block of Président unsalted in an uneven rhythm on my countertop, hoping nothing would break. Once it was flat, I knifed off the ragged edges, then slid it back into the fridge, and waited ten minutes for it to reharden.

Out came the cold dough, which I rolled into a long flat rectangle. Then, as Frances had shown me, I placed the cool butter (a third of the length of the pastry sheet) in its centre and flapped both ends of the dough into the middle, so that the butter was entirely covered. I rolled this package flat. In the bakery, Frances had done this in seconds with the sheeter. Here, I had only my pin. Still, I tried to work fast, for with every second outside the fridge the two layers wanted to seep into one another; to become not croissant, but that other thing.

When the package was the same length the dough had been before, I folded it, bringing the two ends back to the middle, then folding it in half again where the two ends met. A book fold, as it's called. That went back in the fridge.

This was going OK. Was it going OK? Another thing about this long and precise process: if one of the many things that could go wrong went wrong at any point, I would not know until the end.

Twenty minutes later, it came out of the fridge again.

Now, I was flattening those four precarious layers. Back again into the same length strip of dough, which once again I folded. This time in thirds – a letter fold.

'You can't fold any more than that,' Frances had warned, 'or the butter gets too thin, and you get—'

'Brioche?'

'Exactly.'

The letter-folded dough went – you've guessed by now – back in the fridge.

Twenty minutes later, at last, I was at the shaping stage.

I rolled out the dough into a thin rectangle once more and began to slice it widthways into long, narrow triangles. Two days ago, I'd shaped maybe fifty of these into croissants. Stretch and roll, stretch and roll: training my hands to be an ingredient. Was fifty enough training? Well, at least what I was left with at the end looked, for the most part, like croissants.

Now, the final round of proving. Of all the tricky things to get right when making croissants at home, Frances had said, this was the trickiest. You want a moist, warm environment, so that the yeast can at last really go to town: puff up the croissants like pastry balloons. Her advice was to boil water in a pan, then place the pan at the bottom of my oven, and shortly after slide the unbaked croissant trays in above. This I did – rewarding the yeast after all my previous strictness, fattening it before the kill. Just like in the bakery, the fattening took three hours.

It was now nearly eight in the evening and the boulangerie across my street was shutting up for the night, its own stacks of croissants depleted. Though even now I spared a thought for its fridges, freezers and proving cabinets, and for the hundreds of others across the city, where croissants in all their various stages of evolution were quietly slumbering, their taste and texture and potential gathering infinitesimally with each passing second.

It was the moment of truth.

I preheated the oven. Lightly applied egg-wash to my creations, slid them inside, and again, waited. This time, not for long.

My God, the smell! The scent of baking in general is the scent of home and daily life – the creative expression of the hearth. Croissants overwrite this with luxury: the odour of pure sustenance wrapped in indulgence. It is also the smell of the Parisian dawn. Seriously. The Parisian day might be scented with car fumes and piss, but there is a short golden hour when all the ovens are on, when the still-shut boulangeries exhale.

The next day, I cycled a couple of my croissants to Frances at her bakery way before sunrise. I wanted to witness the morning shift. It was one of the best shows I've ever seen in Paris.

In under two hours, in that tiny underground space, tray after tray of pallid gloop was transformed into ornaments of living bronze. The speed at which the bakers worked, crowding the ovens like a rush-hour train terminus, all with bags under their morning eyes, was staggering. They were tired, passionate, precise. I gave up any thought of wanting to prove myself, knew that I couldn't, was happy just to watch in awe. At a certain point, one of Frances's colleagues, a heavy-set man called Romain, beckoned me to see the day's first croissants come out. He didn't even know that croissants were ostensibly why I was there. He was simply proud, wanted to share the smell and his joy.

'This,' he said, 'is why I get up at four every morning. This is what makes the job worthwhile.'

After the rush was over and the boulangerie was about to open its doors to show off the new magic of its bountiful shelves, Frances and I took a moment to review my own creations.

Failure. It felt like a big word when the only success would have been perfection. My croissants *looked* like croissants.

But as Frances said, that's the strange thing about the pastry: the bar to making them well is almost unattainably high, while at the same time they're so distinctive that even a bad one can never be mistaken for anything other than what it is; or what it's trying to be.

They tasted the part, too; had that familiar, impossible flavour of unctuous light. But by then, as I had learned, taste isn't really the aim. The aim is texture and sculpture. The aim is art. On these measures, we agreed my croissants were not entirely, but partly lacking. They flaked less than they ought, and their interior was only honeycombed in parts. Somewhere along the way some things had gone slightly wrong. I'd rolled too hard or clung too long to the dough as I'd shaped it. In places, the butter and *détrempe* had combined. Oh well. Thank you for letting me fail.

For, in the end, making my own croissant was really an act of appreciation for the abundant perfectionism of Paris pastry, and for the people who make it. For the things that gentrification has not yet taken away. If brunch was a kind of capitalism in food form, then the croissant was its opposite. A French resistance. Unprofitable, high-minded, beauty for beauty's sake. *Égalité* in luxury for all.

16ème arrondissement

The mass in Passy's Église Notre-Dame de l'Assomption was a perfunctory enchantment. In my life, I mostly only find myself in church for the major rites, but here was Catholicism just getting on with the weekly business of being itself, transubstantiating once again.

I considered the congregation. Middle-aged and well groomed. The women with their hair in neat ponytails, the men in freshly pressed, sober suits, and all with an aura of such reserve that it had an almost physical presence, shielding their true nature from the world. Even at the moment of salutation, when we were invited to embrace our neighbours, the wishes of peace bore no warmth, only the same stiff obligations of ritual that had come before.

And I had thought I could get one of these people to invite me to dinner – who was I kidding?

Well, they had done once before. People like them, at any rate. There had been a time, when I first moved to Paris, when I was welcomed deep into the world this congregation of the 16th represented: as rich, refined and stuffy as the liver of an overfed goose. That had been a long time ago, however, and while just standing among such people again was enough to convince me that their culture endured, so I was reminded too how far from it my life had strayed. It was all very well joining them in church, but to accompany them to their true Sunday altar, the family table, would take a miracle.

Nevertheless, once the mass was over I did my best. I approached these well-turned-out strangers to tell them about my project and ask what they were about to go on to eat, all the while secretly hoping for Christian charity – that someone might suggest if I was really curious I could join them. No such luck. I was greeted with brusque suspicion.

'Yes, we are having Sunday lunch ... Ingredients? We get them from the markets ... Sorry, we really have to be going, we must buy our *poulet rôti* ... Yes, of course we have a starter and cheese course. Dessert? Naturally ... But please, we have to be on our way ...'

Back out on the streets of the arrondissement, alone, I found myself caught up in the last-minute rush of a soon to be domestically cloistered world. Here were chic crowds jostling in the boulangeries and wine shops of the avenue Mozart, and queuing from local butchers whose windows showcased beautiful, bronzed chickens crackling and turning on spits, smelling like divinity.

The 16th is Paris at its most bourgeois, bloated and prosperous in the city's west. Like many of the outlying arrondissements, it was once a conglomeration of villages that grouped together to become part of the city proper during Napoleon III's restructuring. It was rich right from the start, so much so that it was originally slated to be called the 13th arrondissement before its affluent population complained about that number's negative connotations and had the designation shifted to the poorer east. Perhaps that's what the wealthy mean when they say you make your own luck.

It is also the least densely populated arrondissement and accordingly the most suburban corner of inner Paris, scored by long residential boulevards of large, secretive apartment blocks and gated communities. The 16th has always felt to me a place apart from the rest of the city. The focus of life here is the apartment interior as opposed to the streets, and as such, harder to penetrate; even if – as I say – I had known it once, a long time ago.

The shopping crowds on that Sunday in November were thinning. While the families retreated past the concierges of their Haussmann mansions, I remained out in the cold, trudging over wet, long-fallen leaves and past expensive, empty cafés in the spitting rain. Eventually, I slunk into one of these cafés, accepting defeat.

Of the people I had once known in the 16th, none now remained. I had hoped to reconnect, to see again first-hand how they lived and ate behind closed doors. But all the emails and messages I had sent had been answered with a litany of tragedy and departure: heart attack, cancer, Belgium.

My trip to this service had been a final, desperate throw of the dice, not least because it had been in this very church that, at a funeral five years before, I'd experienced my last true contact with the world of the *haute bourgeoisie*. Some irrational impulse had brought me back, told me I might find someone from that distant sombre occasion still waiting among the pews. I had been wrong.

I had to accept that this most private part of Paris worlds was fully closed off to me. It made me feel sad, brought up again those thoughts that had caused me to embark on this project about how shallow my connections to this city were. The only path I had left now was to remember. I stared through the café windows onto the quieting urban grey of the avenue and tried to retrace my memories.

I was introduced to Antoine at a Christmas party in his large ground-floor apartment on the rue de Ranelagh, which cuts a straight line from the eastern edge of the Bois de Boulogne to the river as it curves round by avenue du Président Kennedy. It was 2002, and I had been invited over with my parents on an almost unheard-of break from the bakery during the festive season. I was a spoddy, suburban teenager adrift in an *haut-bourgeois* sea.

I'd heard all about Antoine already, of course; this suave Parisian gentleman who had met my parents while they were on a holiday in Normandy and charmed the *pantalons* off them. I knew that he was six foot six, silver-haired and elegantly handsome; that he had studied in Georgetown and done military service in Djibouti; that he spoke fluent English with an accent so flawless you'd never know he was even French.

'So you are *le Crâne d'Oeuf*,' Antoine declared at that first meeting, pressing my hand. He was enormous under his Savile Row suit, peering at me down a long Gallic nose that seemed to have evolved as a weapon of condescension. And his voice! It was baritone and blasting, an impression of Britishness that belonged to another age. I was too intimidated to ask the meaning of the term *crâne d'oeuf*.

A dozen oysters had been ordered for every guest. I ate mine at a side table next to Antoine's middle daughter (he had three but no sons), made dry-mouthed by her Parisienne beauty, while she teased me about how the slimy grey creatures in front of me were still alive. That my unaccustomed palate made it through all twelve still remains among my greatest gastronomic accomplishments. It was at the end of the evening, though, that Antoine had a conversation with my parents that would change the course of my life.

'A young man must learn a second language,' he pronounced like it were scripture.

My parents nodded along.

'So your *jeun'homme* will come to stay in my house in the Dordogne this summer. With me, *bien sûr*.'

As with nearly everything that would come to characterise my relationship with Antoine, I had no say in the matter. But so began my education into the people of Paris's 16th: how they eat, and how they do many other things as well.

I learned, for example, that it is normal for the French to take a long break from work for almost the entirety of August, and many of them decamp to another part of France for that period. Often, generations of their family have gone to the exact same part of France each year. For working-class families, this can mean a particular campsite; for most families in the 16th it means a second home. In Antoine's case, it meant his ancestral manor in the Dordogne.

I was told to expect a round of endless soirées, sophisticated socialising and some of the best food I had ever tasted. Oh, and I'd probably have a love affair and come back speaking fluent French.

It didn't turn out like that. Antoine's middle daughter was conspicuously absent, for a start, as were any other people my own age, and for the most part I became a de facto babysitter for his youngest, who at eleven already spoke such precociously good English it didn't even help my French. Meanwhile, Antoine and his frighteningly elegant wife headed to a round of endless soirées, presumably sophisticated socialising and some of the best food I never tasted.

Still, there were moments that stood out. Antoine's 800-year-old house in the medieval hilltop village of Domme with its warren-like corridors of cool stone. His mother, who, though suffering from dementia, was wheeled in front of me ('You will now talk to Mother') to speak in more precise and aristocratic English than even her son. His Algerian manservant, Dreese, a tiny, sad man who was nevertheless always smiling, and who slept in a cupboard under the stairs. The local *vin de noix* (nut-infused red wine) drunk with single cubes of ice on sweltering summer nights. The foie gras that we ate in quantities so vast I felt any moment we could expect a PETA raid, or the dinner party at the farm where they bred hunting dogs, hosted by the ex-army colonel, which had to be cut short because of a row about Charles de Gaulle. And more than anything, Antoine himself, who was kind and bullying and funny, and who treated me with a filial affection, as if we were sharing a constant joke about the stuffiness of his world and the gaucheness of mine.

The experience was sufficiently formative that when I left university several years later, I decided to move to France. My French still needed improving, though, so I called up Antoine to ask if I could spend another August in the Dordogne.

'It is about time!' he boomed.

And that summer, well, it was the best one of my life.

For the first week of that August, it was only Antoine and me in his Domme mansion, which meant he looked to me for both company and servitude. He still referred to me with the nickname he had coined on our first ever meeting, *le Crâne d'Oeuf*, which I learned meant the Egg Head. What had begun as a reference to my supposed bookishness had now been reinforced in Antoine's eyes by my being a recent graduate of the LSE. I'm sure he would have preferred Oxbridge, but some things can't be helped.

Every morning at eight he would stand in his flower-strewn courtyard and yell up to the window of my tiny bedroom annex: 'It is time to get the bread, *Crâne d'Oeuf*.' Knowing that my presence here necessitated playing by his rules, I would dutifully shrug on shirt and shorts and head into town, under strict instructions to buy the precise sliced *boule de pain* from the exact same boulangerie on Domme's main tourist strip, just before the first busloads of tourists arrived.

Antoine was fastidious about standards.

'If we are slovenly just because no one can see us,' he said, 'it will show that we are no better than the animals.'

The way he spoke, it seemed the very future of civilisation rested on the success of our lifestyle for those five or so days. Antoine and I spoke French over breakfast, or at least

I tried to; and we always ate the same butter and honey on bread and drank a loose-leaf blend from a teapot jacketed in its own cosy, which made it stay hot for hours. Then, it was off to the market – always the same market, but following its shifting location in towns across the region.

Antoine declared I should be the one to drive. He liked the idea of having a chauffeur, even if it was only of his old Peugeot 605, which had holes in the footwell and an engine note like a bronchial donkey. The radio and tape deck were broken, too, so Antoine would sing opera, deep and well trained, as I drove.

I'd park up on a crowded verge, and armed with straw tote bags we'd make the rest of our way on foot. The shopping list was always similar: tomatoes and cucumber; potatoes and lettuce; fruit and cheese. But Antoine always found something new to say to the stall holders, his liver-spotted hands squeezing, weighing, judging each day's produce in turn. The only variation was the lunchtime centrepiece, which ranged from Toulouse sausage to sardines to, yes, *poulet rôti*.

Our shopping complete, we'd sit at a pavement café to have the first drink of the day, our lunchtime aperitif. This was white wine, usually, chilled with ice. Often as not, we would be joined by other holidaying Parisians, their straw bags filled with much the same produce as our own.

Lunch was taken at the chateau of Antoine's brother, which was not really a chateau but just a large house, standing alone in the countryside about ten minutes' drive from Domme. It was ugly underneath its wisteria, surrounded by an overgrown meadow and littered inside by a tangle of redundant kitsch and tattered antiques. Its kitchen, once meant for servants, was now the only room that saw any real use. Our market haul, overflowing from the straw bags, would be placed to teeter amid the disorder of its wooden tabletop, while flies flitted back and forth in the dim. Lunch was eaten outside, amid ankle-tickling grass, on a plastic garden table in the western shadow of the great, ugly house, just beside the kitchen door.

The brother, Jean-Marian, as tall as Antoine, looked like an unhealthy French Sean Connery; the younger of the two, he had a rougher, more lascivious quality, accentuated by being a recent divorcee, whose former mistress had now become his fiancée, to whom he now joked he had to find a new mistress in turn.

He shared the house with Robert, a stocky five-foot-nothing manservant, bald and missing teeth. There was also a family friend staying, Nicolas, who was not from quite the same high social milieu as the brothers – he lived in the 18th – but earned his place at the table by having visited every country in Africa.

Though I shared many lunches with these four men over the course of that August, and sometimes with other guests too, there is one in particular that remains clearest in my mind.

On the Friday, Antoine announced to me over breakfast that on that evening the Baron de Bastard would be hosting the first soirée of the season. Because Antoine was speaking in French, however, and the words contained such strangeness and unlikely glamour – the Baron de Bastard! – they knotted together in my head. Antoine spotted my confusion, so continued in English:

'From now on, there will be a soirée almost every night. You didn't think we were here just to get drunk with Robert, did you?'

The rest of the day, anticipation fizzed between the men at Jean-Marian's chateau. It was noticeable even before lunch by the fact that Nicolas had decided to join our trip to the market. He was a small, frail man, but full of passion for all things – specifically, and in no particular order: women, France, Africa and food.

Today, he led the market charge, determined that our lunch be a special one in advance of our collective seasonal debut that evening. He wanted a *cèpes* omelette and as we wandered between the stalls, he rhapsodised non-stop about the fungi.

To the uninitiated, *cèpes* are the Incredible Hulk to the Bruce Banner of field mushrooms. They are super-sized and brawny, of an almost cartoonish aspect, and taste like the forest. Nicolas explained how much their quality was affected by the most minute changes in weather; there must be rainfall, *mais pas trop!* and there must be sunshine, *mais pas trop!* They're also a fleeting magic, sprouting of an August dawn, but barely able to withstand more than a couple of sunsets before they sour and die. Foraging spots are guarded more closely than national secrets, passed down through generations: Nicolas was taken to one once, he said, but blindfolded lest he give away its location.

Back at the chateau, Robert cooked the *cèpes* omelette. When he marched it out of the kitchen, a great bronzed loaf still steaming in its iron skillet, the table burst into spontaneous applause and Robert beamed with toothless pride. But on tucking in, the omelette was oily and overcooked, the *cèpes* cut too small, their flavour smothered by salt. We were just a bunch of blokes eating mushroom and scrambled egg. The mood sagged, all Nicolas's rhapsodising come to naught.

'What do you think, *Crâne d'Oeuf*?' Antoine demanded, and I realised it was up to me, the Englishman, who by definition should never have eaten food as good as this in my life, to save the day. I saw it mattered less how any of this food actually tasted, more the story that we could tell about it.

'*C'est superbe!*' I said, and the table was again all smiles.

Nicolas started talking about French wine – '*La terre en France, Christopher, c'est magique*' – and a red was uncorked to accompany the goat's cheese course that came next. We swilled dregs of rosé from our glasses with thimbles of water and chucked them onto the weedy grass. The red was smoky and old. Too good for the occasion, it finally pushed the meal beyond reproach.

Peaches for dessert. We ate these in silence – their taste of ripe youth – each of us alone with our own thoughts. Jean-Marian lit one of his extra-long cigarettes, dropped ash on his emptied plate. I fetched more rosé from the fridge and we drank it quietly, looking out over the overgrown garden that throbbed with cicadas and afternoon heat.

The meals and memories go on. There was indeed a soirée almost every night. In real chateaux and enormous converted farmhouses, glamorous and heaving with food and wine. Of course we ate some fantastic things, but the spreads laid on were never about showing off. Flavours were traditional, the multi-course structure always rigidly observed. The meals were a way of expressing belonging, both in how they were served and how they were appreciated. By following the codes of the table, by being able to discuss wine and know the origins of a particular dish, so this elite group tacitly affirmed their culture and their right to exist within it.

I also met other people my own age. The next generation of the 16th, here in their collective country seats, with whom I grouped at the soirées and soon started heading out with on adventures all of our own. We raced out in beat-up old cars across fields of sunflower and maize, past guttering sprinklers, alongside limestone cliffs and under the shadow of castles to barbecues, nightclubs and midnight swims. Even among all this youthful fun, however, disciplines were observed. We would still always have an aperitif, still *sit down* for dinner, still have more than one course; and I was still treated like a heretic if I sliced the brie in the wrong direction.

It was delightful. And for me, fresh from completing my degree in anthropology, as fascinating and distinct a culture from my own as some Amazon tribe. I learned then the true pleasures of ritual in eating, of how a meal correctly observed can be much more sustaining than a mere indulgence of whims.

And regardless of how late I'd been out, regardless of how much alcohol I'd consumed the night before, there would be Antoine resolutely booming up at my window at eight in the morning, demanding that we share breakfast and I drive him to market. Every morning, I obliged, though maybe with less spring in my step than I'd had at the start of the holiday.

Soon, Antoine had found a new nickname for me, one

that delighted him even more than *Crane d'Oeuf*. To him I now was, and would forever remain, the 'Lazy Drunk'.

Once I moved to Paris, to begin with I would see Antoine over lunch every couple of weeks or so, so that he could check I had not begun to let standards slip. These lunches were bistro affairs, taken across the road from his office in the middle of the workday, though we never forewent wine or had fewer than three courses. Most of the lunches ran close to two hours. As my own life in the city became busier, however, so these meetings became more infrequent, to the point that I was surprised to receive a phone call from Antoine early one December, asking if I could help serve the wine at his Christmas party. As always, refusal was not an option.

Serving the wine at Antoine's also meant helping to reorder his cellar, which I was to do on the afternoon before the party. It felt so different from the first time I had been to the stylishly shabby ground-floor apartment on Ranelagh. I had graduated from being a foreign guest to the help. This may not sound like an upgrade, but I realised among this culture it in fact implied a kind of drawing closer. And Antoine was now leading me to his own holy of holies: the place where he kept his wine.

Down in the basement of his building was a whole room, dry and warm, and kept under lock and key; flanked by similar rooms that no doubt housed the wine collections of other 16th residents. My job was to take the bottles we would be serving that evening upstairs, then replace them with a younger vintage that had just been delivered to be used for Christmas soirées to come. Close to sixty people were expected that evening, and to each at least one bottle was assigned.

'Three in your case, I imagine,' said Antoine.

The cellar was stacked floor-to-ceiling, mostly with wines from the same Saint-Émilion vineyard, stretching back in vintages to 1993. It was the oldest bottles that were to be drunk tonight, and Antoine started giving me precise instructions as to when to uncork the first batch, and how many should be left before I started opening the second. It was essential, he said, that this wine be given time to breathe.

Once I'd taken tonight's bottles upstairs, I started to restock the shelves with the new delivery: a 2008 batch of the same wine. Antoine and I did this together, in silence: the satisfying crack as crates were prised open, the clink of glass against glass. Until finally, ceremoniously, Antoine took down the slate above the newly stocked shelf, rubbed out the old date and replaced it with the more recent one. Then, for a long minute, he stood back and observed his wine.

This is who I am, his features said: it's what I've achieved with my life. It wasn't the wine, I think, but what it represented: pleasure, a certain refinement, a sense of belonging in this world, of being a man of means. Plus, I imagined, some small certainty for the future. There were enough bottles in the cellar to last another fifteen years of Christmas soirées, and even if he did not make it that far himself, there was a guarantee that at least the wine I was unloading now would; and even if the world was tangibly worse, it – the wine – would be better. Antoine's face, I felt at that moment, was that of a man looking at his own mortality and not being displeased with what he saw.

The guests started to arrive just after seven. It was the same *haut-bourgeois* crowd I had first encountered during my excursion here as a teenager, though after my Dordogne summer and several months in Paris, I was able to regard them more as individuals rather than a singular, elegantly dressed mass. Here was Nicolas, looking tanned and at ease, freshly returned from Senegal, he said, where he had eaten mangoes like I would not believe. And there was Jean-Marian, dashing in a lemon-coloured jumper, with a much younger blonde woman on his arm – was she his fiancée, or a new mistress? I couldn't be sure. There were Antoine's daughters too, less intimidating now, but still just as teasing, calling me 'Lazy Drunk' like their father.

I was not to serve the Saint-Émilion first, I'd been told, as it was to accompany the food; to serve it first would have been sacrilege. Instead, there were bottles of champagne in a great tub of ice water beneath the makeshift bar at which I worked. I took them out, popping and pouring with as much speed and grace as I could muster, as suddenly more and more guests began to arrive.

Soon, there was a queue trailing away from my table, and no matter how fast I poured or expressed that yes, I was settling in nicely in Paris, and hadn't it been fabulous that summer in the Dordogne, the queue just didn't seem to be going down. Before long, there were also people arriving for refills.

'Lazy Drunk!' Antoine's policing voice sounded over the clamour, and he was advancing towards me; he looked more on edge than I'd ever seen him. 'Come on, you can't spend all night talking. You are *monsieur le barman*! You have a job!'

But now he was at my side, uncorking more bottles and

serving fresh champagne to the queuing guests. With two of us, it did not take long for everyone to get a drink, and when the line was finally gone, Antoine turned to me and laughed.

'What were all these people doing turning up at once? No one has the manners to be late! It's bloody ridiculous, *n'est-ce pas*? I think you are allowed to have one *coupe* of champagne for yourself now,' he continued. 'But not too much. Soon you will have to start serving the red.'

I worked hard all the rest of the evening. Antoine had got caterers in to prepare dinner, but I still had to spend my night waitering, collecting empty glasses and bottles, uncorking more Saint-Émilion in anticipation of demand, wandering out among the crowds to offer top-ups and catch threads of conversation.

The soirée ended just after midnight, the last guests swaying drunk and satisfied to their homes on the quiet Christmastime streets of the 16th.

Antoine was slumped in a tattered armchair, surveying the silence and the mild disarray in which his guests had left the apartment. The energy of the party still vibrated faintly on the air. He had a glass in his hand, and on the table beside him, the last, emptied bottle of the 1993 Saint-Émilion. His expression was one of tired satisfaction.

'Well done, Lazy Drunk,' he said, looking up as I approached. 'If you were to work like this every night, we would have to again rethink your name.'

I sat down on a chair next to his, exhausted, realising how important these soirées were for him; a chance to prove his civilisation and his worth.

'Did you try the wine?' Antoine asked, eyeing the ruby liquid in his glass. '*C'était magnifique, non?*'

I was about to say that it was, though it occurred to me then that I had not found time to try even one glass.

Antoine died from cancer in 2018. I had known he'd been sick for a while, and though I spoke with him on the phone, I could not quite bring myself to visit him in hospital over his last weeks.

Life had already taken me in a different direction from the 16th set by that time. I saw the friends I had made there sporadically during my first couple of years in the city, and though I went to a couple more of Antoine's Christmas parties (as a guest this time), gradually we drifted apart. But there was more to not seeing Antoine in his hospital bed than just that.

He was a man of pride and physical stature who relished his social position and the respect it brought him. I was afraid he would not want me to see him so diminished, plugged into who knows how many tubes, vulnerable and dying. To be sure, there was also something selfish to my not going as well: I wanted to preserve the playful, robust image of him, enjoying life, laughing, getting his way.

Back, then, to the Église Notre-Dame de l'Assomption, where that year, Antoine's funeral stood as a dour opener to the *rentrée* season, when Parisians come back to the city from their August pause, and the city's real life gets under way once again. Antoine's coffin was almost comically large, and it made me smile to think how even in death, his presence almost inappropriately dominated the space.

His three daughters were there, weeping freely throughout, and his wife too, who retained a calm poise. There was, though, no sign of Jean-Marian, and it was only through the priest's eulogy that I learned that he had died, too, of a heart attack the year before. There was no Nicolas either, and I wondered if he was dead too. It was possible that he just hadn't been able to make it, that he was back in Africa, eating mangoes, but there was no one to ask.

I cried as the oversized coffin was carried from the church. In part, I was crying for myself, for the part of my life that Antoine's death took with him. But I was crying also for the man, for the loss of a human soul who had been passionate and sometimes difficult, and who seemed to have found the life he wanted and yet also, I fancied, only ever fleetingly felt content: in the midst of a good meal, when people's behaviour matched exactly what he asked of them, contemplating his cellar of wine. I was crying for the man I had loved.

Red Wine

Serves 4

Ingredients:

2 bottles vintage red wine (pref. Saint-Émilion)

Serve with:

Aperitif (saucisson and nut wine suggested)

1 litre simple rosé wine

A five-course meal (*Entrée, Plat, Salade, Fromage, Dessert*)

Bread

Ritual

Time

I gazed out at the wet autumnal avenue. My 'meal' for the 16th had to be wine, I realised. A foodstuff that could strad-dle decades, and inspire ritual. Even among heathens. For

84

the 16th arrondissement is primarily about just that: ritual. Within that ritual is a deference to the world that has come before and that will outlast the present moment. The food is important, yes, but more important is how you speak about it, the order you eat it in, how it is not a fleeting carnality but the performance of an enduring world.

Better, then, if it could be a bottle of the same 2008 Saint-Émilion I had once unloaded in Antoine's cellar, which I realised now would be the same age as the 1993 vintage we had opened that evening. It was an uncorked summer that I dreamed might taste of belonging. And I dreamed and I dreamed ... Not just of the Saint-Émilion, but of how to drink it ...

Open the bottle a good hour ahead of time, with a gathering of friends. And while it is breathing, serve a *vin de noix*, just like the ones they drink in the Dordogne, chilled by single cubes of ice, plus a little *saucisson* sliced as thin as silk. Then, seat your guests at a large wooden table to eat thick slices of beef heart tomato, herb-speckled and lashed with balsamic sauce. With a little rosé? Why not? Now, clear the plates but keep the same cutlery; serve *poulet rôti* and roast potatoes with well-buttered green beans. Now serve the Saint-Émilion: a wine heady and thick with all the tasting notes it's meant to possess. Next comes the salad course, eaten with fresh vinaigrette off plates still cluttered by chicken bones. Then the cheese, ripe as autumn. Open a second bottle of the Saint-Émilion. This one will taste even better. Thanks to the cheese, thanks to being a little drunk, thanks to being sated. Thanks to dining slowly, in the way that you're meant to, in the way that makes you part of a bigger world. Dessert. Not much. A peach, a little cream. Then coffee, and a cigarette ashed languorously into an emptied glass, over the tannin of the past. *Fin.*

Except something told me, as I sat staring from the windows of that empty, expensive café on the avenue Mozart, that I was not yet ready for this meal. I was too near the start of my journey. Here was a feast to look forward to, which I was still working my way back to earning. For the time being, then, it remained a dream.

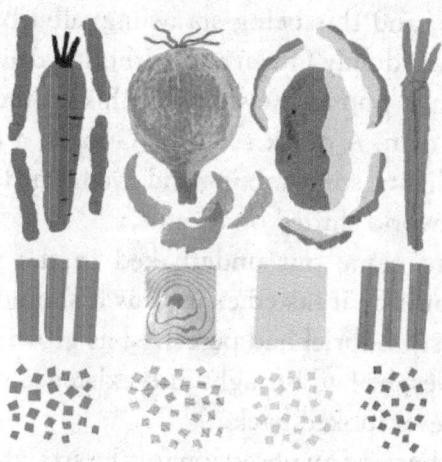

15ème arrondissement

Should Gabriel Hernandez one day be numbered among the best chefs in the world – and I wouldn't bet against it – then let it be known that it started with banana bread.

That's what the American culinary student told me when I met him at a cooking demonstration in Paris's 15th, at the headquarters of Le Cordon Bleu, the school where he had enrolled just a few months earlier to pursue his dream.

It was a dream born one humid summer's day in Florida in the mid-2010s, Gabriel said, when he was bored and more importantly, hungry. Sometimes when you're in that mood only a very particular snack will do. He longed for banana bread, except there was none of the usual store-bought stuff in the house, and this being sprawling suburban America and Gabriel aged only fifteen and without a driver's licence, he couldn't just pop to the shops. So his mother suggested he make his own. A quick scour of Google, a raid of cupboard ingredients, some mixing and oven time later, and for Gabriel, the world shifted on its axis.

The bread came out underbaked in the middle, but around the outside it tasted exactly as it should. A product that previously Gabriel had perceived as growing on supermarket shelves, he had brought into existence with his own hands. He never looked back.

Cooking became an obsession for the straight-A student. He was a good kid, the son of Peruvian immigrants who'd been brought up to understand that America owed no one a living, and he didn't shirk his studies. He even won a scholarship to study marine biology at Florida State. But all that time Gabriel was either making or thinking about food. He found a side job at a diner, spent his mornings slicing avocado and frying eggs by the hundred. It was thankless, gruelling work, but his worst day at the grill was better than his best in class. He tussled between ambition and responsibility – there were kids who'd kill for that scholarship. After two years, however, the writing was on the kitchen wall.

Gabriel quit university to work full time at a Sicilian restaurant in Tallahassee. He put his head down and started to set money aside – because now that he'd decided to fully embrace his ambition, there was only one place he could think of to go.

Named after the blue ribbons worn by an elite order of Renaissance knights known for their decadent feasts, and founded by a cooking magazine in 1895, Le Cordon Bleu is now the largest network of hospitality colleges in the world. Paris's 15th arrondissement is its ground zero.

Opinions are divided about this most populous of Paris neighbourhoods. For most residents of the French capital, it is a byword for dullness, home to middle-class Parisians who are, on the whole, not quite as wealthy or stuck in their ways as those living in the neighbouring 16th. It is also, however, extremely varied, with pockets of modern commerce, distinctly lower-income areas, as well as some of the most expensive real estate anywhere in France . I've known people to really get their backs up defending the 15th's reputation for being boring. 'The whole of Paris is there,' a French friend told me once, though I suppose another way of expressing the same idea would be to say that the 15th is Paris neutral. In any case, for my purposes, the fact that the arrondissement is home to the world's most famous cooking school meant that, when it came to searching its streets for culinary knowledge, like Gabriel, I didn't hesitate for an instant.

I'd imagined the Cordon Bleu would be housed in a building steeped in history, full of tall hats, copper pans, white tiles and naked flames. What I found was an airport lounge, with better catering.

The new, purpose-built premises opened in 2016, when the school moved from a 15th backstreet to the Quai André-Citroën, just a few hundred metres down the Seine from the Eiffel Tower. From the outside, the building is a three-storey jumble of concrete, metal and glass – lightly postmodern; unmistakably corporate. Inside, this aesthetic continues. Before I even made it to the front desk, I had passed a gift shop and a practice kitchen. The latter is a glass-walled display tank occupied by tourists who pay upwards of €200 per head for a half-day's tuition. The Cordon Bleu has not got where it has by selling itself cheap.

In the high-ceilinged lobby, a UN's worth of international flags signalled the continued pre-eminence of French cooking's philosophy around the world. No matter how many bemoan that food in France is not what it was, there remains no argument that, when it comes to the principles of fine dining, French cuisine is still the mother, and Paris the source. The superabundance of the natural French larder, the provenance of culinary superstars from La Varenne to Escoffier, and the forces of colonialism all played their part. More than anything, though, it seemed to me here, the secret was the French willingness to take as high-minded an approach to food as they do to many other pursuits, both in regard to eating and making. The French perfected and codified techniques not just for individuals but for the whole teams it takes to make a feast. So today, when kids from Mumbai to Glasgow to Tallahassee dream of kitchen glory, Paris remains the marinade in which they want to soak.

When I sat down next to Gabriel at the public cooking tutorial that morning – unusually, I thought, dedicated to Ecuadorian cuisine – he was just another fresh face among a fresh-faced crowd. In fact, aside from being noticeably well groomed, his most distinctive trait was how undistinctive he was: average height, average build, gelled black hair and dark eyes, a complexion that could do with more Vitamin D. We offered each other polite smiles, then it was all eyes front.

It was the most beautiful classroom I had ever seen. A cool aluminium worktop ran stage-like across the front, its surface overlooked by a mirror so that it could be seen anywhere in the room. And as though this wasn't visibility enough, a panopticon of cameras were trained on the hands of the performing chefs, each broadcasting live feeds to six ceiling-hung screens.

The effect was of a dizzying multiplication of images, and what images they were! The chefs in their pristine whites, the rough texture of uncooked produce against the worktop sheen, and the serried sharpened tools of the kitchen trade hanging behind. I imagined a photography series: '*Haute cuisine* in the Age of Mechanical Reproduction.'

Despite this slick appearance, the demonstration was chaotic. Delivered almost simultaneously in Spanish, English and French, it taxed my concentration, and those of the others in the room, many of whom kept up a low murmur throughout. It turned out to be a corporate endeavour by a firm trying to sell Ecuadorian produce in Europe. Well, no such thing as a free lunch.

Still, we did get fed. Crab crème brûlée, a stew built from a plantain-based *mirepoix*, dragon fruit sorbet and Arriba chocolate mousse. How French it all was at its foundation: another country's ingredients were having their flavour and meaning awoken by the Gallic culinary mind.

When it was done, I overheard Gabriel and another student talking about what they had just seen with the enthusiastic pretension that is characteristic of those early in their life's vocation. It was how I'd spoken once upon a time, when I talked to my friends about books.

'I liked the *mirepoix*,' Gabriel was saying, 'but I felt it was playing safe. Like it was comfort food pretending to be *haute cuisine*.'

I had my in.

*

Since starting at the school, Gabriel's days begin at 4.45 a.m. Up, shower in his tiny apartment in Issy-les-Moulineaux, a suburb just south of the 15th. Then, an hour ironing his uniform and readying his mind for the day ahead.

If he hurries, he can make the walk to school in forty minutes. Gabriel said he is on too tight a budget to take the metro. The money he earned from that Sicilian restaurant, even augmented by the small loan his parents could afford, will only stretch so far. Fortunately, he likes Paris at that hour: the city not quite awake, the boulangeries filling the street with their smell. It's too early to buy a croissant, though, which is OK. Gabriel prefers to keep a light stomach. Breakfast is a Red Bull, which he drinks as he walks.

He gets to the Cordon Bleu when it opens at 6.30, and changes into his whites. Students are strictly forbidden from wearing the uniform on the streets. It's a question of respect, of the kitchen's sanctity, of hygiene. Then, there's another twenty minutes hanging around with other students before heading to class for seven. Lessons start at 7.30, but it's obligatory to turn up fifteen minutes before. Gabriel likes to be there fifteen minutes before that so he can bag a seat near the front.

'Are the other students as keen as you?' I asked.

'Oh yes,' said Gabriel. 'Just not all of them.'

He was telling me all this about himself with an unguarded innocence that felt more the product of good manners rather than any particular desire for self-promotion. His words were precise, even slightly robotic.

'There are also some very wealthy people who just want

to be better home cooks,' he said, 'but anyone who wants to go on to become a chef, you have to get ready. Because these are the demands of the real world.'

First class is instruction. In a classroom like the one I'd sat in, with its mirrors and its screens, and banks of white-coated students sitting in groggy morning silence, a professional chef takes them through the paces of assembling luxuriant evening fare.

'That's when the stress starts,' Gabriel said. 'You're following the trussing, the seasoning, or whatever, and you're desperately trying to make notes. Because you'll have to make this later, and you'll only have one shot.'

Most demos last three hours. They consist of two recipes drawn from the great vault of French classics, from *saumon meunière* to *oeufs cocotte*. And for Gabriel, it's all observed on an empty stomach. The lesson doesn't end until 11 a.m. Six hours awake, and he still hasn't eaten.

Then, it's up to the test kitchens to make for himself the dishes he has just seen. Kitchens that are more like laboratories: overwhelmingly silver metal, obsessively pristine. (I blagged a free tour of the school to see for myself. Easy enough when even the shortest, most basic courses start at €12,800: my guide was as enthusiastic as an estate agent on commission.)

Assessment starts the moment Gabriel crosses the threshold. Even the cleanliness of his uniform is judged. Any stain is a stain on his performance. He has only three chef's jackets and only time to clean them on Sundays; that's three strikes a week to avoid spatter, but so far Gabriel's mark is near perfect in this field.

'It's all about upholding the standard,' he told me with

an uncommon flicker of pride. 'If you're a messy worker, you're never going to get far in a kitchen.'

The practical is like TV game show cooking: rushing to the store cupboard, working against the clock, constantly being observed by teachers who circle like pedantic sharks. It's not enough to make food that tastes and looks like what's just been shown; you have to make it in the correct (French) way. There may be plenty of ways to *dépouiller un chat*, but only one is accepted here. And you have to keep your workstation clean, maintain a positive attitude, not forget even the smallest of details.

'You get used to working ahead,' Gabriel explained. 'I'm planning three, four steps past whatever I'm doing, looking at my notes, praying I get it right.'

Sometimes, his prayers are answered. Everything comes out as it should. More often there is a minor flaw. Less than beautiful plating, a split in a chicken breast's skin, a forgotten oyster: Gabriel related these mistakes to me as if he wanted absolution for his sins. Such flaws can ruin his day, his week. There is no praise in Cordon Bleu for good enough. At least Gabriel gets to eat what he has made. Most days, the only proper meals he has come from the test kitchen. Though if he hasn't cooked them right, he is also eating his defeat.

Classes end between 5 and 6 p.m. Gabriel makes the forty-minute trek back to the tiny apartment in Issy where he will watch further tutorials on his laptop, which are about three hours long, though Gabriel likes to pause, rewind, make notes. Most nights, it will be nine at least before he has time for himself. And with that time, he practises what he has learned.

Gabriel's home set-up is the truest Parisian artist's garret

I have known. The apartment came with an electric stove, but this trips the fuse for the whole place when he turns it on. So he has bought himself a hotplate and a table-top oven. He uses his desk as a work surface, and has only the tiniest of sinks. For saucepans he has five ancient copper pots that he picked up from an antiques market the week he arrived, and for knives ... suffice it to say, Gabriel has a few.

'I love knives,' he told me, 'and more than anything, I love making them sharp.'

This impulse was born partly out of the love for perfection that runs through everything Gabriel does; and partly because good knives are the foundation to all professional cooking. Knife skills are both the first lesson taught at the Cordon Bleu, and the one that must be returned to most in the students' spare time.

'The principle is simple,' Gabriel said, 'whether you're sharpening or cutting. You start slow, and only when you've got the technique exactly right do you speed up.'

Gabriel spends endless nights in that tiny apartment, tirelessly flipping knives against his honing steel in firm diagonal sweeps; each lightning pass making full contact with the whole length of the blade. Then, he loads up some ignorable TV show on his computer and works through different cuts.

'I use potatoes,' he said, 'because they're cheap and easy to practise on.'

He pronounced the names for these different cuts that he'd been taught with precise reverence: *carré, julienne, paysanne, brunoise*. He had not yet learned French, but these old kitchen expressions tripped from his tongue with familiar ease.

How many potatoes did he get through in a week?

95

Hundreds.

And what did he do with them afterwards?

Some he ate, he said, the rest he threw away; literally thousands of perfect potato cubes or batons or discs discarded into the trash: the collateral damage of Gabriel's journey towards mastery of his ephemeral art.

'So, then,' I asked at last, 'why Paris?'

It was the only question that Gabriel had trouble answering.

'It's the quality of the chefs you get here that is completely different,' he said after a pause. 'I ... I don't mean that the chefs you get in America are bad, but ... It's also the exposure you get to the city and the language. The inspiration you get from just eating the food.'

He looked at me imploringly, like this was the answer I'd wanted; the words sounded like they'd come from the Cordon Bleu prospectus. But we both knew by now how little Gabriel had seen of Paris, that he could not speak French, and that the only restaurant he'd been to since moving here was a Thai place he'd visited the week he arrived.

'I mean, it's the Cordon Bleu!' Gabriel concluded. 'You're learning French cooking techniques in France. What could be better than that?'

Few are the nights when Gabriel is in bed much before one. He sets his alarm for 4.45 a.m. so he can repeat all this again tomorrow. Then, he crashes into a sleep too short and deep for dreams.

Gabriel Hernandez does have dreams, though, of the waking kind. They are for the future, for the kinds of things he is going to learn, for the kitchens he will work in, and, whisper it, for the kitchen he might one day run himself.

It will be a place that encompasses elements of American, Peruvian and French cuisine, and perhaps other ways of cooking that Gabriel has not yet discovered. Whatever he cooks, though, he knows it has to tell a story.

He told me this in no uncertain terms.

'Cooking is about story.'

And he knows that studying at Cordon Bleu, though important, is just one chapter of his own story, just as he knows that there are many years of hard graft ahead. But that's OK; he's more than willing to put them in. Because even the most basic narrative enchantment of cooking has not yet left him. Every dish he makes is still a wonder – that he brought something new into an unsuspecting world.

Whatever Gabriel Hernandez's story turns out to be, let it be known that it started with banana bread.

Ratatouille

Serves 4 as a main

Ingredients:

2 aubergines

Olive oil

Salt

2 red onions

1 carrot

1 celery stick

2 green peppers

3 garlic cloves

500g fresh medium tomatoes

Pepper

2 sprigs of thyme

2 courgettes

1 sharp knife

It wasn't Gabriel who suggested I make ratatouille.

Listen, I wasn't going to insult the kid by bringing up the dish that the majority of non-cooks now associate with Parisian cuisine for no good reason apart from that Pixar film about a preternaturally talented rat. A film that, while brilliant, speaks far more about the general challenges of an artist than it does the laborious graft any chef must go through before they start to create. Furthermore, ratatouille is not, as at least is made clear in the film itself, fine dining. If you don't fancy throwing away a hundred potatoes, though, it's one of the best dishes there is with which to practise knife cuts.

When I had set out to discover the Cordon Bleu, I had imagined that I might learn some complex and rarefied expression of the great Gallic larder. The secrets behind a Hollandaise sauce, perhaps, or how to stew the perfect *coq au vin*. My time with Gabriel, though, had been humbling, and returning to the sorry wedges of metal I called knives in my home kitchen, I realised I had to go back to basics. So first, I sat with those so-called knives and a block of seldom-used honing steel, making the same hard diagonal strokes Gabriel had spoken of, moving slowly, getting it right, until at last I had tools fit for purpose.

Then, I applied myself to *carré* (literally 'square') two aubergines.

In simple terms, this meant dicing them into large cubes. For this cut, Gabriel had counselled first slicing off the aubergine's rounded edges, so that they resembled two white bricks on my chopping block. My newly sharpened blade cut through their flesh like, well, a knife.

I chopped in three directions. First, three horizontal swathes, then coming down over the top, length and width-ways: piercing the aubergines with the tip of my knife, then moving it through towards its weightier hilt, fingers mindfully clawed in that grip which chefs will tell you prevents you from cutting yourself – if you get it right. I'm fairly sure this is a lie, though on this occasion I did not cut myself slicing the aubergines.

I fried them off in olive oil and salt and set them aside. This was my one concession to the Cordon Bleu-sanctioned way of making a ratatouille, which states that all the elements should be cooked separately, before being combined. Tonight, however, was primarily about the knife skills, plus a winter storm had blown up outside; I wanted to cook my vegetables into a well-acquainted stew.

Next – and ratatouille purists look away now – I sliced a *mirepoix*. This is the technical way of saying I diced two onions, a carrot and a stick of celery. The essentials of this were the same as the aubergine. I followed Gabriel's advice to make sure I could at least lay each of the ingredients flat before chopping, and this time made my cuts as close to each other as I could.

Mirepoix is not traditional in ratatouille, and there are whole essays that could be written about it in its own right. In essence, though, it is a combination of sliced vegetables (usually, but not always, the three I was using; in the Ecuadorian cooking demonstration, of course, they'd used plantain) cooked as the base of a stock, soup, stew or sauce. It was invented – or at least codified – by a chef working for the Duke of Mirepoix in the eighteenth century, and must be cooked slowly so that the vegetables' sweetness is released.

I threw this into my casserole dish, and placed it over a low heat.

Next, I julienned two green peppers, which is to say deseeded and cut them into long, thin strips. No one knows where the term *julienne* came from, but its first recorded use was in a 1722 cookbook called *Le Cuisinier Royal*. Usually, it's used to add texture to salads; here, I just wanted another cut.

There was no special trick to all this knife work, no magic key that Gabriel had revealed. It was just a question of a sharp blade; slow, careful progress; and keeping my fingers out of the way. And then, practice. I thought of the speed he could work at. All that time he had spent in the pursuit of saving time. The julienned pepper went into the pot.

Next came three cloves of garlic. With a smaller knife, I cut this into a fine *brunoise* – near-microscopic cubes – so that its pungency would seep more evenly through the dish. Then, I 'rough-chopped' a half-kilo of tomatoes – a codified term, meaning cut any which way, but making sure all the slices are more or less the same size.

I threw the rough-chopped tomatoes, the fine *brunoise* garlic and my cooked *carré* aubergines into the mix; sprinkled in salt, pepper and thyme; glugged in some more olive oil, and waited for it all to reduce.

My two dinner guests, Albert and Alberto, were both being uncharacteristically polite about my literal butchering of this southern dish. Well, Albert, who was born in Provence, mentioned that this wasn't how his mother made ratatouille, and Italian Alberto said he only really knew the Sicilian version, caponata, but apart from that ...

Finally, I paysanned a courgette. This 'peasant' cut

prescribes following the natural shape of the vegetable, slicing it out as thin discs which, in a personal flourish, I laid out in a swirl on top of my sauce, splashed over more olive oil and thyme, and then I slid the casserole into the oven to bake.

I told Albert and Alberto about my encounter with Gabriel. I had set out to search for someone who had come to Paris chasing its myths in the way the three of us once had, I explained, but instead I felt that I had found a person who was wrapped up in a different dream.

'How do you mean?' asked Alberto.

There was the fact of how much it was costing him, how hard he was working. It wasn't some abstract lifestyle choice he was chasing, but a concrete, all-encompassing skill. It needed a less subtle fantasy to sustain it – particularly given that, from an outsider's perspective, it was hard not to believe the students at the Cordon Bleu were getting screwed.

There are plenty of other catering colleges in Paris with equally prestigious lists of alumni that can be accessed for almost a third of the Cordon Bleu's price. True, they might not have the live-feed TV screens, or the swanky building, or the famous brand, but they teach the same cuts. And €33,400 – as Gabriel's course was costing – is a lot to pay to get into an industry where starting salaries aren't much higher than minimum wage.

'So it's not just Paris that I think Gabriel's here for,' I said, 'it's something bigger.'

'Bigger than Paris? It's impossible,' Alberto mocked.

'It came together for me when I asked him which was the best make of knife to choose,' I continued. 'He said that everyone was different, that chefs choose the knife that speaks to them. He said it was like Harry Potter and wands.'

Alberto laughed, 'So you mean, for him, Cordon Bleu is a sort of Hogwarts?'

'I do,' I said. I could see how, for Gabriel, there was an alchemical magic in cooking – every time he took something out of the oven, he felt he might have turned lead into gold.

'Ah, so these different words for knife cuts are like spells,' Albert added.

Was it stretching the metaphor? I don't think so. There was little spectacular in what I had just done; even the most average of home cooks knows how to slice vegetables in different ways. Yet by learning those shapes' specific, sometimes archaic, unexplained names, and training yourself to carve them as fast as they can be spoken, the whole dish is elevated: its deepest qualities known only to a select few. And knife cuts were just the beginning. Paris was a place to imbibe the language and ritual and history of cooking: those same things that Antoine and the other people I had known in the 16th still so respected; the story that lives latent in dishes before they are even cooked. The name Cordon Bleu, thanks to its background, its location and its relentless self-promotion, is among the biggest incantations of them all.

Out came my ratatouille, crisp on top, bubbling beneath. We ate it with the hurly-burly wind howling outside, its sharp summer flavours thickened to wintertime warmth; its geometries still separate but also, magically, one.

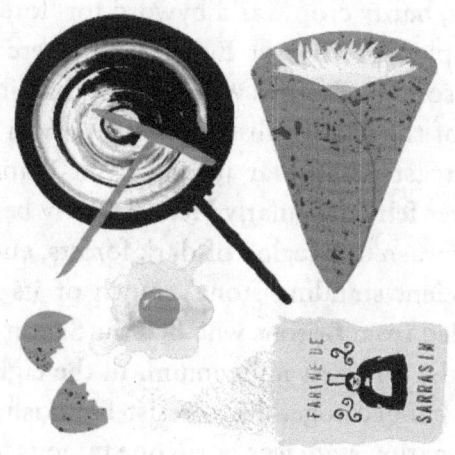

14ème arrondissement

Sometimes it's harder to know when a story starts. For the crêpes of Montparnasse, in Paris's 14th arrondissement, it was somewhere between the 1850s and the mists of time. Splitting the difference, I'll say the Crusades.

The holy wars of the twelfth and thirteenth centuries were not only about Western Europeans exporting genocidal Christianity and poor hygiene to the Levant: they stole stuff and brought it home too. Along with the knock-off crowns of thorns and Templar gold that filled their saddlebags on the return journey, there were seeds. Some claim that buckwheat is still called *sarrasin* (literally, Saracen) in French because of these origins, and though the very name of this fast-growing, hardy crop was a byword for 'foreign', it was soon being planted all over Europe. Nowhere did it find more fertile soil, the Bretons will tell you, than in Brittany – on account of the relative absence in Brittany of fertile soil.

This overcast peninsular jutting from France's north-west has never felt particularly French. Partly because, for a long time, it wasn't. A region of dark forests, endless coast-line and ancient standing stones, much of its population was descended from Britons who fled the Saxon invasion of England in the mid-first millennium. In the eighth century, these exiles banded together to resist Frankish expansion, and a proto-nation state was born: one famous for its Celtic customs, its own pantheon of pagan-inflected saints, and its crêpes.

The legend goes that not so long after *sarrasin* was intro-duced to Brittany, one of those happy accidents occurred that have dominated tales of culinary invention from coffee to the Flaming Homer. A young peasant girl was taking her *sarrasin* porridge from the fire when some of it slopped over the side and spattered onto a hot stone. There, it began to crisp, and for the first time ever that hot, earthy scent, which can still be smelled today both across Brittany and on certain streets of the 14th arrondissement, was birthed into the world. We can fill in the moment when the peasant girl peeled her new creation off the hot stone and thought: I bet this would go really well with some ham, egg and cheese.

Except, obviously she didn't. Because it's only a legend. Human beings have been cooking batter on hot rocks since the start of civilisation (see: the mists of time) and in their early days, *sarrasin* crêpes were probably treated as more of a bread-like accompaniment, to be dipped in stews rather than eaten with a filling. While I'm at it, I should mention that the Crusader origin story is also disputed. Other scholars/food historians claim that *sarrasin* was introduced to France from the Far East several centuries later through more traditional patterns of trade, its name being a reference to its dark colour rather than its literal origin.

All this to say that, at some point after the twelfth century but before the nineteenth, *sarrasin* crêpes became a part of the Breton diet. And when the first railroads were built in the mid-1800s, and Bretons started migrating to Paris in large numbers, they brought their staple food with them. This was also, by complete coincidence, the same time that a particular watermill, deep in the Breton hinterland, not far from the castle town of Josselin, first started to grind.

The bus dropped me off at a lonesome shelter under skies the colour of wet slate. A cold country wind gusted through the empty street, buffeting the compact stone houses and dragging sodden leaves over the cracked tarmac. In the distance a couple of tractors were beetling across fields of black earth. A grapeshot of starlings whorled overhead. I wasn't in Paris any more.

I checked maps on my phone, the screen mottled with drops in the thin rain. I'd come as far as public transport would take me, and now had three miles to walk over farmland.

It had seemed like a good idea at the time – back when I was nestled in the extreme cosiness of La Crêperie de Josselin on the rue du Montparnasse, kilometre zero for Breton culture in Paris. Every inch of the restaurant's wood-panelled walls was decorated in regional ephemera: portraits of Duchess

Anne – Brittany's most beloved historical figure, seducer
of the king and defender of Breton independence – doily-
covered lampshades, porcelain figurines in traditional dress.
I'd had a bellyful of cooked *sarrasin*, the doors were snugly
closed on the winter weather outside, and the restaurant's
owner – a second-generation Parisian Breton, gym-bodied
and enthusiastic – had agreed to talk me through the art of
the crêpe.

They were simple things to make, he'd insisted; the trick
was in the ingredients, really. Good Breton flour was essential, preferably sourced from the Moulin de Carmenais, not
far from the town for which La Crêperie de Josselin was
named, which provided the *sarrasin* not only for his establishment but for nearly all the proper crêperies in the 14th.

'If you're really interested in making crêpes, you should
give them a visit,' he said. 'See the full process.'

The moment we'd stopped talking, I checked ticket
prices to darkest Brittany and found a journey in just two
days' time that was almost criminally cheap. So what that it
would take close to eight hours and require two changes? So
many of Paris's food traditions have been brought into the
city from elsewhere; here was a chance to follow at least one
of them back along its provenance. Not just the tradition
either, but the principal ingredient and the process behind its
creation. I could consider the journey of *sarrasin* flour as a
mirror to the journey of Breton migrants themselves.

I tried calling the Moulin de Carmenais to see if anyone
there would be interested in showing me round, but got no
answer. Hmm. I checked the tickets again. They weren't
going to stay this cheap for long. Ah, hell. I booked them.

So now here I was in the middle of a freezing nowhere,

with a hike across quagmire fields ahead and no guarantee of a welcome when I reached the other side. I zipped up my coat and strode into the spitting rain.

As I walked, I considered the fields around me, fallow now, though still littered in places with dead traces of the crops they'd grown: husks of maize, the shorn stems of corn. There was no *sarrasin* to be seen. Buckwheat is a plant of the high summer, producing its yield in under twelve weeks; resilient, in part, because it grows faster than weeds.

I imagined this landscape of gentle undulation in high summer, alive with the massed pretty green stems and white flowers of *sarrasin*, the clouds reduced to just a few puffs of scudding shadow, and the distant farm buildings flashing bright in the sun. Well, I had to do something to keep my spirits up. Today, the vista was as bleak as nature could make it. Grey on grey, becoming very grey later.

The town of Josselin had hardly been better. It was a beautiful town, yes: built on the bend of a river and dominated by one of the most opulent chateaux in France – no small boast in a country of opulent chateaux – it was nevertheless marked by an out-of-season desolation. Its streets deserted, its shops shuttered. I'd hoped to grab a crêpe for lunch, to try one close to the source. But no. All the crêperies were closed until the spring and the tourists returned. I'd started to get a feeling for why so many Bretons might want to leave.

They hadn't had it easy when they did. Not at first. Relative latecomers to Paris in terms of migration from other parts of France, the first Bretons in the city fast became the most marginalised of classes. They were separated from the

Parisians by their Celtic-derived language, their religion, which tended towards the brutally devout, and their reputation: Brittany was regarded back then as a savage and mysterious land, its people not much better than barbarians. Added to this, many of the better paid, skilled jobs had already been filled, leaving Breton men to search for whatever unskilled labour they could, and Breton women to work in domestic service.

Yet still they came. Lured for the same reasons that migrants have been in the past and will continue to be in the future, by the great shining dream of Paris: the opportunity and freedoms that it promised. Unusually, the majority of Breton migrants were women. Less bound to the land by agriculture, many also sought an escape from the shackles of marriage. Paris offered a refuge, of sorts.

When they arrived in the city, however, they did not travel far.

'For the same reason that explorers first settled in their landing port before going further,' write local historians of the 14th arrondissement, Sylvie Bonin and Bernadette Costa, 'Bretons set down their suitcases near the station where they got off the train. At the end of the iron umbilical cord which tied them to their home country.' That station was Montparnasse.

Inexpensive, hilly, near city parks, full of artists' studios, and with an embarrassment of well-run cafés, Montparnasse, about a mile south of the rive gauche of the Seine, was also the area which in future decades would become the hub not only of artistic Paris, but the world. It was the stomping ground of Hemingway and Stein, latterly Baldwin and de Beauvoir. There was a forty-year period in the mid-twentieth century when you'd have struggled to walk down the area's main boulevard and *not* bump into a titan of culture. Today, though, evidence of the area's heritage is mostly confined to its famous cemetery, the final resting place to many of the greats who used to prop up Montparnasse's bars.

Everything had changed in the 1970s, when much of the neighbourhood's old studio space was demolished to make way for modern developments as part of then President Georges Pompidou's plan to transform the face of Paris as Baron Haussmann had done before him. The fifty-nine-storey Tour Montparnasse, which now dominates the area like a huge brown obelisk, was intended to be the first of many such structures around the capital. It was, however, met with such resistance— my favourite jibe against it is that it was the box the Eiffel Tower came in – that any similar buildings were put on pause, and a law was passed, which remained in place until 2015, that no new buildings in Paris were permitted to be built more than seven storeys high. This came too late for the artists, who'd long since fled to the *rive droite*, or further afield to Berlin. I remember it as one of my great disappointments when I first wandered the capital in pursuit of its literary legends: how the mythic stage set of their exploits had become part tourist trap, part shopping centre. Many of the Bretons, however, remained.

The mill had clearly grown since its foundation, though was still relatively small. A central stone building at the foot of a gully and backing onto, of course, a river. The original structure, which was perhaps ten metres wide and four storeys high, was now flanked by two corrugated iron extensions each of roughly the same size again. Strange to consider how many crêpes it must account for, how there was a whole Paris industry reliant on what it produced.

The gates were open, which was good. Less good, there was an enormous dog blocking my way. I'm no expert in breeds, but at a guess I'd say Dobermann crossed with lion. And it was barking at me. Possible newspaper reports flashed through my head. 'Englishman, 37, horrifically mauled while trespassing in remote corner of Breton countryside. When asked what he was doing, he said he wanted to make a crêpe.'

I did not, however, stop walking. The barks grew more insistent, the dog's eyes on me like I were a steak dinner. 'Englishman, 37, researching Paris food becomes snack himself.' But then, I was alongside him, and as I'd hoped, he didn't seem to know what to do. Eventually he offered an embarrassed growl and slunk away. The way to the mill was clear.

The reception was a quaint stone cottage just next to the main structure. I knocked on the blue wooden door and soon found myself in an office space staffed by two middle-aged women, both of whom looked understandably surprised.

'I, um, hello. I'm trying to find out more about food in Paris,' I said, which seemed suddenly a bit absurd, and it was tempting to follow up with, 'and I seem to have got lost.'

'How did you get here?' the woman closest to me asked, still suspicious. She was glamorous, in a French bob haircut, full make-up and an expensive-looking blouse. I figured she was in charge.

'I, uh, walked,' I said.

'From Paris?'

'No, no, I got the 6 to Saint Servant, then walked from

there,' I said, hoping that the mention of the number of the regional bus route might make me seem more like a local. 'But I wondered if I could ask a few questions. About the mill. If you've got time?'

'Ah, time,' the woman started performatively arranging papers on her desk. 'Time's something we can always have more of, no?'

It was a very analogue office. There was a computer off to the side, but the main tools of mill administration still seemed to be an in-tray, an out-tray and a landline.

She sighed and held out a hand.

'*Je me présente*: Madame Ricaud, owner of the Moulin de Carmenais,' she said. 'What do you want to know?'

I began to tell her about my endeavour to learn recipes from the different arrondissements, to ask her about the history of the mill, about *sarrasin* flour, and their connection to Paris. The longer she spoke in response, the more effusive she became. She forgot that there were other things to do, and eventually seemed almost unwilling to let me leave.

As she spoke, my eyes were opened to the vast cultural and economic significance mills had held in the past, for they were not only the cornerstone of the crêpe industry, but of all baking in France. The original watermill on this site had been a local government initiative – a public utility for the surrounding farms.

Because mills could only be built in certain places, they were often located outside of town, and so represented outposts of civilisation in the remote countryside. Most important, they were one of the three 'pillars' of local lordships, along with the castle and the church. It was through mills that village life was maintained.

In its distant past, the Moulin de Carmenais served only local farmers, who would come to transform the product of their labour into foodstuffs that could be consumed and preserved through the winter.

'We didn't only mill *sarrasin* back then,' Madame Ricaud said. 'It was anything the farmers wanted us to grind.'

'Sorry, when you say, you,' I interrupted. 'Has it always been your family running this mill?'

'Since 1890,' she said. 'That's my great-grandfather.' She turned to indicate a sepia photograph on the office's stone wall of an old man in worker's overalls bent under the weight of a sack of flour. 'Back then, he would walk the flour back into the village by hand: 100kg bags, can you imagine?'

I thought of my walk across the fields.

Her parents had taken the mill over in the 1960s, adding to and changing it so that it was no longer powered by water. It was not long after that time when they were contacted by a woman who had just left from the nearest village to establish a crêperie in Paris. La Crêperie de Josselin. It turned out it was this woman's son who had sent me here.

From that point on, a link was forged between the Moulin de Carmenais and the capital. The fortunes of Bretons in Paris had begun to improve by then, thanks to the booming economy of the city, an emergence of politicised members of the Breton community, and the arrival in Paris of new waves of immigrants onto whom xenophobic prejudices were transferred. Perhaps most significantly, though, they had learned French – the result of a sometimes brutal nineteenth-century government policy dubbed 'the war on patois'. La Crêperie de Josselin was the first of more than a dozen upmarket crêpe places to open around the old Breton quarter. They all wanted high-quality Breton flour, and it made sense for the mill to deliver to them all. Not that Paris is the mill's only market – to succeed in this business of very tight margins, they have to deliver far and wide; and the raw grain they process now comes from all over too.

'The *sarrasin* comes in like this,' Madame Ricaud said, pulling me a sample of uncrushed seeds like small black lentils from a display cabinet beside her desk. 'We turn it into something that can be cooked.'

Eventually, Madame Ricaud offered me some *sarrasin* to take home.

'It's not every day we get English tourists here,' she giggled, leading me from the office and into the mill itself.

It was a cavernous, dry space that rattled with the sound of machinery and smelled of nutty earth. A circular conveyor belt like a rustic baggage carrousel kept delivering a rotation of different sized sacks towards the nozzle of a big funnel, which inflated them with flour, while a couple of men – who looked at me with *Deliverance*-like suspicion – heaved them onto pallets by hand. Somewhere way above, I knew, there must be a millstone constantly turning, pressing sustenance from seeds.

'Here,' Madame Ricaud found a crate of 1kg flour bags in a corner and placed one heavily in my hand. 'Use that to make your crêpes.'

It was my final absolution. Like grain from the fields, I'd arrived at this mill for preparation. Now, I was ready to cook.

Sarrasin Crêpe
Ingredients:

For the batter (makes around 8 crêpes):

¾ cup sarrasin flour

1 egg, beaten

Dash of olive oil

Pinch of salt

1 cup water

For the filling:

Grated Emmental

Ham

Egg

(or whatever you want)

The secret of a good crêpe, according to the owner of La Crêperie de Josselin? 'We always save some of the day's batter over to put in the next day's mix. It makes the cooking more even. The longer batter's been standing for, the better it's combined.'

To make crêpes as well as I could, then, I realised I would be best off leaving all my batter to rest overnight. What a long time all this was taking me. Indeed, the pack of *sarrasin* flour I'd been gifted at the Moulin de Carmenais had already sat on my kitchen shelf for a week. It was a beautiful thing, boasting an image of a traditionally dressed Breton woman printed in block primary colours, and it had begun to take on a talismanic significance for my journey to Brittany. I had been loath to open it. But you can't have your pancake and eat it too.

Carefully, using one of my recently sharpened knives, I

sliced through the Sellotape that had been used to hand-seal it, and let the odour of the Moulin de Carmenais into my kitchen. That smell of the edible earth. The flour inside was sawdust fine, and the grey of the Breton sky. I portioned some of it out into my mixing bowl.

There are several different recipe options for crêpe batter, from the very basic – just flour and water – to the more unctuous, which include milk and eggs. Tradition dictates that the recipe varies according to its place of origin within Brittany – the basic variety is found in the north of the region, while most places in the south favour a more deluxe blend. Josselin was southern Brittany, just about, and accordingly La Crêperie de Josselin made their batter with egg, water and a dash of oil. This, to hazard a personal opinion, is the superior combination.

I cracked a single beaten egg into the *sarrasin* and gently stirred, then the dash of oil, a pinch of salt and half of the water, stirring the concoction into a thick paste, whisking out any lumps before adding the rest. Now, the mixture was fluid and silken, clinging to my fork when I lifted it from the bowl and cascading back in a single emulsion stream. I let this stand for twenty-four hours, dreaming of its flavour as the water fully absorbed into the flour and leeched out its starch. Eventually, it was time to cook.

Crêpe-making is also a game of kit. To make a crêpe properly you need the circular cast-iron hotplate called in Breton a 'bilig' on which they are directly cooked; the small rake-like 'rozell' to evenly spread the batter; and the 'spanell', a long, thin spatula for flipping and folding your creation. I had none of these, though had been assured this need only make for an almost negligible difference in my finished product: my crêpe's thickness would be a half-millimetre short of perfection.

Making do, I ran a knob of butter about my largest frying pan. Not too much, but enough that every inch of the pan's surface was sheened. I poured a single ladle of batter inside, let it flow flat, centre to edge. Suddenly, though, as I contemplated the classic ingredients of egg, ham and cheese I had set aside with which to fill my creation, an almost sacrilegious thought entered my mind. How Breton, really, are crêpes?

Historically, there's not a whole lot of evidence to support the notion that Bretons ever ate much more *sarrasin* than any other regions in the west of France. And certainly the way we eat crêpes now, with the multitude of possible fillings, is a blatantly twentieth-century development, contemporary with the supercharged abundance brought by industrialised agriculture.

The spreading ladleful of batter that I had poured into my pan had now crisped on one side, been flipped, and started to crisp on the other. It was time to add my filling. I cracked the egg in the crêpe's centre, pierced its yolk and drew it out to all sides. Next, the scattering of cheese – grated Emmental, of which I made sure to let some fall beyond the batter, so that it was touching both the crêpe and the hot pan. And at last, a few slices of cut ham.

As the ingredients began to commingle and steam, my blasphemy persisted; I couldn't help but notice how redolent of Paris it all was. How different was this to an *omelette jambon fromage*, a *sandwich mixte*, a *croque-monsieur*?

The success of Bretons in Paris is to be celebrated, no doubt. They are no longer maligned or mistrusted and have long moved away from the job market's lower echelons. It is an inspirational tale, a triumph of multiculturalism. Yet this assimilation has come at a cost. The Breton language is no longer spoken in the city and much of Breton identity has been repackaged as branding. I thought of the kitsch interior of La Crêperie de Josselin, surely more 'Breton' than anywhere in Brittany had ever really been. Even the region's 'traditional' dress was a nineteenth-century invention. And as to crêpes themselves, it seemed clear that they were hybrid, rather than singularly Breton, creations. History had been replaced by legends that sell.

Except.

There was a persuasiveness to the smell now emanating from my pan. That wholesome scent of fields. One that said 'Brittany', despite anything rational that I told myself. And I realised that, like all legends, the crêpe had made its own reality.

So what if Bretons had not been eating *crêpes complètes* since the thirteenth century; they had brought the *idea* of their having done so to Paris more than a hundred years ago, and the world had believed them. From that belief had come truth. Through the Moulin de Carmenais, the link La Crêperie de Josselin and the other crêperies of Montparnasse now had with the Breton countryside was as authentic as it's possible to be.

For the final stage, I folded my still-cooking crêpe in half. Some of the cheese was fraying brown at its edges, while the batter continued to crisp and caramelise underneath, and the packaged insides started to stew. Then I folded it again, making something not so unlike a croissant: a neat triangle of impermeable French layers that I could hold in my hand.

I took a bite. Through that imagined taste of Breton earth and the rich, simple trinity of Parisian fast food that filled it, I had a final revelation: the power of legends is formed by the pleasure they bring. By that measure, I'd give crêpes at least another eight hundred years.

13ème arrondissement

Imagine, for a moment, that you were tasked with reinventing Paris architecture for the future. The most important question, surely, would be what to keep. What talisman should be preserved that still announced your new buildings as belonging to the City of Light? A nod to the mansard roofs? To the cream-grey limestone? To the cafés and cobblestones of the streets?

Michel Holley, being a modernist architect inspired by Le Corbusier, had little interest in any of these things. Taking a mid-century intellectual (i.e. pretentious) view, he decided that the single most definitive attribute of the capital was uniformity of height. Not any particular height, just wherever several adjoining buildings reached an equal distance into the sky, that was Paris for him.

So when, in the 1960s, Holley got the brief to redesign the 13th arrondissement for the modern age, he began by creating Les Olympiades: a self-contained mega-complex of eight brutalist tower blocks sitting atop a huge concrete plateau, each one exactly 104 metres tall. It was a fantastic, sparsely beautiful structure, but no normal person was ever going to look at it and say: You know what? That really reminds me of the boulevard Saint-Michel.

Les Olympiades was a disaster. Especially with Parisians who, give or take a few revolutions, are not renowned for their embrace of the new. The complex was intended to lure young professionals but they failed to come, put off by the very uniformity Holley had hoped might charm their conservative Parisian hearts.

Les Olympiades seemed doomed to architectural ignominy – until events on the world stage took a turn. The end of the Vietnam War heralded one of the biggest mass migrations the world had ever seen as many who had fought on the side of the South, along with members of Vietnam's ethnic Chinese minority and intellectuals, fled overseas. Cutting a long and depressingly familiar story short, after much hardship, resistance and political wrangling, many of these refugees found their way to France. More liberally minded politicians managed to prevail in their view that the country owed these imperilled people asylum on account of having ruled over them for the first half of the twentieth century, when not just Vietnam, but Laos and Cambodia had been French colonial possessions.

The underused Olympiades seemed almost purpose built

to accommodate this sudden influx. Not only were there hundreds of empty apartments, there were acres of vacant commercial space where the more visible markers of community, from supermarkets to restaurants, could take root. Within a matter of years, a whole area of Paris had been created that encompassed not just Les Olympiades, but also several surrounding blocks – and which, despite being home to a predominantly South-East Asian community, would soon become known as Europe's largest Chinatown.

In all my time in Paris, I had never visited. I realise this is unforgivable. Paris is small for a capital city, after all, and in more than a decade here I had failed to set foot in one of its most culturally and architecturally fascinating corners. There were always other, closer Chinatowns. Belleville, up in the 20th, for example. Even my street in the 19th is a small one. Which is to say that what might have been my primary reason for visiting Les Olympiades – the food – was literally catered for elsewhere. To me, then, it was unknown territory. If I were to have any chance of understanding the 13th, of discovering some definitive food from its endless menus, I needed a guide.

Aurore Nguyen was exactly the kind of young professional Les Olympiades had been built to attract: a blogger and food consultant in her early thirties. When I met her on the blustery pavements of the avenue de Choisy, she was mid-negotiation with a recipe book editor, talking rapid-fire French into her smartphone, which at all other times was to hang on a lanyard about her neck.

'Sorry,' she apologised the moment she was done, 'they're wanting me to do photographs too, and I said, sure, I can do photographs. I'm a good photographer, but it's not what I was hired for.'

I had found Aurore via an online article about the tours she used to lead of the 13th back in 2019, and I was a little surprised she'd even agreed to meet. The tour guide gig was long over, and Aurore was now a Paris food insider – friends with all the hot young chefs, au fait with the trendiest new restaurants, invited to their openings. Just getting in contact with her had given me cause for reflection. I was worried I'd be revealed as an *ingénu* or a fraud in my project to learn about the city through its food. Who was this English outsider who thought he could say anything about Paris cuisine? However, Aurore said she liked the sound of what I was trying to do, and as the daughter of Vietnamese immigrants, she'd enjoy the challenge of trying to decide on what should be the representative dish of the 13th arrondissement.

'I didn't grow up here, by the way,' she said as she led me at pace towards the Olympiades complex. 'I'm a *banlieue* girl. But me and my family would come into the 13th every weekend.'

'I see,' I said, running to catch up.

'I hated it.'

'You ... what? Why?'

'It was so boring.'

'It doesn't seem boring,' I said. It was just ... normal. On its outskirts, Europe's largest Chinatown looked much like any other part of middle-class Paris. Wide boulevards, mostly Haussmann-style buildings, plane trees drab in the late-winter gloom. This was not, however, what Aurore meant.

'But it was thinking about how boring it used to be that made me realise what *had* to be its representative food.'

'You found the food boring?' I was stunned.

'What? No! Are you kidding! The food was the only thing that saved those weekends.'

'Ah,' I said. 'Of course.'

'One particular food above all.'

'Which food?'

'I'll tell you later,' she said. 'First, I have to show you what those weekends were like.'

The queue to Les Olympiades car park was a thing of nightmares. Not exciting nightmares, but the ones where you have somewhere to be that you can never reach.

'This was how they started,' Aurore said, breaking from a stream of advice about the five literal best restaurants right now in Paris, each of which I absolutely had to go to. *If* I could get a reservation. Which I couldn't. Now she stopped speaking to survey the bumper-to-bumper snarl in front of us and sighed.

'After the drive from the suburbs, we could sit here for hours.'

At least the kerb was busy with motion: shoppers and hawkers, shawled older women selling Asian herbs and Buddhist kitsch over box-crate stalls. All of Les Olympiades was in front of us, but we were too close to appreciate its dimensions. As we had drawn near, I'd seen those huge towers cutting their dull uniformity onto the horizon, but at the foot of the mountain, the complex's visible scale was reduced to a brown steel-and-glass edifice not even as tall as a Haussmann block.

'Obviously we did a lot of Asian cooking at home,' Aurore was saying. 'I must have rolled kilometres of spring rolls. But we couldn't get the ingredients we needed where we lived, so we'd come here to stock up.'

The crush of families around us today, she said, had come to do the same. Trolley-wielding groups who'd escaped their queuing purgatory were now making their way towards the maw of Les Olympiades' largest Asian supermarket, Tang Frères. My gaze fell on a young girl hanging heavy from her mother's arm, her face scrunched into a ball of useless protest. We'd all been there once.

Tang Frères is probably the single best-known business in all the 13th. Founded in 1976 as a soy and rice cake import concern by two brothers from Laos, in 1981 they opened a supermarket that became an institution. Indeed, despite the firm's continued expansion – it now operates ten outlets in Paris and is moving into other business domains – Aurore told me that its flagship store retains an old-fashioned, almost august reputation. It is a global business so enmeshed in its place of origin that French Asians all around the capital still refer to it as if to an old friend.

For such a major hub, however, I was surprised to discover that Tang Frères is no bigger than an average inner-city supermarket. Produce was packed as tight as it could fit. As Aurore led me down the narrow aisles, talking about the themed dinner parties she liked to throw, I eyed luminous pink jellies jostling for space with mystery preserves, great sacks of dried mushrooms squeezed alongside more flavours of instant noodle than I knew existed. Next, vacuum-packed vegetables, huge troughs of frozen river fish, heaving counters of offal. And these were just the products I could see: the frenzy of exchange taking place was giddying, as an army of shelf-stackers replaced goods from what must have been enormous storage rooms as fast as the many buyers could take them.

'Here ...' Aurore paused from talking about a chef I should meet and took a bottle of black liquid from one of the shelves. 'Maggi sauce. This is what all Asian families in France used back when they couldn't get soy. Now it's part of our cooking tradition. Egg with Maggi sauce. Amazing.'

Both the sauce's bold red and yellow label and its sour-umami flavour were hazily familiar to me. But what it actually *was*, I had no idea – a brand of soy? I later learned that Maggi sauce is a Swiss invention from the turn of the twentieth century – a hydrolysed vegetable protein, which means ... I'm not sure. But despite how questionably chemical it sounds, the sauce is actually delicious and, accordingly, insanely popular. It's the secret seasoning of dishes from Mexico to the Philippines, and Aurore liked it on her eggs.

We quit Tang Frères to take a narrow escalator into the belly of Les Olympiades proper. It felt like shimmying back through time. The escalator carried us up into a labyrinthine shopping arcade: chip marble floor scuffed by decades of footfall, low ceiling mottled by fire sprinklers, air thick with the smell of boiled rice. Few of the outlets here had changed their decor in years; they were visions of the future from the past, neon signs buzzing anachronistically above their doors. A good half of them were restaurants, and the biggest, most popular of all was right at the entrance: a great festival of a place called Chinatown Olympiades, which already had crowds milling outside.

'We'd come here all the time,' Aurore sighed, 'birthdays, marriages, christenings ...'

Sure enough, many of the people crowding outside

Chinatown Olympiades were still in their wedding best: suits for the men, bright figure-hugging floral gowns for the women. They were lining up to have their names checked off multiple guest lists, to be led past fibreglass lion statues into a great rambling interior that was like a Ming Dynasty theme park.

'So is this where you got the food that rescued those childhood weekends?'

'Ugh, no! There's no good Chinese food in Paris,' Aurore snapped. 'None that I know of. Most Chinese people in Paris come from a town called Wenzhou. It's a place known for its business, not its food. So, they're good at opening restaurants but bad at cooking in them.'

'Really, though?' I pushed, 'no good Chinese food *anywhere* in Paris?'

'It'd be like a French colony in China populated only by people from La Creuse,' Aurore said, referencing the sparsely populated department of central France, often used in the country as a byword for a cultural void. 'I always tell people who ask where to find the best Chinese restaurants in Paris: the Eurostar! In London, it's all Cantonese food. You guys are so lucky!'

Happily for us, the other restaurants in the arcade were all South-East Asian: Thai, Cambodian, Laotian and Vietnamese, most filled to capacity. Their overspilling 'pavement' tables were crammed with gossiping older women in big coats and perfectly coiffed hair, families with children, and ancient men squinting at foreign-language newspapers.

'So, do *you* like Vietnamese food?' Aurore asked abruptly.

Now, I *love* Vietnamese food. Since coming to Paris, I have probably eaten more Vietnamese food than any other single global cuisine apart from French. The only means I could think of to convince Aurore of this personal truth was to start on an elaborate display of my knowledge of Vietnamese dishes.

'Did you know that the bo bun was invented in Paris?' I said.

Secretly, I'd already been thinking that for this reason, the bo bun might end up as my representative dish for the 13th. The birth of this combination of beef and vermicelli noodles in Paris was surely Les Olympiades' greatest culinary triumph – for it had become so iconic of Vietnamese cuisine that when President Obama had shared a table with Anthony Bourdain in Hanoi this was what they ordered.

'I hate it when people say that,' said Aurore.

'What?'

'Sure, maybe the *name* bo bun originated here,' she continued, 'but it literally just means beef noodles. The idea of having spring rolls with vegetables, vermicelli and marinated meat. You could find that in any village in Vietnam.'

'Oh,' I said. 'It is nice, though.'

'What, bo bun? Yeah, I love it.'

'So was bo bun the food that saved—'

'No.'

We'd reached the end of the arcade now, and Aurore pushed open the scratched glass doors that led outside onto the plaza. Here was a cityscape that was completely distinct from traditional Paris, all traces of Haussmann eclipsed. The huge concrete space was enclosed on all sides by those perfectly aligned tower blocks and dotted by one-storey commercial outlets with what appeared to be traditional Chinese pagoda roofs. This last design feature was pure serendipity.

Holley had intended the free-standing commercial premises to resemble Parisian market stalls. The incoming South-East Asian migrants, though, had reinterpreted his art.

'Here.' Aurore pointed to one of the units, a restaurant called Pho 86. 'We'd spend hours in this place. Ugh. My dad would come here to hang out with his friends for hours after we'd done the shopping.'

'So it was pho, then?' I said excitedly; of all Vietnamese food, I love the noodle soup dish most of all. Its steamy, sinus-blasting richness, the zing and crackle of its added herbs, the thrill of—

'No,' said Aurore. 'The pho here is terrible. In a lot of the 13th, the pho is terrible. The restaurants use such cheap ingredients.'

'I always imagined the 13th did the best pho in Paris,' I said, disappointed.

'You imagined wrong,' said Aurore. 'The best pho in Paris ...' for a moment I swear I saw her eyes misting over, 'for that you want to go to a place called Mam From Hanoi. It's in the 2nd. They use the same beef supplier as the Élysée Palace. It's just ...' she made a chef's kiss gesture. 'But it's pho from the north of Vietnam, so maybe it's different from what you've had before. Fewer herbs.'

'Right,' I said, 'fewer herbs. Got it.'

'And don't start saying pho is a French dish either.'

'*Do* people say it's a French dish?'

'Pho. *Pot au feu*,' she said. 'Some people say that's how it got its name.'

'But it didn't?'

'It didn't,' said Aurore firmly.

I looked into the restaurant now. At the handful of

leather-jacketed men still chatting at its bar. The tables busy with families, the karaoke screens. I wondered what, if anything, had changed since Aurore's childhood more than twenty years before.

'I looked into living in one of the towers recently,' Aurore said, a little wistful as we walked on.

'You did?' The 13th was a long way from the Paris social-ite world Aurore seemed to love. But maybe I'd misjudged her. I cast my eye up at one of the enormous structures, at its elegantly proportioned windows and clean, concrete lines: much more beautiful on close inspection than at a glance. 'And?'

'Too expensive,' said Aurore. 'Not the apartment. The building charges. This place is a nightmare to run.'

It stood to reason. Les Olympiades was a city within a city, a man-made geographical feature, an egalitarian attempt to reach the stars. Such visions do not come cheap.

'Anyway,' Aurore continued, 'time for a banh mi.'

A sandwich? After all that build-up, we were just getting a sandwich?

No, Aurore retorted, this banh mi was not *just* a sandwich.

The queue pouring from the front of Khai Tri suggested that the people of the 13th did not think so either.

It was the kind of never-ending queue I'd associate with the latest fashionable restaurant, the kind that ought to consist of people with thick-rimmed glasses, line tattoos and, well, probably Aurore. Of course, Aurore actually was here, but then, so was everyone else. Old women with their shopping carts, kids dancing impatiently at their parents' side, Tang Frères workers on their break, all waiting to get into what seemed to me to be a second-hand bookshop. No, wait, it *was* a second-hand bookshop ... but it also sold banh mi.

Standing directly over the road from one of the main thoroughfares of Les Olympiades, Khai Tri was perfectly placed: a trap for hungry shoppers. Founded in 1984, it made, Aurore told me, something quite spectacular: the best banh mi in Paris, maybe the best in the world. Here was where we'd find the food – the reward – that had made her mundane childhood trips from the suburbs bearable over all those years.

The queue moved fast, but not so fast that Aurore didn't have time to explain a little of the history of the banh mi, which it turned out *was* a true fusion cuisine.

The French introduced baguettes to Vietnam in the nineteenth century, though for a long time they were eaten in the same way as they were back in France – as an accompaniment to meals, for breakfast, something to wrap around *jambon* and *beurre*. But when, in 1954, the country was partitioned into north and south administrative departments, a wave of migrants arrived in Saigon, mixing up the city's food cultures. The idea of stuffing baguettes with Vietnamese ingredients began to gain ground. A food phenomenon was born.

Of course, Khai Tri did not simply sell 'banh mi', which in any case is just Vietnamese for 'bread'. There were multiple sandwiches on offer, and Aurore instructed me that I must order the *dac biet*. This literally means 'special'. I'd have to come back to find out the details of the recipe, though: Saturday service was no time for chit-chat. Our order was passed to the assembly station, and I watched our sandwiches take shape in double time. Three kinds of meat, carrots, cucumber, mayonnaise, a drizzle of Maggi sauce! Then we were being shepherded outside, to eat our prize on the kerb.

No, it was not just a sandwich. It was a revelation. A whole party of textures and tastes. Chewy pork, crisp chicken; the fizzing, generous crunch of pickled carrot; the quenching cool of cucumber; the fresh coriander, the sweet minerality of the Maggi – all laid on a decadent bed of mayonnaise quickened by rising chilli heat, and contained in the very cheapest of baguettes. It was fusion food, true, but it was also an announcement from the Vietnamese ingredients to the French, one that stated quite plainly: We've got this one. *We* are the main event.

It was also, I realised, the taste of memories. Not just Aurore's, but those of the whole neighbourhood. The queue we had stood in had been a Saturday constant here for forty years. Hundreds of thousands of visitors, young and old, satiated by the same recipe for more than a generation. The antithesis of a trend.

Banh Mi Dac Biet
For 1 sandwich
Ingredients (all in equal ratios):
Glazed Pork
Chicken *'de la poste'*
Cha lua
Pickled cucumber
Pickled carrot

½ cheap baguette

A few drops of Maggi sauce
Diced chilli peppers (to taste)
Mayonnaise

Neighbourhood memories are not easily made, still less so sustained. Even so, when I returned to Khai Tri a couple of days later to find out what I could about their banh mi recipe, I was shocked by the croissant-like level of dedication it required, by how much work hid behind every bite.

'We close at three,' the shop's owner and son of Khai Tri's founders told me, 'so we can start work on the next day's ingredients.'

Middle-aged, with a high brow and permanent grin, he was only too happy to divulge the secrets of the banh mi. If I was willing to put in the same amount of time as they did, I was welcome to them. It fast became clear that I was not.

First, there was the julienning of carrots and the bâtonetting of cucumber, both to be lightly pickled in a solution of vinegar and sugar. At Khai Tri they also mixed their own mayonnaise, but all that was relatively easy.

The real work was in the preparation of the meats. First, the *poulet de la poste*, a recipe brought by the owner's mother from Saigon. There, it was sold on the street; in Paris, they made it themselves. Effectively, it was a kind of twice-cooked pulled chicken. It meant marinating more than a dozen birds in ginger, garlic and fish sauce, then letting them roast very slowly for five hours so they became tender enough to pull to ribbons, which could then be baked crisp into beautiful, umami gold.

Then there was the glazed pork. Marinated overnight for twenty-four hours in honey, sugar, hoisin, five spice and rice wine, it required roasting for half an hour, then basting in its own juices, more roasting, then flipping, basting, roasting; flipping, basting, then roasting again. At last, the meat was sliced into thin strips to give the banh mi tug and tension at its core, laced with wonderful, spiced sweetness.

Finally, the cooks at Khai Tri make their own *cha lua*, a kind of Vietnamese pâté: they pound pork together with fish sauce, garlic, pepper and salt, then wrap it in banana leaf to boil. This tasty paste is spread onto the baguette to give the banh mi an underlying smooth flavour that holds the whole together – like the rhythm section in an orchestra.

'You can buy all these ingredients in a shop, though, right?' I asked, thinking of my own oven, of the space in my kitchen. I wasn't sure I wanted to spend two days and more than a hundred euros making a sandwich. Some things are better left to the professionals.

'Oh yes,' Khai Tri's owner chuckled. 'In Tang Frères, definitely, you'll get all you need. Apart from the *poulet de la poste*. But look for dried chicken flakes instead.'

Resolving to start my own banh mi preparation a good few steps further along the process, I returned to Tang Frères to source what I needed. In the supermarket, I observed the same families gathering their goods as they had done for a generation, and would do for generations to come. And I realised that, however different this *quartier*'s buildings looked from the classic Haussmann boulevard, and however much the food on offer strayed from what you might find in the traditional French kitchen cabinet, Les Olympia-des guarded one of the purest essences of Paris that still existed: here was the city as community, as shared history and marketplace, mostly uncorrupted by global commerce or tourism or really any outsiders at all.

When it came to assembling my banh mi, restraint had been the other main counsel. Don't put in too much of any one ingredient, I'd been told. The essence of a good banh mi was in its balance. Every flavour should hit the same heights.

12ème arrondissement

'You want to know what I eat?' The old man's weather-grooved face slackened with confusion, but only fleetingly. For then I saw a mask of mischief descend, a glint in his frost-blue eyes. 'I am sorry,' he said. 'It is a secret.'

'A secret?' I repeated, casting my gaze across the mouth of his forest shelter, where the few possessions of his life were sorted in neat piles on the compacted mud. There were J-cloths, dented cutlery, even a small camping stove, but no trace of food.

'You have seen the horses in the *Bois*?' the old man continued, his voice wavering a little.

'I have,' I said, in a riding school less than a hundred

metres from where we stood, but invisible from here through the surrounding trees. Horses being ridden in circles. Prim, healthy creatures with plaited manes and mincing hooves.

'Human beings now are like those horses,' the old man said. 'Horses that have forgotten that they are wild, that have forgotten the world they live in – how they must be curious if they want to survive.'

Maybe I should have seen it coming. I was in the Bois de Vincennes, in the furthest reaches of the 12th arrondissement, to learn about the eating habits of the park's significant number of homeless people, and I had met a philosopher. Typical France.

'So, you want to know what I eat?' he asked. 'Before that we must learn more about each other. First, I tell you my name, which is Bolec. Then, you tell me yours. Afterwards, we talk …'

The Bois de Vincennes, a vast 995-hectare park that bulges from Paris's eastern flank is a prime example of a city edgeland, those unfettered, liminal spaces where the city proper gives way to something less well defined, and where the rule of law might be subject to negotiation. It is a place of sex work and casual outdoor hook-ups, of circuses and zoos, and of late-night partying at illegal raves, where you may not be hallucinating should you hear the roar of big cats on the wind.

Vincennes started as a royal hunting preserve, then became a military training ground and finally a park under Napoleon III. At the turn of the twentieth century, it played home to something more sinister. When France staged an exhibition celebrating its various colonial territories, a number of pavilions were constructed in the east of the park, each representing a different foreign possession. And to these exoticised reproductions of vernacular design were brought not only local artefacts and flora, but the actual people of those territories. Tuaregs were taken from the Sahara, tribespeople from Congo, Kanaks from Melanesia. They were clothed in their respective 'traditional' dress and displayed as part of the exhibit: a literal human zoo.

The pavilions are still here, in varying states of decay. With thatched roofs long since caved in, bamboo smashing through glass, and faux Maghrebin tiles graffiti-scrawled and flaking, they are the ruins of kitsch prison cells that the French government cannot make up its mind either to pre-serve or fully destroy.

The most ubiquitous, visible strangeness of the Bois de Vincennes today are the tents between the trees. There are an estimated 3,500 people living rough on the streets of Paris, referred to by French society, and by themselves, as 'sans domicile fixe' or simply SDF – without fixed abode. Of these people, around 200 have established themselves year-round in the Bois, with numbers spiking dramatically in summer. It may be technically illegal to camp for the night here on non-designated camping grounds, but local author-ities, from a combination of pragmatism and compassion, have long looked the other way. So semi-permanent encamp-ments have proliferated and bedded into the geography of the place, clinging to the park's main thoroughfares and around its handful of public water pumps.

To call these dwellings 'visible', however, does not tell the whole story. For though they are literally all over Vin-cennes – flashes of synthetic fabric screaming through the underbrush – they are also ignored. Looked *through* by most of the park's visitors who come to jog down forest paths, picnic on green spaces, shag in the bushes. The Bois de Vincennes is surrounded by some of the most expensive real estate in Paris, and the occupants of the mansions that overlook the park don't much care for human suffering that might spoil their view.

Most city dwellers are culpable of this kind of heedlessness. I certainly have been. And perhaps I only noticed the lack of noticing that goes on in the Bois because I had gone specifically with the park's homeless population in mind.

Paris may be a centre of world gastronomy, but it is also, like everywhere, a place where people simply have to eat. It felt wrong, in my journey through the city's food, to look through this significant section of its population. The SDFs of Paris are as in need of sustenance as anyone else. What does the capital of *haute cuisine* look like for them? The 12th, a varied and historically working-class district from which the Bois de Vincennes grows like a giant lung, was where I set out to answer that question.

From the moment I crossed into the Bois, I felt its strange, eerie weight. It was mid-February, late afternoon, under a low sky of characterless white; the park's north-western edge was deserted. Just a couple of old-fashioned carousels – a frozen belle-époque menagerie of horses and birds grimacing for children who would not come – and beyond them, a small artificial lake, landscaped in the English way, its mud-brown surface rippled by a couple of mucky swans. Beyond that, there was forest. Most of the trees were thin, stood less than three metres tall, and were winter naked, like so many upright twigs. But it was a forest. Soon it swallowed me. I could still hear the city: the distant wash of traffic, the sirens, the occasional rhythmic clunk/clack of trains. But I could see only woods.

After less than ten minutes' walk, the tents began. Dozens of them. A-frames and domes, geodesics and tunnels: a whole suburb of canvas that edged the forest path. Some were camping-store fresh, others dusted lichen green. Most had more tarpaulin strung taut above them, and signs of life in their surrounds. There were bicycles and bins, clothes draped over lines, and yes, barbecues and camping stoves. But they were silent. No signs of movement. Their inhabitants were nowhere to be seen. I left the main path and started to walk capillary tracks between encampments.

I had a sense of a village peeping at me from behind closed blinds. As the minutes ticked by, a new thought nudged its way into my head: What if the people here did not want to be seen? What if the only thing worse for them than being looked through was being looked at?

'*Eh, mec!*' the voice came suddenly, sharp as garlic. '*Mec!*'

I looked around, my heart thumping from surprise.

'*Tu veux une clop?*'

Wanna fag?

I did not know where the voice was coming from. The tent suburb was as still as before.

'*Ici.*'

From under the shadowy awning of a tent not ten metres from where I stood, someone was waving. I approached.

He was a very large, very hairy man, wearing only a sleeveless puffa jacket. Seated alone at a grubby picnic table, he was smoking an enormous hand-rolled cigarette in front of a half-devoured plate of *mousse de canard*.

'You want?' he gestured towards his pack of feathery rolling tobacco.

'Sure.' The man offered a welcoming grin. I reached to roll myself a – much smaller – cigarette. 'Thanks. How's the *mousse de canard*?'

'What?'

'The duck pâté.'

'Pfft.'

He was Bulgarian, in his early forties. He had left his home country because there was no work, and because he was European. He emphasised this point over and over: for him, Paris was the heart of Europe and he was a member of the European brotherhood, so Paris was where he belonged. At least, I think this is what he said, for his French was erratic, full of – I assumed – Bulgarian phrases, and punctuated by explosive coughs of laughter as he cackled at jokes I had not understood he was making. His gold teeth flashing in the gloom.

I asked him what the people of the Bois tended to eat.

'Different things,' he said. 'We are many nations here in the heart of Europe. We eat many different things.'

Academics love a liminal space, and with the Bois being on the doorstep of numerous Paris universities, I'd found an embarrassment of scholarly papers on its residents. According to them, the population of these tent villages is diverse, as you might expect, though a majority come from other EU countries, often from Eastern Europe. Study after study questions the inclusive notion that anyone can find themselves homeless – many subjects make their way to the Bois following 'difficult' childhoods, migratory journeys, or personal economic catastrophe; often a combination of all three. They are attracted to Vincennes by the reputation of local authorities for being relatively tolerant, by the park's tranquillity, or to mitigate the exhaustions of life on the city streets. There are advantages to Vincennes living, but it also requires a particular set of survival skills. One thing these academic papers often remark on is that, unlike the SDFs elsewhere in the city, the residents of Vincennes are less likely to patronise the city's *restaurants solidaires*, or soup kitchens.

'I love the *restaurants solidaires*,' the Bulgarian declared, sucking away merrily at his enormous fag. 'Otherwise, I'm just raiding supermarket bins. Sometimes it's good,' he indicated the *mousse de canard*. 'Sometimes it's *la merde*, you know. And you have to be careful, eh? If the food goes bad …' He let out a long, raking cough. 'But the *restaurants solidaires* …' he trailed off into Bulgarian, and gestured effusively with his hairy-knuckled hands, '… but they can be a long way. Sometimes it's too much effort to walk.'

'Is that where you think people are now, then?' I asked.

'What?'

'All these other tents, they seem empty.'

He shrugged. 'I don't know anyone in the other tents,'

I would learn that this was frequently the case here. The Bois de Vincennes is peopled by those who often had cause to be suspicious of others.

It was growing darker now, and the encampments seemed as quiet as before. My encounter with the Bulgarian had been entertaining, but it hadn't answered as many of my questions as I might have liked. I was about to leave, to reorient my search. Then, I heard the drumming. A rapid, insistent rhythm echoing off the trees. It was coming from one of the tents. Attuning my ear, I made my way to its source.

As I approached the tent, I saw old packets and cartons of organic produce dangling from the trees. Herbal tea, oat milk, quinoa: they hung like so many magic charms in the dying light. The tent itself was black and very clean and neat, to the degree that it lacked any of the surrounding domestic detritus that had betrayed other encampments as people's homes. There was only this strange display of organic produce, and the drumming. It was not a place I could pass by.

I called out a greeting several times until the drumming stopped. The front of the tent unzipped a crack; a young woman's face filled the opening.

'*Oui?*'

She was so private that at first she would not tell me where she was from or how she had ended up in the woods. She did, though, seem excited to talk, saying she seldom had a chance to speak to anyone and certainly not to her neighbours in the woods.

We chatted for a long while, and slowly she opened up about her shame, the difficulties of her life, her rage against the government and eventually, yes, about how she had ended up in this place, where she was from, her name. To honour the anonymity that she so valued, however, I will not write those details here.

She explained the organic packaging in the trees.

There were often volunteer groups that left food outside her tent, but it was not 'good' food, not 'healthy', not what she wanted to eat. So she had started hanging the organic produce outside her tent as a sign, protesting her choice to refuse their charity and her freedom to eat what she wanted. And it had worked; the volunteer groups had stopped bringing her unwanted food.

When I got home that evening, the conversation stuck with me, not least because it underscored that many of the residents of the Bois had chosen that place precisely because it offered them independence from the standard, more regulated SDF experiences that they were likely to encounter elsewhere in Paris. To gain some insight into what that might look like, though, to see what they were refusing, I needed to visit a *restaurant solidaire*.

'CAP, *bac*, BTS,' Chef Yann Coudare reeled off his qualifications with shy modesty. 'Then I worked in commercial restaurants for years. But truly, here is harder, more rewarding work.'

It was the day after my first visit to the Bois. We were sitting at one of the tables of the Restaurant Solidaire Saint-Eloi, the only state-run soup kitchen in the 12th, talking in the empty calm before service. There was a pot of coffee steaming between us and morning sun flooded the room, bounced warmly from its pristine vinyl floor. Despite the hospital-like simplicity of its decor, the Saint-Éloi was a cosy, welcoming space, complemented by the broad smile of Chef Coudare.

'We do around three hundred covers at each service,' he continued, hands folded loose over his tattooed forearms, 'and 90 per cent of what we make is cooked fresh.'

'Three hundred covers?'

'*C'est beaucoup, eh?*' he laughed. 'Most restaurants won't do half that.'

'And it's all free?'

'Of course,' he said. 'You just have to be registered with Paris social services.'

Familiar myself with the horrors of French bureaucracy, I had a feeling that this registration was probably not as easy as Chef Coudare made it sound. But that was hardly his responsibility.

His team did their best to uphold the principles of French dining, making sure that all the food they served was varied, good quality, and of course always in that holy French service trinity of *entrée*, *plat*, *dessert*. 'Plus a cheese course,' Chef Coudare concluded.

Two other members of the kitchen staff bustled in — women in their fifties, both with the same heavy make-up and dyed black hair, laughing, joshing and demanding to be introduced.

'You're English?' one said. 'Ah, but you know, it's not terrible, English food.'

'Just not as good as French food,' I countered – not above a little charm.

'This is true,' she agreed, a little too quickly. 'It doesn't have the depth, the variety, the history.'

Perhaps I should have stood up for my country's cuisine, for my own family's traditional English restaurant, but I was aware that I found myself in a soup kitchen that offered a cheese course.

I asked if they only served French cuisine.

'Not at all,' said Chef Coudare. 'We do an international cuisine. It's necessary. Because we try not to do the same meal twice in one month.'

'In the whole month? So, you're not told what to make by the town hall?'

'The town hall decides the ingredients,' said the chef, 'but I choose what to do with them. In fact, look,' he pulled a notebook from the pocket of his whites, 'I was just working on the menus for March.'

He slid the book over to me, indicating its neat grid of *entrées*, *plats*, *desserts* for the coming week. It looked as promising as the specials board at any Paris bistro: *oeuf mayonnaise* and *boeuf bourguignon*; remoulade and paella; *carrottes rapées* and couscous ...

'Come,' said Chef Coudare. 'I'll show you the kitchens.'

He led me through a pair of heavy aluminium doors into a workspace that was almost the same size as the dining area and just as spotless. At that moment, there was only one chef in there, tending to a couple of buckets of whole frozen fish (hake, I think) which he was laying out on baking trays.

'Normally, we are fourteen in the kitchen,' Chef Coudare explained. 'A big team.'

He pointed out all the usual furniture of the cooking trade – the ovens, the knives, the stoves – taking pride in the evidence of his kitchen's authenticity. This was no reheating factory, it was an artisan workshop where every onion had to be chopped. And the *pièce de résistance* of his tour: the banks of refrigerators, as brimming with fresh produce as a Dutch still life. Lettuce, tomatoes, carrots, leeks; not a Turkey Twizzler in sight.

'*Hélas*, there's no table service,' he concluded. 'That's perhaps the biggest difference between us and commercial restaurants. We serve our dishes straight at the pass.'

He pointed back towards the dining area, to the empty buffet – 'the pass' – that looked like a stage waiting to be filled. But it was something else that caught my eye. Underneath stood a crate filled with bottles of red wine.

'You serve wine?'

'Of course,' Chef Coudare replied, nonchalantly.

He didn't spell it out, but I knew well enough that the French consider wine essential to any even half-decent meal. It's practically a human right.

I was enamoured. A little by Chef Coudare and the Saint-Éloi, but even more by the system of which they were a part. There could do with being more *restaurants solidaires* – currently there are only eleven state-funded ones in the whole of central Paris – but the quality of food, the centrality of the very best French values, and above all the dignity they represented, seemed well worth celebrating. When it came to choosing a meal for the 12th arrondissement, one from Chef Coudare's meticulously planned, doggedly inventive menus for the city's SDF community seemed the optimistic, humanity-affirming choice.

And yet.

In Vincennes, there is the law and there are the conventions of how it is administered. Much of France is a bit like this, from jumping the metro to cycling through red lights, to working under the table – after all, this is a country where even undocumented workers can unionise. But in the Bois, what is legal and what is permitted exist in a Byzantine tension.

Take prostitution, which is legal in France, though soliciting is not. Whatever the law says, though, soliciting is tolerated in the park the majority of the time, but 'banned' on Wednesdays and weekends, when children are off school.

With the park's inhabitants, things get more complicated.

Anyone who arrived after 2016 is only allowed to pitch tents; any more permanent dwellings will be destroyed. For those who came to the park before that year, however, when its SDF population could be numbered in dozens rather than hundreds, their homespun cabins, shacks and even fenced-off gardens are permitted to remain. I had read about a longer-standing group of residents, mostly concentrated in the south of the park, and I was curious to hear more about their approaches to finding and preparing food.

Bolec, the old man with frost-blue eyes, was technically one such elder. As I sat down to convince him of my curiosity, he told me he had been living in the park for almost ten years, not that his dwelling suggested such permanence. It was not even a tent; more a sofa piled in blankets and protected by a couple of tarpaulin lean-tos. But Bolec knew what he was doing.

'You don't want to live in a tent,' he said, his voice growing more confident – we spoke in English, which was better than his French, and later he told me he had learned it from Google Translate. 'You sit all day in a tent, it's bad for your lungs. The Bois is very humid. In summer it's humid, in winter it's humid. In a tent you become ill.'

He was from Poland, raised in a Warsaw orphanage. Tired of the obstacles that life continually threw his way as a young man with no family, after turning forty he made a deliberate choice to become homeless and quickly embraced the freedom such a life offered. He was now sixty-five. In that time, he had tramped gradually west across the Continent, or more accurately cycled – there was a bike leant up against his bed. He had done many things to get by: sketched caricatures, begged, foraged for mushrooms.

'Mushrooms?' I stopped him at this mention of food. 'Here?'

'No, in Poland,' Bolec smiled. 'There are no edible mushrooms in the Bois. I have never understood why. Perhaps the French ate them all. Many years ago. When they were poor as well.'

He was a small man, with a thin, athletic build; his voice was lilting, dusted with mischief. And without wanting to glamorise his life choices, which had often been born of alienation and sadness, there was a mystical quality about him that was hard to deny.

As we spoke, the sun began to break through the whiteness above, casting wonderful silver light through the grey-brown trees. I thought how calm much of Bolec's time here must be, for his encampment was a long way from any others, and there must be little to do but contemplate the slow changing of the seasons. He avoided Paris as much as he could, only going in when he absolutely had to, for food or to charge his phone.

'For food?' I asked.

'Ah, yes,' Bolec smiled, 'I said that was my secret, did I not? Well, I have decided you are curious, so I will tell you. But perhaps it won't seem so interesting after all. I eat healthily. And in moderation. When you are homeless, moderation is important.'

'But where do you get it from?'

Again, that smile: 'People ask me sometimes, is it difficult living in the Bois de Vincennes? I say no. What is difficult here, is dying.'

I waited for a less cryptic answer.

'To find food is easy,' he sighed. 'People give it to you,

just like they will save you if you are unwell. They won't give money, but if all you want is food and survival, it makes them happy. So, I go with them to supermarkets, and get rice, sandwiches. There is a Chinese hoisin wrap from Monoprix that is very good.'

'So you never go to the *restaurants solidaires*?'

'Never,' said Bolec. 'I dislike the *restaurants solidaires*. I dislike all the restaurants in Paris. They are so formal, so restrictive. The bars as well. You see all these people sitting on terraces, their arms in like this.' He did a mime like a person trying to eat in a straightjacket and we laughed. 'There is only one that is good. A bar. Not a restaurant. Perhaps you have heard of it? Called La Liberté.'

La Liberté is one of Paris's truly legendary bars, though of the sort whose reputation is hard to understand until you experience it in person. Hardly more than an entrance passage and a single room of about thirty square metres, there should be nothing more to it than countless other tiny neighbourhood joints. Its secret is that it is a constant party at which not only is anyone welcome, they are embraced. It is less than a block from the Saint-Éloi, and I ended up writing much of this chapter at one of its tables, where I heard half a dozen life stories and felt like I made twice as many friends. (It is not, perhaps, the best of bars to work from.) Bolec went there only occasionally, and yet I couldn't help wondering if part of its appeal for him lay in its name: a bar called Freedom.

After a good hour of chatting, it was time to say our farewells, as I continued even deeper into the Bois.

Nikolai and Avryll were from the countryside around

Bucharest, though they had been in Vincennes for more years than either could remember. Their home – for a home it indubitably was – consisted of a whole complex of tents and self-built shelters, focused around a smouldering fire pit hearth with an enormous coal-blackened cauldron, alongside which was a sturdy marquee which served as a kitchen, hung with pots and pans, plates and knives. A drawer overflowed with mismatched, presumably found cutlery. Huge jerrycans of water stood nearby. They even had a larder: a metre-deep hole covered by a home-made A-frame of wood and tarp.

'It was how my family kept things fresh in our village,' Nikolai said, 'so why not here?'

In the larder were a couple of shelves stacked with store-bought perishables, plus a whole crate of potatoes, which Nikolai and Avryll grew right here in the forest.

In some ways, they seemed a mismatched couple, each of them existing, or so it seemed, in different epochs of time. Nikolai had work in Paris as a construction labourer. He was fifty, but he could have been younger, in a neat plaid shirt and fashion-ripped jeans, with his golden hair styled in a long Mohawk. Avryll was probably younger, but her sallow complexion suggested the years had been far harder on her. She wore a long, loose-fitting skirt and shawl; her hair was bound up in a headscarf. She almost never left the forest, barely left this encampment, which she said she had to protect when Nikolai was away.

Nikolai did most of the talking, keen to justify his right to this piece of land. Colonialism was the reason they were here, he said. Because big countries bullied small countries, because the world was run by a business mafia, it was only right that he came to where the money was.

'Countries,' he said, 'what are countries? You want to know my country?' he pointed to the twin edges of his encampment. 'It starts there and ends there. It has a population of two.'

It had taken me some time and nerve to cross their border, marked as it was by a knee-high bramble fence. But as soon as I did, I was welcomed with extraordinary warmth. There was coffee brewing in a blackened pot on the fire, and straight away a mug was poured for me. A chair was proffered and then a cigarette – hand rolled, but out of a Marlboro pack. Like everyone else I'd spoken to in the park, Nikolai and Avryll said they did not know their neighbours. As close as many of the tents were pitched to one another, however similar their occupants' situations, Vincennes was not a community.

There were bad people here, Nikolai told me, addicts and thieves you couldn't trust. But I was a writer, he said, and he knew I would tell the truth. Possibly he was not above a little charm himself, but I hoped I could prove him right.

While we spoke, one of their pet cats – they had four – arrived and began to rub itself affectionately against Nikolai's leg. He scooped it up, began to stroke its chin.

'I wish I'd been born an animal,' he said. 'Animals are so much better than human beings, you know why?'

I said I did not.

'Because humans enslave each other. I see it in the city all the time. And they enslave animals. But animals would never enslave each other. They would never enslave humans. The worst thing,' he said, 'is to be enslaved.'

Eventually, we got around to talking about food.

'We cook normal things,' Avryll told me. 'Like anyone,

really. Rice, potatoes. Tonight, we're having pasta. Sometimes we have barbecues. But on special occasions,' she smiled, 'we will do something Romanian.'

'Something Romanian? Like what?'

'Do you know *sarmale*?

From the start, I had been anxious about trespassing on the inhabitants of Vincennes. In particular, I felt the dark shadow cast by that colonial exhibition held in the park just over a hundred years before. Was I really so different from those gawping belle-époque tourists, seeking out the cheap thrill of gazing at people whose lives were so different from mine? Who, likely as not, had had little choice about their circumstances.

My visits, however, had confounded my ideas about the place. I am not denying that for many in Vincennes, life is both physically and mentally exhausting. Yet for many of them it represents a protest against various kinds of captivity. From Bolec's and Nikolai's points of view, their state was one of freedom, removed from the bonds and obligations of the settled, capital-driven city dweller. Both had made comparisons between human beings and animals, and claimed the rest of us were blinkered and enslaved – notwithstanding that Nikolai's freedom looked very different from his partner Avryll's, and that there is a paradox in celebrating a freedom into which one has very nearly been forced.

Just after my encounters in the park, Paris experienced nearly two straight weeks of rain. Every day I thought of the residents of the Bois: their tarps filling with water, the ground of their encampments turning to mud; clothes perpetually sodden; fires hard to light.

However, taking Bolec and Nikolai – and to a degree the drumming woman – at their word, freedom, *la liberté*, was the most precious thing they had. And for that, when it came to finding a meal to best represent their lives, it had to be something they made themselves, which they ate when and how they wanted to eat it. Food that made them feel at home.

Sarmale
Serves 4–6
Ingredients:
1 cabbage
4 onions
2 tsp paprika
Tomato paste
1 bunch of dill
200g rice
400g pork mince
400g beef mince
1 cup water
500g tinned tomatoes

Avryll's instructions to make *sarmale*, the national dish of Romania, were perfunctory, as if barely worth her effort to give. Surely everyone knew how to make *sarmale*! Knew that it was a meal of spiced pork, beef and rice wrapped inside cabbage leaves and boiled. I did not. When I got home, then, I had to cross-check what I thought Avryll had told me with recipes online.

First, the coring and boiling of a whole cabbage, letting it wilt in the bubbling water so that it could be peeled apart as individual leaves. This was a satisfying task: the cabbage became more forgiving; its crisp hardness was made malleable, something that could be shaped in the hand.

Setting aside the softened leaves to cool, I prepared the filling.

'Lots of onions,' Avryll had told me, while pointing into their earth-dug root cellar, which was filled with onions that she was proud of having grown herself. I finely diced four to sweat out in my pan. To this pungent bed, I added paprika, tomato paste, dill, uncooked rice and then the raw meat. As instructed, I removed the pan from the heat while I combined the ingredients. Turning the mixture over and over, it took on the air of a slightly uncanny substance, for it looked like food to the eye but would not be to the tongue – it still awaited heat.

Now, I sliced the wilted cabbage leaves into triangular swatches, spread them flat in my hands, and began to wrap a tablespoon of the meat filling in each one. Rolling and folding. Rolling and folding. It was slow, calming work.

After a good half-hour of patient wrapping, I had nearly two dozen parcels of cabbage-wrapped meat. I diced what remained of the cabbage to layer the bottom of my saucepan like a forest floor. The parcels went on top of this, and over them went water and tinned tomatoes.

I put the pan over the heat to come gradually to a simmer, so that the cabbage parcels of spiced meat and rice would steam and steep. It was a gentle cooking. A way of preparing meat that was suitable for outdoor cooking, and yet the opposite of a barbecue. I thought of Nikolai and Avryll's campfire. How tempting I would have found it over that open flame to grill up sausages or steaks, to have them singe and crackle. I knew that they did this from time to time, but saw how the novelty of such an approach to cooking can quickly fade. In this dish, each mouthful had been given its shelter, shielded several times over from the heat, transforming unseen from raw to cooked.

I left it all to bubble away for an hour, let it steam up the apartment windows. It was raining outside. At last, I spooned a hugely generous helping onto a plate and I sat down to its bosky warmth, its faintly bitter comfort.

11ème arrondissement

Philippe was an unemployed intellectual and heavy drinker whom I had seldom seen without a Gallimard paperback and a glass of white wine in hand. He was one of the encrusted locals who propped up the bar at Au Chat Noir, the Oberkampf dive where I too had misspent more nights than I could count. And now he was practising Ramadan? Queuing with men in thawbs and black puffas for the bounty of fast-breaking pastries that had sweetened the narrow pavements of the boulevard de Belleville for the past two weeks? It was a surprise, to say the least.

He seemed equally shocked to see me. The bar we frequented may have been less than a block away, but this street corner where we bumped into each other was another world:

a thin strip of North African restaurants, kebab joints and *alimentations* (corner grocers), most of which were too local even to have names on their frontage. Such proximity of different communities is a key flavour of the 11th, the most densely populated urban district in Europe.

When I enquired politely about the background to this unexpected turn of events, Philippe explained that he was Tunisian Jewish. 'On my mother's side. I spent the first nine years of my life in Tunis. These sweets,' he gestured to one of the trestle tables heaving with honeyed snacks, 'were the taste of my childhood. But you can only find a lot of them around Paris during Ramadan. Though it's dangerous,' he patted his belly, which given he was well into his fifties was impressively slender, 'because there's no fasting for me.'

I was startled into a brief silence. This new knowledge of his origins was a reminder that it's not only cities but also people who have their hidden corners.

'Would you like me to explain the snacks to you?' he asked.

'Absolutely!'

Truth be told, I was already several days deep into trying to discover more about the 11th's North African cuisines. My sights were set on one dish in particular, couscous, which more than any other epitomises Maghrebin cooking at home and abroad, and is hugely popular across Paris but particularly in this arrondissement. Yet, it being Ramadan, people making and eating couscous outside of their homes had been hard to find. I had had more luck exploring the sweet pastries that are stocked up on during the day for the evening's fast-breaking feast – though, due to my diabetes, I was not able to sample them. This was not for want of trying from the shop owners, whose generosity had been life-threateningly insistent.

'Come now, a free sample. Just one, my friend. Here, try this one, a *banane*, it does not have so much sugar, it will be fine.'

I suppose relatively it did not have so much sugar, not compared to, say, sugar, but it was still made up of about 60 per cent of the stuff, plus a couple of teaspoons of honey. This was all mixed up with flour and saffron then deep-fried into a shape like a Spanish churro. It was tasty as a drug and pinch-the-bridge-of-your-nose sweet. I only had one. Another might have killed me.

The shopkeeper explained the long hours demanded by Ramadan – catering for people who could only eat and drink before sunrise or after sunset.

'I start before six every morning, and don't finish until ten at night. Because it's not only selling. When we shut, I have to help make all of tomorrow's pastries as well.'

He was Algerian, he told me, from the 11th.

'So you were born here?' I said.

'That's right.'

'And you've lived here all your life?'

'Always in the 11th,' he said, with no small hint of pride. I would have been proud of that too, though I could not help but notice how he had introduced himself as Algerian, not French.

Philippe was a more enthusiastic than knowledgeable food guide. The main thrust of the tour he gave me was him pointing at things and declaring, 'That, wow, I loved that. I can't remember what it's called.'

As a style of food criticism I wasn't against it, but it added little, aside from the endorsement of an individual stomach, to what I already knew. But that was OK, because now we were getting on to bigger subjects, as we spoke about the thorny discourse surrounding North African/French identity. I'd been hesitant about asking the men I spoke to directly where they were 'from'. I'd asked about family backgrounds (the majority were Algerian or Tunisian, rather than Moroccan descendants), and where people had been born (mostly in Belleville itself), but as to which nationality they identified with, that just wasn't a question to ask strangers sharing their sweets.

Along with just straightforward politeness, I was also keeping in mind things I knew from having lived in France for ten years and what I'd read. In Jean Beaman's book, *Citizen Outsider*, about the assimilation of North African immigrants in France, the sociologist cites statistics that while 70 per cent of those actually born in the country do feel French, close to half feel their Frenchness is denied by others. Just asking questions about identity would have been an accusation.

Philippe, though, had brought the subject up himself. As it happened, in regard to couscous.

'Do you remember the news story about Florian Philippot (a major *Front National* politician) getting in trouble for eating couscous?' he'd asked.

'I can't say I do.'

'It was quite funny, I suppose. They called it couscousgate. Maybe five, eight years ago Philippot was in Alsace and he was photographed eating couscous, and it made all these FN guys angry. They were saying, you're in Alsace you should be eating choucroute.'

'Jesus …'

'Except what *he* said was that these days couscous was just as French a dish as choucroute because North Africa had been a part of France for so long, its cuisine had become French cuisine.'

Instinctively to me this actually seemed quite a reasonable perspective from a far-right politician. In Britain, the idea of imported foods, such as curry, now being part of our national cuisine has become a deeply ingrained source of liberal pride. In France, though, I wondered if things were quite the same.

'So,' I asked, 'do you agree?'

Philippe puffed through his lips, 'It's difficult, eh? Like the identity of the people.'

'What do you mean?' I said.

'Well, there are so many contrasting identities at stake,' Philippe explained. 'When we talk about North African assimilation into France, it's not even like there's only one kind of North African we're talking about. As you know, there are Tunisians, Algerians, Moroccans, and some of them are also Jewish like me, as well as Muslim. Also, there are the children of colonisers who had lived in North Africa for generations before they migrated back. And that's before you even get into questions of class. That's a lot of things to negotiate before you layer French identity on top.'

'I see …' I said, frowning; what did this have to do with couscous?

'How much do you really know about the history of

France in Africa?' Philippe continued, an excited edge entering his voice. It was the tone of someone who'd spent half his life reading, but didn't get enough opportunities to demonstrate his knowledge.

'A little,' I replied, 'I mean, I did a course on the Algerian war of independence at university, but ...' I saw a cloud of disappointment cross Philippe's features, 'but that was a long time ago.'

'Excellent,' he brightened. 'So I will tell you about it, then. From the beginning. We can do it over a drink!'

We headed back to our usual haunt, Au Chat Noir – this scruffy, hipster joint epitomises another aspect of this formerly industrial arrondissement, which is most widely thought of as Paris's Williamsburg or Shoreditch. Philippe ordered us each a glass of white wine, then led me to his customary seat where there might as well have been an indentation of him in the vinyl. Then, just like that, he began to talk about French colonial history. I have no doubt that there were other ways of telling his story – history is a constantly moving target and full of modern agendas – but I did make sure to do my own research after we spoke, and verified several historians as agreeing with Philippe's version of the facts.

When France invaded Algeria in 1830, he said, their first wave of attack was conceived as spectacle. The French fleet was packed to the gunnels with new weapons of war that they wanted to demonstrate, so their landing ground, a place called Sidi Ferruch, was chosen less for strategic purposes and more for its perfect half-moon bay, which resembled an amphitheatre or a stage. Bourgeois Parisians were invited to make their way out across the Mediterranean on government ships for the show, to watch state-of-the-art cannon light up the dawn as they thudded ordinance indiscriminately into the unsuspecting Algerian town designated as France's bridgehead in Africa.

It was an invasion ostensibly based on an insult. Algeria's then ruler had swiped at France's consul to the country with a fly whisk. Admittedly, this was because that consul had demanded a series of crippling trade tariffs, but this was glossed over in the French press where the whole incident was drummed up as an inexcusable attack on the honour of France.

'What it really was, was colonial ambition,' Philippe said, sipping gingerly at his glass – a professional barfly, I'd known him to nurse the same drink for hours. 'The French had seen the success of the British in India, they wanted a big overseas territory of their own. But they didn't want just another protectorate. France was looking at Algeria as potentially their version of America, or a way of creating more of France. Algeria wasn't a single country back then, you see, but a place of squabbling tribes only loosely governed by the Ottomans. You'll still get people today saying it was a haven for slavers and pirates. Perhaps it was. But more importantly, to the French, it was a kind of terra nullius – do you know this term?'

'A land with no master,' I said, perhaps a little too pleased with myself.

'Very good.'

The invasion was not as straightforward as its arrogant first salvo suggested, he continued. It took France almost twenty years to conquer Algeria in a particularly bloody, violent war that would characterise many of the Franco-Algerian conflicts to come.

When settlers began to arrive, which they did in huge numbers, many were not from France at all, but rather from territories within its orbit. Catalans and Corsicans, Sardinians and Italians. Because of their black leather shoes, different from the local footwear, they became known as the black feet or *pieds noirs*. Meanwhile, Philippe said, France itself was falling in love with its new possession, glamorising and appropriating its customs and aesthetics.

'You know the cancan?' Philippe said. 'That was claimed to be based on an Algerian tribal dance. If you believe that kind of thing.'

He went on to explain how Tunisia and Morocco were conquered later, in the late nineteenth and early twentieth centuries respectively, and seen as natural strategic expansions to France's North African territory. Their submission was less bloody, relatively, which is not to say that thousands did not die.

'You have to understand that although these were conquered peoples, French was becoming their dominant language, the structures of their states were the same ones we have here. By the twentieth century, people born in North Africa were considered by law to be French nationals. And this particularly suited formerly marginalised communities of the region, like the Jews, as well as of course the wealthier classes who helped administer what was effectively now just part of the French state, and so saw most of its benefits. I could put it another way. When I said that I was part Tunisian, that's not exactly true, because when she was born in Tunis, my mother was legally French. It means when we talk about North African immigration to France, which by the way started properly in the First World War, it wasn't technically considered to be immigration because they were already *of* this country, even if they weren't treated like it.'

'That sounds complicated.'

'Then, eventually colonialism starts coming to an end around the world,' Philippe went on, 'but after more than a hundred years of rule, there was a sense in France that particularly Algeria wanting independence was equivalent to ...' he waved his hand about looking for inspiration, 'Brittany trying to secede. And that's not to mention the *pieds noirs*. There were more than a million of them in Algeria by then, one quarter of the country's population. Try asking one of their descendants if couscous is French.'

By now, I'd almost forgotten how the mention of couscousgate had kicked off this lecture.

'They'd say it is?'

'Many of them would. More than that, a lot of them still have no shame around colonialism itself either. How could they? Without colonialism, who they are would not exist. But the repercussions of the Algerian war of independence were felt in France for years. They still are today. There's been so much police brutality down the years. Personally, I sometimes wonder how some Algerians can stand to come and live here at all.'

'So, did you eat couscous growing up, then?' I asked, trying to bring the conversation back to something more concrete.

'Of course,' said Philippe. 'I think my grandmother's couscous was one of the best in all of Tunis.'

'Really?' I was suddenly excited. 'And do you know her recipe?'

'Not at all,' Philippe laughed, finishing his wine. 'For

that, you would have to ask my grandmother. But she is a long time dead, *hèlas.*'

The Medina is not one of Paris's famous couscous restaurants – for that, you would have to go to the celebrity-frequented Ruche à Miel in the 12th, or the old-fashioned institution Chez Omar in the Marais – but that is no slight on its quality. It is a local place with a simple, Moorish-style interior and complimentary olives and dates set out on all the tables, deeply ensconced in the life of the *quartier*, serving to an almost exclusively North African crowd.

I'd got talking to its manager, Mohamed, while he was distributing free lunch bags to the neighbourhood poor, white and African. He and his friends did this every day of Ramadan as part of the charitable practice known as *zakat*, which is one of the five pillars of Islam and particularly undertaken during the holy month. If I wanted to know how they made couscous, he suggested I return at around six, just before their chef started to prepare the evening's feast.

Hamed did not look like a chef, which is to say he was much more fresh-faced and sprightly than many I've met in that profession. He was also distractingly handsome, tall and lithe with deep-brown eyes, full lips and a generous, teasing smile. He was from Tunisia, he said. Well, he was born in Paris, but his family was Tunisian, which was why in the restaurant he made couscous the Tunisian way.

Before I go any further, just to be clear exactly what I'm talking about, in France, couscous is a catch-all term referring to both the semolina grain and the spiced stew it is served with. It dates back at least a thousand years; some people say longer – some even like to believe it was invented by a desert djinn. And it is not only its theoretical identity that is complicated, I was learning; in some respects, asking someone how to make couscous is akin to asking how to make spaghetti: varieties and methods differ by region and by individual.

Tunisian and Moroccan couscous recipes were more popular in Paris than Algerian varieties, Hamed explained, though he couldn't say why. Later, I discovered that there had been a historic resistance in Algeria to considering their traditional couscous a restaurant food – it was fiercely domestic. When Algerians began opening eateries in France, the most famous being Chez Bébert, founded in 1956, they tended to cook to a new, public-facing recipe, the *couscous royal.*

'The main difference between Moroccan couscous and Tunisian couscous,' Hamed said, 'is that Moroccan is *jaune* [yellow] because of turmeric, and it usually contains nuts and dried fruit, while Tunisian couscous is *rouge* [red] because of tomatoes and harissa paste. And we like it spicy.' He winked at me, though I don't think he even realised he was doing it – he was just effortlessly charismatic and effervescing with uncomplicated niceness. The kind of man you'd think twice about introducing to your girlfriend. Not that he'd do anything, mind you, he was far too nice.

'So where did you learn your recipe?'

'Back in Tunisia,' Hamed said, 'I went for two months to study with my grandmother.'

'Oh really?'

'Yes, that's who looks after our couscous recipes,' he continued. 'You ask anyone who makes their favourite couscous, they'll say their grandmother.'

That sounded familiar.

'So, what's the recipe?'

'They make it differently over there,' Hamed went on, those deep-brown eyes looking off briefly into the middle distance, seeing, I imagined, some sunlit shore framed by Mediterranean blue. 'They prepare the semolina fresh ...'

He explained this process. Later, I hypnotised myself watching YouTube clips of how it's done. Water is sprinkled onto ground semolina flour and the mixture massaged between practised palms until it starts to form into small grains. Next, it's rubbed and tossed in a rolling motion in a tight-woven basket to break up lumps, and after that, sifted to separate any loose flour that has not yet formed into couscous grains, so that the leftover flour can be subjected to the same process again. Finally, the couscous is left out to dry under the hot Tunisian sun.

'That's why we can't make it fresh in Paris,' Hamed said. 'We do not have the sun.'

I wasn't sure this sounded totally scientific, but I understood what Hamed meant.

'What about the sauce, though?' I asked.

'For us here it can be different every day, depending on what ingredients we find at the market.'

'You buy from Belleville market?'

'Of course. And I make it the Tunisian way, except less spicy – because we serve to people from across the Maghreb.'

'I see,' I said. 'But the recipe?'

'Oh, you shouldn't listen to me about the recipe, I am not a chef.'

'But you're the chef at this restaurant,' I said. 'Aren't you?'

'I do the cooking at this restaurant,' Hamed corrected me. 'It's not the same.'

Don't think it was lost on me, the deep Frenchness of those words.

'If you really want to learn how to make Tunisian cous-cous,' he continued, 'you'd be better off talking to a Tunisian granny.'

OK, but where was I going to find one of those?

'Hold on,' I countered, 'but you said that here you made things less spicy than in Tunisia, and really what I want to learn is that. A Parisian couscous.'

Hamed laughed then, lighting up the room. 'There's no such thing as a Parisian couscous,' he said definitively. 'It would be like saying an English pizza, or an Italian curry. Couscous can be Moroccan, it can be Algerian, it can be from Mauritania. But it cannot be French.'

I did not press the point. Nor did I continue to ask for the recipe, which it seemed Hamed was too humble to try and teach, but I promised to take a seat in the restaurant and taste what he made.

'It will be my delight to serve you,' he said, suddenly switching into perfect flowing English – our conversation until this point had been in French.

My eyes widened in surprise.

'I spent some time in London,' Hamed shrugged. 'But you're in France. You have to practise your French.'

Dinner in the Medina was one of the calmest eating experiences I have ever known. Islamic chanting music was playing low over the speakers when I went to take my seat, and the half-dozen other men in the restaurant – there were only men – were either dining in silence or conducting inaudibly murmured conversations of warm intimacy over the paper-clothed tables.

I was served a jug of mint-infused iced water, which I sipped on while chewing at the alternate sweet and salt flavours of the complimentary olives and dates. There was no printed or written menu, just a list of dishes that the single, unhurried waiter relayed to me with practised ease, as if reciting a prayer. It was still Ramadan, and all the other tables were piled high with different foods: savoury pastries, steaming soups, copious fish salads. For me, however, there was only one thing I was going to be ordering.

'*Le couscous, s'il vous plaît.*'

It came in two separate bowls. One of fantastic turmeric-golden grain, brightened by a single crescent of roasted green pepper, the other a lamb stew of vivid scarlet – the colour of an ageing star. Moving at the relaxed pace of the restaurant, I spooned some of the latter over the former, and I began to eat.

Now, I should make a confession here. A little late in the day, but here it is: I am no great fan of couscous. I don't mean to say that I dislike it, only that I would seldom order or cook the dish for myself. To me, couscous somehow lacks the showy, look-at-me flavours of, say, Vietnamese cuisine to have won over my palate. And yet this was easily one of the most enjoyable, munificent meals on my Paris food journey so far.

It was deeply redolent of home cooking – seeking to comfort rather than to impress. That melange of subtle, building spice and chewy, salt-rich lamb, perfectly cushioned by the fragrant, pillowy restraint of the grain. A dish of the hearth, above all.

*

I was put in contact with Nicole by my long-time Parisian friend Albert. She was virtually his grandmother, he explained. Well, technically, she was the girlfriend of his step-grandfather, but both had filled their quasi-familial roles for so long, it no longer seemed to matter that they were not related by blood. And she made an amazing couscous – the best couscous, Albert claimed. 'But then, your grandmother always makes the best couscous.'

Albert is *pied noir* on his father's side and couscous was the central dish of the household in which he grew up. *He* wouldn't go so far as calling it a French dish, he said, though in my continued research I discovered that the *couscous royal* now served in many Algerian restaurants around the capital was literally an invention of *pied noir* communities who had migrated to the city back in the early fifties. Because of this, I half expected the recipe Nicole would give me would be for a couscous of this variety, which includes a mixed grill of meats – chicken, lamb, merguez – arranged into a crown shape atop the sauce, hence the dish's regal name. I ought to have learned by now that things would not be so simple.

Nicole did not correspond to a typical image of a grandmother. Rather, she was a portrait of Parisian elegance, dressed in an oversized cashmere jumper and with subtle, perfectly applied make-up. Meeting her in the Seine-side café she had suggested for our interview felt like a rendezvous with the city's past. Except of course she had not always lived in Paris, though neither was she *pied noir*. She was born in Tunis into a Jewish family that had been in Tunisia for almost two thousand years.

'How long?' I asked, with a note of incredulity.

'My father could trace his family in the country back to the first century AD,' she told me, leaving lipstick marks on her espresso cup. 'I moved to Paris for university, but you have to understand, I grew up speaking French, feeling I was French, being taught in French schools. Paris was where I always wanted to be. That was in 1961.'

For a moment, I forgot about couscous; was captivated by the idea of the woman opposite me having experienced the Paris of the 1960s – the era of Nouvelle Vague cinema and student revolt, when Sartre and Camus still smoked in the cafés, when the central market at Les Halles still stood.

'Was it very different?' I asked lamely.

'Oh yes,' Nicole said. 'So different. So incredibly different.'

'How?'

'It was black.'

'Huh?'

'All these buildings that you see,' she gestured out of the window with a delicate, perfectly manicured hand. 'They were covered in grime. All of Paris was. You have no idea how much cleaner it is now.'

'Oh,' I said, my romantic vision of the past tarnished.

'So, you wanted to know to how I make couscous?'

It was not a couscous recipe that you would find in restaurants, Nicole told me, and certainly not a *couscous royal*. Nor was it the couscous she cooked for Albert, who is vegetarian. No, it was not typical, she said, but then, what was typical anyway? This was a Tunisian *Shabbat* couscous, in other words a filling feast for many hungry people on a Friday night, and one of its main elements was fried meatballs.

'I don't know how far back the recipe goes,' she said. 'A long way.'

'The first century AD?' I smiled.

'A long way back.'

Couscous-Boulettes du Shabbat

Serves a small neighbourhood (10–12 people)

Ingredients:

For the meatballs:

500g beef mince

200g stale bread, chopped

3 onions, diced

1 tsp ground cinnamon

½ bunch of flat-leaf parsley, chopped

½ bunch of coriander, chopped

Harissa (to taste)

2 egg yolks

Oil for frying

For the batter:

2 egg whites

Flour (to coat the meatballs)

1 tbsp water mixed with ½ tsp tomato concentrate

For the meatball sauce:

2 garlic cloves

300g tinned tomatoes

For the couscous sauce:

1.5kg beef

2 tomatoes

3 carrots
3 leeks
6 turnips
3 celery sticks
500g pumpkin
½ white cabbage
2 onions
5 garlic cloves
300g tinned chickpeas
Water to cover
½ bunch of coriander
10 mint leaves
½ bunch of flat-leaf parsley

For the couscous:
1kg dried couscous
1 litre boiling water
½ tsp tumeric powder

To make the meatballs I combined the beef mince in a large
bowl with stale bread that I'd chopped and soaked in water,
diced onion, ground cinnamon, chopped parsley and coriander, harissa, and finally the yolks of two eggs: I rolled it
all together in my hands, then started carefully shaping it
into little orbs on my kitchen countertop, while I thought
of how Nicole had learned how to do this in Tunis with her
mother; how her mother had learned from her mother in
turn, and so on.

Next, a thin, pancake-like batter in a shallow bowl: flour,
egg whites, a little tomato concentrate mixed into water. I
rolled the meatballs in this coating, remembering the motion

Nicole had inadvertently made when she explained this step to me. Her hand hovered over the café table, its index finger curving right from arthritis, an affliction I remembered in my own grandmother's hands.

'My mother used to cook for the whole neighbourhood,' Nicole had said. 'Huge amounts. She would start on the Thursday, then on *Shabbat* itself, people would just start calling by. They never said they were coming, just turned up.'

I fried off the coated meatballs, watched them spit and sizzle and brown in my shallow pan. Next, in a separate saucepan, I thinly sliced and lightly fried the garlic, to which I added the tomatoes, making a simple sauce in which the meatballs were to be fully cooked. It was peculiar: at this stage I felt I could have been prepping a simple spaghetti and meatballs, rather than couscous.

But this was only the start. Here was a mammoth dish for my tiny kitchen. The meatballs I set in my oven to keep warm while I focused on making the second broth. This I started by searing beef, then throwing in the enormous quantity of vegetables all at once as I'd been instructed (the recipe I have listed above, which was the one Nicole gave me, feeds ten people; I had cut its ratios in half, but even so my kitchen counters overflowed with produce). I had roughly chopped all of them to more or less the same rough two-centimetre-thick size, apart from the garlic, which had been crushed. They sat, sweating away in my crowded saucepan, seeming remarkably European.

There was no spice in Nicole's couscous sauce. None at all. Only the addition of chickpeas hinted at any flavour beyond the most conservative of French kitchens. It made me pause for a moment to think how strange it was that food is nationalised at all. Here were ingredients that grew from Paris to Algiers and far beyond. Who was to say that they belonged to any particular place? Well, people were people. What they say and what they feel is what makes the world.

I poured water into the pot and waited a good hour and a half. Everything was bubbling away now, my tiny kitchen rich with the smells of North Africa, which in this moment, were the same as the smells of northern Europe. It was time to make the couscous.

'Towards the end of her life, even my mother used dried couscous,' Nicole had said. 'I always use dried couscous myself. There's no space for making it fresh in Paris, and dried couscous these days is almost as good.'

Technically, I should have used a *couscousier*, a two-tiered saucepan, in which the top is like a flat-bottomed sieve which can be filled with the dried grain so that it will be cooked and flavoured by the steam rising from the stew underneath. But *couscousiers* were expensive, and where would I store it afterwards? The pots and pans I had already filled the small space almost to the rafters.

So instead, I cooked the couscous as I always do. Boiled a kettle, submerged the grains in a 1:1 ratio of scalding water, then left it to soak and engorge. Finally, in a flourish that was more a tribute to the meal I'd had at the Medina than integral to Nicole's recipe, I stirred in bright yellow turmeric powder, fluffing it with my fork. All that was left was to slice the herbs: coriander, mint and parsley, a bright garnish for the sauce.

Nicole's *Shabbat* couscous was excellent. Warming and hearty, full of energy and life. A feast for a neighbourhood that felt ill contained in my apartment. And then, there was that wonderful feeling of tasting a recipe that stretches back centuries, that crosses borders, that had been carried and developed by the many grandmothers of a single household for years.

Perhaps, I considered, couscous was too complicated and fraught with politics to talk about its national identity. Better to say that of all the cultures in modern France, it belongs to the family, and to whatever culture those families belong to in turn.

10ème arrondissement

A completely normal Saturday in Paris: rain and riot police, the sound of drums. Do you hear the people sing? I could, and they were in fine voice. Or at least one of them was, which was probably why she'd been given the loudhailer, marching at the front of the *gilets jaunes*, all two dozen of them. It was a procession with all the grandeur of a defeated army. Not just defeated, massacred.

I remembered when the *gilets jaunes* numbered in their tens of thousands, making a battleground of France. In its heyday, back in the winter of 2018/19, this grassroots, largely rural movement that rose up to protest fuel tax and the cost of living seemed both an existential threat to, and the potential salvation of, the Fifth Republic. Today, they were already an anachronism. Following their procession through the narrow backstreets of the 10th, the main emotion I registered in the ordinary Parisian faces coming to gawp from the windows of their apartments was surprise: the *gilets jaunes* were *still* a thing?

I mean, barely, but here they were, nevertheless. The survivors. The ones willing to die for the cause. Middle-aged men with beards and badges, women with weather-reddened faces, sucking on a steady stream of fags. They had the outward scruffiness of the marginally employed. Several had the dates of their previous marches inked on their yellow vests, from the heady start right up until now, when they still assembled in ever-dwindling numbers once a week, more social group than insurrection. It was not as though the things they were fighting for had been resolved, just that their symbols had run out of steam. Only the *tricolore*, fluttering proud at the front of the march, spoke of how they were still part of a bigger debate.

I had marched in plenty of demonstrations in my time in this city, where as well as being an agent for change, revolution is also a spectator sport: *la manif* is practically an institution as well as a national pastime. I recalled the sinus-burn of tear gas and the triumphant pollution of flaming bins; the semi-ritualised charge and feint with riot cops; the flash of grenades and the press of bodies. How fun it all is, electrified with romance, righteousness and sex – that's right, apart from actual sex it's one of the more erotically charged activities that goes on in this city, for protests are a regulated risk, and no matter the cause, you can't help but soon feel connected to the people you are marching with, part of the eternal good facing down injustice. And because food is a soft corollary of the erotic, I also recalled what I ate.

To any large protest, its profiteers. More often than not, these are people who could not care less about the cause but know well enough to capitalise on the Napoleonic dictum that an army marches on its stomach. In Paris, they take the form of men cooking merguez on shopping trolley grills. How many movements have been sustained by those spiced, fatty beef sausages, served between cheap baguette and doused in the kind of mustard that gives tear gas a good name? But this was not the protest meal I was remembering.

On the two prior occasions when I had marched with the *gilets jaunes*, sheltering on side streets off boulevard de Magenta, fellow protestors had unshouldered backpacks to share the food they had brought for the march – food of the home regions from which they'd come to make a stand in the capital.

The first backpack had yielded dried sausage and Comté cheese, washed down with a flask of young wine. The second, something more elaborate. This *gilet jaune*, a gangly, bespectacled man who worked as a hotel concierge in the Alps – had made us *tartiflette*, cooked at home and packaged in individual portion-sized plastic tubs. The palpitatingly calorific cheese, potato and lardon dish from the Savoie region might have been laboratory-designed to impart the energy to withstand mountain winters or fight a rebellion. He had even brought spoons.

As I write, a new battle line has been drawn. Now, it is the country's farmers articulating the struggle. Where the *gilets*

jaunes came to represent more general working-class con-
cerns, here the fight is specific, targeted on EU environmental
regulations and the French government's attempt to force
down food prices, which the farmers say are making their
already underappreciated and precarious lives even harder.

The yellow vests have given way to new symbols, and the
main tool of protest has become the blockade. Tractors have
been used to clog the arterial roads to Paris, and there was
talk of trying to cut off Rungis, the city's wholesale food
market, a siege on the bellies of all of us who live here. In
some respects, though, it's the same fight as it always is. The
people against the state, individuals against the world, hope
against despair.

I had known early on in this project that the food of Paris
protest would be my dish for the 10th. Home to two of Paris's
major railway hubs, the Gare du Nord and the Gare de l'Est,
the 10th is better connected than any other arrondissement
to the places from which much protest comes. Also, it was
where I had been offered sustenance by my fellow marchers.
Both times, I had been making my way towards the agora of
the French state, the place de la République. This gloomy,
functional square with a statue of Marianne at its centre
is where France's citizens congregate when they want to be
seen. It is the meeting point of three arrondissements, but in
my experience has been most often approached by protests
from the 10th, and so the arrondissement has become the
crucible of Paris *manifestation* in my mind.

Unfortunately, the regional farmers had not got this
memo. Instead, they were making a stand in the city's south,
where they were bringing their tractors from across France
to breach the Périphérique ring road that surrounds central

Paris. So, a few days after following the sad remnants of the *gilets jaunes* in the 10th, I jumped on the metro and headed south, to witness whatever was about to go down. This time, I packed my own spoon.

As it turned out, however, there was no food being shared at this march. That was, in part, the point.

All the way there I was even more acutely aware than normal of things being eaten – the huge quantity of produce weighing heavy on bistro tables. The salads and steaks and literally thousands of fried potatoes that were being consumed on this, just another average Paris lunchtime. And all those urbanely dressed Parisians grazing with the same day-to-day nonchalance we all exhibit, unlikely to be giving much more than a passing thought to where their food had come from; how it had all at some point been farmed from the mostly French earth. France remains one of the few countries in the world that could sustain itself entirely off the food it produces, but how often did any of us living in this city stop to consider how the whole place and the 'civilisation' it so proudly guarded was maintained off the backs and work of others so distant from ourselves. Who, likely as not, would hold divergent political views, who laboured under big skies and in circumstances alien to our own. And who, justifiably enough, had not come to Paris on this occasion to bring us any more to eat.

Under the railway tracks at Sèvres-Lecourbe I encountered a great gathering of beardless, ruddy men, cigarettes squeezed in their large hands. Over their jumpers or beneath weather-scarred coats, they wore T-shirts bearing the slogan of the march: '*On marche sur la tête*'. More men poured out of coaches that had driven to the capital from all corners of France. Many carried handmade signs that declared in no uncertain terms that they had not come to Paris for the sights.

The statistics around French farming are dire: two fifths of farmers make less than €5,000 a year and would be unable to survive without subsidies; one quarter have no romantic partner – twice the number of the rest of the population. Somewhere in France, a farmer takes his or her own life every two to three days. No wonder, then, that the righteous indignation was as palpable as the cigarette smoke on the air. It was an atmosphere I knew well from other protests: the hope, and the collective certainty in the cause.

There were journalists too, dozens of them. Sticking out as obviously as, well, me. They thrust microphones under farmers' faces, soliciting their views.

'If the people of France want to eat well, they have to pay for it,' one farmer was asserting. 'Or they can have bad food from Eastern Europe for cheap. It's their choice.'

To start with, I decided I was better off keeping my motivations for being here quiet. Better to play the bumbling, curious foreigner than the snooty, city-dwelling writer working on a book about Paris cuisine.

'So, what does the T-shirt slogan mean?' I approached one farmer to ask. '*On marche sur la tête.*'

'*Bah … C'est une expression,*' he replied. He was from Hauts-de-France, wearing an HDF bandana, and smelled richly of beer.

'Right, yes, but what does it mean?'

He looked at me like I was an idiot. 'It means we're walking on our heads,' he said.

'No, I mean, I understand, but—'

'We're turning things upside down,' he continued. 'Changing the order of things so we get heard.'

I can't say this made a lot of sense to me, but it was a slogan to get behind: a new branding for a new movement. Branding has long been one of the great strengths of French protest. From the Phrygian caps of 1789 – so ensconced now in the national identity that they were borrowed for the Paris 2024 Olympic mascot – right up to the master stroke of the *gilet jaune*, indelibly transforming the practical uniform of the working man – the high-vis tabard – into a symbol of resistance. For this farmers' protest, too, people have been turning town signs upside down right across the country, a simple gesture to make their cause visible everywhere you go.

'*On marche sur la tête!*' the booze-smelling farmer yelled at me, bringing our conversation to a close.

There was only one farmer I was direct with about my aims, the same one I had overheard talking to a journalist about how the French needed to pay to eat well. He was a brick of a man in a new biker jacket with wire-rimmed glasses and close-cropped curly hair. I told him I was English, trying to learn more about the food of Paris, and—

'I am neither English, nor do I know anything about Paris,' he barked. 'So I have nothing to say to you.' Then he stomped off.

There was an arrogance among the farmers, and a hard-done-by quality, which was neither endearing nor easy to condemn.

At last the tractors arrived, met by cheers as they rumbled in uncanny procession down the boulevard: a battalion of regional pride, of the periphery resisting the centre. Their wheels and cabins were buffed clean, as though despite themselves they wanted to put on a good show for the town. Hung over their plates were the names of the towns and regions they had come from, upside down of course. Meanwhile, over many of their shiny cabs, the *tricolore* of the Republic flew.

Another completely normal Saturday in Paris: more rain, more riot police, this time on the place de la République itself, where the sound of measured speeches and polite, attentive applause had replaced the beating of drums.

Today, it was the turn of the other side of the farmers' protest. The smaller-scale farmers of the Île-de-France (greater Paris area), united under the banner of the Confédération Paysanne, were earnestly huddled under a large marquee, listening to a series of speeches by younger, trendier-looking individuals, who, though ostensibly linked to the larger movement, actually seemed to be championing policies that were diametrically opposed to it. These speakers wanted more control over pesticides, restraints on larger farms, greater international co-operation: all things the *marche sur la tête* protests were marching against. I was put in mind of the General de Gaulle quote about the difficulty of governing a country with 246 different varieties of cheese. (In fact, France has more than a thousand varieties of cheese; I guess de Gaulle was just being optimistic.)

Nor did these farmers have any issue bringing their produce to Paris. In fact, they'd set up stalls. They were selling leeks and potatoes, vegan tartines, artisanal beer. Here was a more urbane, picturesque kind of farmer, whose voice would be heard through sensible, articulate debate rather than bare-faced anger and grandstanding schemes. And yet: speaker after speaker insisted on connecting this specific protest to the larger cause.

There is something in France's national character that makes it want to rerun the Revolution over and over, as French protest expert Eddy Fougier put it in 2019, it's 'as if we're fighting a permanent, peaceful civil war over what our country should be.' By contrast to other European nations, there is remarkable support for protest across the political spectrum. Despite their less than cosmopolitan views, even a year into their movement the *gilets jaunes* still enjoyed the broad approval of 68 per cent of French people. And protest here works; it changes policy. The large number of different parties in France's National Assembly means most causes have a direct political voice.

The symbols of the state are also evergreen symbols of defiance. The national flag began life as the banner of the Revolution, the Marseillaise as its anthem. Almost the only French protests in which they are not commonly used are migrant- and minority-led ones. Even in those, however, the fundamental French value of resistance is being upheld.

Eventually, I tired of the enthusiastic clapping and dreams of a better future – and getting drenched just outside the confines of the Confédération Paysanne's marquee – and went to take a look at the riot police, camped out around the limits of the square. They were having lunch.

The French riot police, the much-maligned CRS, spend most of the time idling around in case things get out of hand. In each of the dozen or so parked vans I saw large, ruddy, beardless men in Kevlar settling down to small, compartmentalised trays. They might have been economy passengers on a long-haul flight were it not for the red gingham dishcloths upon which many of them had laid out their trays.

To begin with, I watched from a distance, amused by the peculiar quaintness of seeing this militarised arm of the state reduced to the aesthetic of a French country kitchen. Then I approached.

The first cop I could find to speak to was a big man, probably in his early fifties, with a pencil moustache and clad in the head-to-toe armour of crowd control. He was standing outside his van and willing to talk – about food at least.

They were given 'normal' things to eat in the CRS, he said, 'French' things.

Did he like them?

Well, yes, in fact they were often very tasty, but in his opinion too calorific.

'Most weekends we don't have anything much to do, but they still want to give us the energy to crack heads,' he laughed.

'And so,' I asked, 'what are you eating today?'

'Today?' he said. 'Today it's *tartiflette*.'

The synchronicity of this was too much to ignore. I had now encountered *tartiflette* as fuel on either side of the barricade. It was rich, sustaining and portable, boasting a hearty simplicity. But more, like the flag, the national anthem and the right to protest itself, it was a symbol that most of France, of whatever political allegiance, could get behind. My choice for a meal of protest, and for the 10th arrondissement, was made, and such was the time of year, I knew exactly where I had to go to learn how to make it.

*

The Salon de l'Agriculture is another instance when Paris is visited by France. Ostensibly a farm show, it is also so much more: an occasion for politicians to press flesh, for the countryside to feel seen, for France to affirm its agricultural soul. It takes place at the city's largest exhibition centre at the Porte de Versailles, where for over a week at the end of February seven pavilions the size of aircraft hangers are colonised by the terroir.

Most famously, there are the animals. The cows and sheep and pigs, most prize-winningly enormous, are nose-ringed into town to stand on golden straw underneath high, artificial light, to be gawped at and touched by people who usually only know such creatures by their taste. People come to see these animals, then, but they stay for the food.

The smell of the catering pavilion was almost worth the price of admission alone. It was partly a smell of people, bustling in their hundreds from the outside cold, but much more it was of cooking. I could see steam rising in the huge, interior distance – multiple columns of it coming from different stalls as if from the separate fires of an encamped army. Each one promised something delicious at its source. The floor plan was divided up by the regional cooking of different *départements* like a scale map of France. What I needed was the Auvergne-Rhône-Alpes region, but it was far from the entrance; there was the rest of the country to get through first. So began a gastronomic odyssey, past Breton crêpes, Alsatian choucroute, and far more than 246 varieties of cheese; and distracted by a whole barricade of booze.

Eventually, I stumbled blearily into the Auvergne-Rhône-

Alpes section, where several cauldrons of *tartiflette* were being stirred. Head spinning, I started to talk to the man overseeing them about how to cook the dish. He was wiry, with tired eyes and a deep winter tan, and put me in mind of one of the farmers I'd spoken to rather than a chef. He was also smoking a hand-rolled cigarette, in a small protest of his own against city rules. He took some persuasion to tell me his recipe, and eventually only gave it up grudgingly, like a man handing over a weapon in a fight.

Tartiflette

Sustains 4 revolutionaries
Ingredients:
1kg potatoes
2 brown onions
250g lardons
1 whole Reblochon cheese

First, I peeled and paysanned the potatoes into discs and put them on to parboil. Meanwhile, I sliced the onions into rings, and threw lardons into a hot pan.

The lardons flinched as they hit the heat. They began to sizzle, leeching their glossy gold fat into the base of my pan. Then, after a few minutes of stirring, and savouring the thrilling, divisive smell of scorching flesh, I lowered the flame, poured in a tiny amount more cooking oil to augment the lardon fat, and threw in the onions, then watched them sweat and soften.

Now, I took the half-cooked potatoes off the boil, poured them out into my colander, and returned them to the saucepan to steam dry. The potatoes went into the pan, hissing in protest at first, then drinking in its sweet/salt oil to their core.

Next came the Reblochon. Another mountain cheese like the Tomme that gives *aligot* its particular flavour and texture, its name derived from the word '*reblocher*', which literally means to pinch the cow's udder a second time. As legend would have it, this came from when farmers would hold back some of the cow's milk from the state-measured first milking, dodging tax on all that was produced. A small act of resistance in itself, and one that yields a far richer second milk.

The Reblochon was soft and pungently nutty, newly freed from the cool, hillside cellars where for two months it had gained its flavour. It was too soft to grate. I took the smaller of my two knives and sliced it into the thinnest strips I could and mixed them, rind and all, into the bubbling pan.

Usually, the next step when making *tartiflette* would be to slip the whole heavy concoction under the grill. It would have made things even better, branding the dish's surface with beautiful brown craters of caramelisation. Except that was not how it had been done at the Salon de l'Agriculture, and it's not how you make *tartiflette* if you are making it in big enough quantities to feed an army, whichever side you're fighting on.

Besides, I could already tell it would be cracking-heads tasty regardless.

Yet another normal Saturday in Paris: riot police, but this time no rain. I took my *tartiflette* to eat from a plastic tub on the place de la République. I found a place to sit on the dais of the central statue in earshot of yet another protest gathering. There were *tricolores*.

I un-popped the lid, loosed the *tartiflette*'s countryside odours into the city here at the heart of the Republic, caught the scent of all the things that had once been grown and cultivated from the terroir. Then I began to eat.

On first bite, I wondered: was there enough flavour here? Had I overestimated the Reblochon's strength, expected too much from the natural salt of the pork? But with every mouthful the flavour built. We are many, we are strong. And it built and it built, the velveteen cheese wrapping those starch-rich, crumbling potatoes became a fist of potential. The lardons were almost a lightening agent, a *relief!*

When I was finished, I felt I was a man with the energy to storm or defend a Bastille. Once I'd digested, at least.

Meanwhile, the protesters in front of me had broken out into the Marseillaise. An agitated, full-throated rendition that sounded, as it always does, a call to arms; a promise of violence in the service of a better world.

It had attracted the attention of a couple of the policeman patrolling the square. I watched them edge closer, backs straightening, hands gripping tightly at the weapons of state that hung by their side. They looked like they might be readying themselves in case the anthem sparked into something more, or perhaps they just wanted to join the song.

9ème arrondissement

There were three of us in the sauna: me in a towel, and two strangers, a man and a woman, both entirely naked, all sat in steamy silence.

'Do you come here a lot?' said the man at last. He was slim, fiftyish, and I noticed now not entirely unclothed; he was wearing an Apple Watch. He was not talking to me.

'From time to time,' said the woman. She was maybe a little younger, though with the contours of her body buttressed by plastic against age. 'Normally there are more people.'

'Too many people,' the man sighed, stretching. 'I was here last Saturday, *c'était le bordel*.'

They both laughed at that, and even I cracked a smile,

though more because I was proud of myself for catching this French pun in this somewhat strained circumstance. '*Bordel*' is a slightly cheeky French term that is usually used to express the idea that something is a mess, crowded, chaotic, but it literally means a bordello, and though we were technically only in a swingers' club, well, I got the idea.

'*Je peux?*' the man asked then.

'*Allez,*' said the woman, and just like that, he reached his Apple-Watched wrist down between her thighs. The woman gasped, and in seconds had brought her hand – taloned with fuchsia-pink nail extensions – towards his groin.

Now, I know what you're thinking: what did any of this have to do with food?

The libertine and the gourmand have long been bedfellows, or table mates: appetite is the gateway to a multitude of sins. And this was Paris's 9th arrondissement, home of the city's red-light district, among the most famous red-light districts in all of Europe, established at the end of the nineteenth century around the grand cabarets and loose-living bohemians who had digs in this northern *quartier*. Pigalle remains a couple of square kilometres of massage parlours and sex shops, peep shows and brothels, most decked out in cheap 1970s neon and hawked by the crustiest *vrai Parisiens* in town, who perch smoking cigarette stubs on old bar stools at their entrances, trying to coax passers-by inside.

Few areas were more mysterious to me. Not least because alongside these centres of vice, normal Paris continued, blithely indifferent to whatever might be going on behind closed doors. Here were tourists and third-wave coffee shops, overhyped restaurants and international flavours. It was where I had lived when I first came to the city. I had seen its more reputable establishments change hands and evolve, had witnessed their gentrification and sanitisation. In that time, the neighbourhood had even gained a new, bougie nickname, 'SoPi', for South Pigalle – a rebranding from its seedy past. Yet the skin joints had remained, frozen in time, and were a reminder that even when you don't dress it up with flat whites and burrata, sex sells. On the other hand, I had never set foot in any of them.

It's not a commonly known fact, but among its other claims, Paris is one of the swinging capitals of the world. According to some statistics, more than a quarter of Parisian couples have shared partners, and one in ten have been to a sex club like the one I was now in. *Libertinage*, as it's known, is one of the city's largest subcultures, yet it was utterly unknown to me. Surely, though, it was more than coincidence that a city so renowned for its gastronomy made such an active pastime of sex as well.

Then I had discovered that Pigalle's largest sex club, Moon City – in fact, the largest heterosexual sex club in Paris – also offered its patrons food. Even if, full disclosure – and there will be a lot more of that in what follows – the club was technically on the 18th side of the boulevard that separates the two arrondissements, I decided I had to go and see how these two pleasures of the flesh combined.

The entrance to Moon City was like a bawdy Balinese temple, a gateway carved from wood and layered over the two lower storeys of a Haussmann block. Peculiar how I'd walked past something so obvious so many times without giving it a second thought. It was right there for all the world to see: on the boulevard de Clichy, between a pharmacy and a neighbourhood bar, with two statues of spear-clutching warriors outside and its name emblazoned in spiky Arabic-style font over the great vent above its door.

I had to buzz to get inside, felt myself being eyed from a closed-circuit television camera for a couple of seconds, then the door opened with a magnetic thunk and a chubby man in a floral shirt ushered me in.

'Do you know what this is?' he asked.

'Yes.'

'And you know for a single man on his own it's €168?'

I knew that too, just as I knew that couples only paid 80, and that for single women it was free. Oh well, at least it would be tax deductible.

'Also, there's no one here at the moment,' the gatekeeper told me.

'Oh.'

'But that should change soon,' he said, 'it's only early.'

It was. Two in the afternoon to be precise, on a Sunday; I had come because this was when Moon City also advertised that it would provide its clients with a meal: brunch. 'Come to satisfy (not only) your taste buds and meet other gour-mands', the website said.

'So, you can come back later,' the man was saying, 'or ...'

'No, it's OK.' It had already taken all the confidence I had to get to this point; if I wandered back into the streets of Pigalle now, I would never return. 'Just one thing, is it true that you're serving brunch?'

The man looked at me quizzically, 'Yes, it's true.'

I paid my €168 in return for a towel, a sarong, a wrist pouch filled with five(!) condoms and a single token for a drink. The towel and the sarong were the obligatory dress code. The 500 or so sex clubs of Paris are broadly divided into two categories, the 'dry', which usually expect guests to come adorned in burlesque-adjacent finery, and the hammams. Moon City was one of the latter.

I ascended to the changing rooms, up a side staircase from the welcome desk, taking care to catalogue every sensation as I went. I had come to observe; so as long as I was observing, I told myself, what I was doing was fine. Except just yet there wasn't much that was particularly noticeable. I'd hoped perhaps for somewhere offensively gaudy, for the stink of semen and disinfectant, but the staircase was just a staircase and the air didn't smell of much at all.

Then I was in the changing rooms, which had wooden lockers printed with images of Hindu gods, and there was nothing much left for it but to take off all my clothes. I might have backed out then, too, but €168 is a lot to sink just to look at a staircase. So I got naked, wrapped the sarong around my waist and threw my towel as rakishly as I could over my shoulder. And I stepped out into the sex club alone. Or so I thought.

The place was huge. I mean, I knew that from the size of the frontage and from having read online about its 1,200 square metres of floor space, but neither had prepared me for the reality. I was in a long, shadowy corridor flanked by multiple side rooms of different sizes and shapes, most with some kind of unadorned slab of vinyl furniture at their centre, a funhouse of mirrors lining their walls and dully lit in red or purple.

It was silent, aside from the whirr of the heating system, and completely separate from the outside world. In terms of adornment, there were a few vague gestures towards the East: carved wooden statues of Ganesh or of lovers wrapped in some Kama Sutra embrace – the kind of pieces that might crop up in a wealthy 'well-travelled' Parisian's home. There was a faint stale sniff of plywood, perhaps, and of dried sweat. What it all put me in mind of most was the smell and feel of the suburban Laser Quest I'd known as a kid back home.

My footsteps slapped nakedly down the hallway as I explored all the way to its end, where I found a tiled, mint-smelling steam room that fogged up my glasses, and which had a couple of dark alcoves intended, presumably, for doing unspeakable things.

Eventually, I went into the sauna, a comparatively homely space at the top of another set of stairs. Brunch was presumably served on the ground floor, but I was in no hurry, and besides, right now I didn't have much of an appetite.

Taking a seat on one of its wooden benches and sinking into the hot, dry heat, my mind started to reel at the prospect of what this place must be like when it was full. There was space for hundreds here – the saturnalian excess of it all!

Just then, someone stalked past the sauna entrance. A man, tall and pigeon-chested, dressed, like me, in a towel and a sarong. I'd guess he was in his early thirties, though he moved with a tall person's hunch. He stalked back, eyed me briefly, then opened the glass door, removed his sarong, and stepped inside.

To begin with, we sat in silence, sweating and staring at the hot coals. Eventually I plucked up the courage to speak.

'Ça va?' I cleared my throat, 'Ça va?'

'Ça va,' came the slightly surprised reply.

'Um ...'

'*Oui?*'

'It's just ... well, it's my first time in somewhere like this, and I was wondering, um, are there any rules?'

'Your first time?' he stared at me. He had a pointy nose and close-set eyes. '*Ça, c'est quelque chose.*' That's something.

'Really?'

'Me, I'm a libertine. I promise you've made a good choice. It's a great life.' He held out his hand. '*Je me présente: Christophe.*'

'Uh, that's my name too,' I said. 'I mean, well, Chris.'

We shared a clammy handshake, and he began telling me the rules of the game. How sex clubs run on respect. You never do anything that anyone doesn't want.

'How do you know if someone wants something?'

'If they touch you,' Christophe said. 'Or if they invite you to touch them.'

'Got it.'

He went on to say that Moon City was one of his favourite clubs because it was guaranteed a large, mixed crowd.

I did not mention that at this point its whole cavernous interior was being occupied entirely by two white guys in their thirties called Chris. But I guess he sensed it.

'Paris is late to bed, late to rise,' he reassured me. 'You'll see. It'll get busy soon.'

He started talking to me about the other sex clubs in Paris, how it was a huge scene, there were literally thousands of people like him. He said he tried to go at least once a week and preferred the 'moist' clubs to the 'dry'.

'I'm from the *banlieue*,' he said. 'There are many sex

clubs there as well. But it's the holidays, and I'll tell you, you should never go to a *banlieue* sex club in the holidays.'

'Why not?' I asked.

'*Trop de mecs*,' he said. Too many guys. 'My local one, the last time I went, there were ten men and only one woman. We just kept following her room to room.'

'That sounds a bit depressing,' I said.

'She ended up picking me, though,' Christophe said. 'I don't know why, I mean there were nine other men she could have gone for, but she picked me.'

'Cool,' I said. It seemed the appropriate thing to say.

'But here it never gets like that,' he added. 'They always ensure a good mix. Because it's so expensive for guys. But it's actually very good value.'

'Oh yes?'

'Absolutely. Because once you've paid, you can stay for as long as you want. And there's a bar and really nice staff ...' I couldn't help but feel he was justifying the price tag he'd just paid to himself, 'and have you seen the brunch?'

'No,' I said, 'but it's actually the reason I'm here.'

'What?'

'No, I just mean ...' telling people I was here in an essentially journalistic capacity did not seem like a good idea, 'sorry, my French. I meant I'm feeling hungry. Do you want to ...?'

'Yes,' said Christophe. 'Let's go and have brunch.'

We headed downstairs past the jacuzzi, which was surrounded by fake vegetation and fibreglass rocks. Spoiling its pretence towards unfettered nature were two large red and white signs warning that it was strictly forbidden to masturbate or have sex in the water. It was currently turned off, a large sink of tepid blue, and despite the signs, there was a single, unmissable clump of stringy, grey ooze floating on its surface.

'The jacuzzi is awesome,' Christophe said in passing.

We continued into the lounge, a big, open space, also decorated largely on the Hindu theme. There were deep leather couches and low tables, and a man in work overalls setting up a sound system. We ignored him, and he ignored us. We headed for the brunch spread.

It was not quite the 'gourmand' experience that had been promised. There was a selection of individually pack-aged supermarket brioche and a plate of desiccated iceberg lettuce, and meat – a lot of meat. Four platters of thin, cheap slices, many still bearing the pressed indents from the plastic packaging from which they had recently been released, sweating in the club's subtropical warmth.

I took one of each variety on offer: the anatomical maroon of a serrano, the inflamed red of a chorizo, the pink and white marble of a *rosette de Lyon*, and finally, the flaccid processed grey of a turkey ham. Christophe contented himself with just a single cut of the turkey, loading it with some lettuce onto his cardboard plate.

'You don't want to feel too heavy,' he cautioned.

I pumped filter coffee from a large thermos into a paper cup and wandered back to one of the leather couches to eat. Christophe came to sit down opposite me, plate balanced on his naked knees, and both of us began to chase the meat with wooden cutlery that was not up to the task.

'So how long have you been a libertine for?' I asked.

'Ten years almost,' Christophe said. 'It must seem

foreign to you, I imagine. I have heard it's not so common in England, no?'

'I don't think so,' I said, with little authority. 'Why do you think it's so popular in Paris?'

Christophe shrugged. 'There's the history, perhaps. Paris has been a home of libertinism for centuries. And I suppose we are just a less inhibited, more sensual people.'

He brought a drooping slice of turkey up to his thin lips and at the same moment the sound system at last kicked in: the opening chords to James Blunt's 'You're Beautiful'.

'I suppose so,' I said, and forced myself to concentrate on the food, piling some lettuce and my own slice of turkey onto a brioche and taking a careful bite.

It was, well ... good is probably too generous a word, but it was cool and salty with the faint undertow of sweetness of the brioche and refreshing watery crunch of lettuce. What it reminded me of were packed lunch sandwiches at school. Perhaps not what you want to be thinking about in a sex club, but I found it grounding: a sensation of the normality that still existed outside the dark walls of this alien world.

As it happened, it was then that someone else entered from the outside, looking every bit as ordinary as the turkey slice in my hand. A woman in her late fifties, she was even dressed a little like a primary school teacher. Yes, she was wearing clothes: jeans and a lavender hoodie, which clung frumpily to her spare-tyre belly. She'd come in to clear something with the barman. I was put at ease by her friendly, grandmotherly laughter about the difficulty of getting here from the suburbs.

Forty minutes later, the club was filling up and Christophe and I were surrounded by couples sipping thermos coffee and scrabbling meat around their paper plates. I started to feel a little bored, the limits of my small talk stretched to breaking, and so I padded back upstairs. I passed a caged window onto a room occupied by an older couple; I realised that the splayed and naked behind pointed towards me belonged to the grandmotherly woman I had seen earlier at the bar. Her partner sat astride her back, facing me like a back-to-front cowboy.

'There's someone watching you,' her partner growled when he saw me – he was entirely bald, like a gurning egg, and wearing a pair of wire-rimmed spectacles.

The granny whinnied.

'You like it when people watch you,' the man continued. 'You like it, don't you, you whore.'

Suddenly I didn't know what to do. I did not particularly want to stay, nor did I want to hurt their feelings. I gave it thirty seconds, which I counted down in my head, looking but not really looking at this act that resembled an enthusiastic medical examination, then I moved on. A turkey slice was not going to be enough to ground me any more; I needed a drink.

Alcohol, Christophe had told me, was not a big part of the libertine lifestyle – 'Too much is bad for performance' – and the bar reflected this. Though large and flashy, it was stocked mainly with syrups and, as far as I could see, no beer or wine. Things were less busy in the lounge now, but the few people who were there – all only in sarongs, of course – were all drinking spirits straight. I ordered Jack Daniel's over ice, fishing my token out from among the condoms in my wrist pouch to pay. I tried to drink it as casually as I could, enjoying the cool fire and faint courage I felt as it settled in my naked belly, trying to listen in to the conversations around me.

I overheard a woman ask the barman if the turkey meat was halal. It was.

This was when I visited the sauna. Things were really starting to heat up generally. Except now, Apple Watch guy and his partner of the moment had started to perform an acrobatic '69' right next to me and I felt obliged to leave. I returned to the steam room, where I realised I was not alone.

My glasses had fogged again the moment I went in, however, so at first I could only hear her. The rhythmic scrubbing of an exfoliating mitt on skin and orgasmic groans coming from the steam to my right. Then, they stopped.

'*Excusez-moi?*' a voice sounded from the mist. '*Monsieur?*'

'*Oui?*'

'*Vous pouvez m'aider?*' Can you help me? (addressed, I noted, with the formal '*vous*') 'I can't reach my back.'

I stood up and moved towards the voice out of automatic politeness. I was brought up to believe that when someone asks for assistance, assistance is what you offer. It did not even occur to me in the moment that when someone asks you to rub their back in the steam room of a sex club, there might be other things they're expecting you to rub as well.

As I neared, the mists parted to reveal a woman in her early thirties, completely naked, and with a quite phenomenal body – whatever that means to you. Just think: whatever your idea of erotic perfection, regardless of your sexual orientation, that's what this person had, to me. She handed me her scrubbing mitt, and turned around, bracing herself against the wall.

'My back.'

I started to scrub. Keeping myself at an arm-locked distance, exfoliating her smooth, tanned skin.

'No,' she said, 'Not like that. *Plus ... fort.*'

Now my mind was catching up with what this meant, and panic set in about whether I was crossing some line of participant observation, not to mention fidelity. The only thing I could think to do, however, was to redouble my efforts. Do literally what she'd asked. I was really scrubbing now, the dead skin coming off her back in ribbons.

'No,' she said again. 'Do it more ... like a massage.'

'Right, um,' I faltered at last, and she turned around to look at me, at the opaque saucers nearly fully covering my eyes.

'I understand,' she sighed. 'It must be difficult. With glasses.'

Then, she left. My heart thumping in my chest like a randy rabbit, I slumped back to one of the benches, only to realise that there were now more people in the room. Wet squelching slaps were coming from another unseen corner, and shrieks. And not just that, there was movement beside me on the bench too. Three bodies – I was pretty sure the one closest to me was Christophe, then a woman, and after that, another man. All of them were having a near-illegal amount of fun.

Despite myself, and whatever attempt at observational detachment I'd tried to bring in here with me, despite the meat platter brunch and the James Blunt and the grandmother's arse, and even despite the fact that it was Christophe's boring, bony behind thrusting up and down near my shoulder, I found myself starting to fall under Moon City's spell. All the flesh and pheromones, and other moans, and how increasingly inconsequential the outside world had started to seem. Yep, no doubt about it, I was getting turned on. It was time to leave.

I emerged blinking into the Pigalle sunshine with a sauna/ steam room freshness perfuming my skin. No matter how clean I actually was, however, I felt much dirtier than when I had arrived.

My journey around Moon City had been eye-opening, certainly, but its entirely functional charcuterie platter – which hardly screamed seduction – hadn't shown me much about the food of Pigalle. Enquiring about the 'design' of their 'menu' a few days later with the man at the door who had welcomed me before, he scowled and said: 'We do not offer cuisine here. Just food.'

'How do you mean?'

'Simply what we offer is just so people can stay in the club as long as they like. To give them strength for the other thing.'

'So is that why there's so much meat?' I persisted. 'Because it's light, but still gives a lot of energy?'

'It's whatever we find at the supermarket that day,' said the doorman. He considered for a moment. 'I suppose we'd never buy cheese.'

'Oh really, why not?'

'Because it's cheese!' he exclaimed, as if that explained everything. 'Most of the people who work here are from Senegal. They just buy what appeals to them.'

Libertinism may have evolved from the same desire for satiation as gastronomy, then, but that did not mean Paris's modern libertines were gastronomes. Theirs was an all-encompassing hobby, and drug-like in its singular pursuit of a fix.

What I saw in Moon City was nothing like sex in the real world. Rather, it was like finding myself inside a live, potentially interactive porno. The pleasures of such an experience – if it's something you can stomach – are undeniable, but they are also broad and intense. Who would spend time worrying about the subtleties of a Béarnaise sauce when they could be tag-teaming a complete stranger in a steam room? Food offers sensuality and contemplation, art and eroticism rather than brute physical satisfaction. But for the habitual libertines of Paris, it is merely fuel.

For all that, then, I decided that the dish that best represents the erotically charged libertine spirit of the 9th should be oysters. I say this not only because of their fame as an aphrodisiac, but because they are also light and packed full of energy. Reputedly devoured by the four-dozen by Casanova every morning, oysters are a French national obsession: the country is the number one consumer of the mollusc in Europe, and per capita, in the world. And though I'm aware correlation does not imply causation, I could not help but read that statistic in light of the Parisian penchant for libertinage. Finally, there is something in the palpitating vitality of an oyster that links it semiotically with the sexual act. The very fact that Moon City's doorman had spoken of an absolute moratorium on cheese was this in its inverse. Cheese is a product of decay. The oyster, when you eat it, is still alive. Energy made energy with only a little death in between.

There was only one place to go to get my hit. Again technically in the 18th but standing on the western edge of Pigalle, it is a place marinated in the area's hedonistic soul: the Brasserie Wepler.

Among the furthest flung of Paris's storied cafés, Wepler has presided over the place de Clichy since the nineteenth century. In that time, it has hosted artists, film directors and writers – from Modigliani to François Truffaut to Henry Miller. The last of these described the café with characteristic seedy affection in his novella of loose morals *Quiet Days in Clichy*: 'The rosy glow which suffused the place emanated from the cluster of whores who usually congregated near the entrance. They fluttered around in the dimming light like perfumed fireflies.'

Wepler is also famous for its seafood, especially its oysters, of which it serves close to a million a year.

That Tuesday lunchtime, the brasserie was doing a brisk service. Nearly all the generously spaced tables that filled its large art deco interior were occupied. True, I didn't spot anyone I took to be a sex worker, but then it was only early, and some things have changed. Like all of Paris's grand cafés, Wepler has become a heritage establishment, beyond the daily budget of most modern bohemians. Still, it smelled wonderfully of the old-fashioned posh restaurant scent of gently heated butter, and the tables were laid with starched white cloths. I was taken to an intimate booth deep in its interior and offered a menu with seven different varieties of oyster to choose from.

There is probably no dish that food writers like more than the oyster, and for good reason. Oysters are both a confrontation and exemplification of what it means to eat. If not the first creature we ever put in our mouths, the prehistory of their consumption is at least the most evident: found in shell middens from New South Wales to Northern Ireland to Nova Scotia. More than that, how we usually eat them today – how the French insist we should eat them – is hardly different from the method of our Pleistocene ancestors: raw, unadorned, straight from the shell.

As to their libido-enhancing qualities, the bivalves themselves are as randy as anything in nature. The males pump sperm from gonads that can constitute as much as 40 per cent of their body, then later in their life cycle change sex to female and spawn as many as 200 million eggs. More to the point, when they are most tumescent with this seed (characteristically in the colder 'months with an "R"') they are also at their most delicious: full of a whole cocktail of nutrients, guaranteed to offer more bang for your buck than any slice of reconstituted turkey ham.

Oysters
Serves 1
Ingredients:
A month with an 'R' in its name
6 fresh Gillardeau oysters
Dense brown bread
Butter
Chilled Chablis

At Wepler, I chose a platter of the Gillardeaus, the Rolls-Royce of oyster varieties, traditionally farmed near La Rochelle. I opted for the No. 5 size. In terms of oyster scaling, the higher the number, the smaller the beast – and size matters. Bigger is considered better, but the only other Gillardeaus on the menu, the No. 2s, were priced at €31.20 for six, and I was still smarting from my Moon City expense. The 5s would do.

Now, I know that my mission in Paris so far had been to learn and replicate the recipe, but it's fair to say that there is no real recipe for preparing an oyster the French way. That's the point. Just as long as you know how to remove the shell (shucking with a firm, slow, wheedling pressure at its base) and how not to lose of any of its juices in the process.

The real knowledge is in how to eat them, and that has already been given – far better than it could be by me or anyone I was likely to meet – by the American food writer M. F. K. Fisher in her seminal work *Consider the Oyster*, which is among the greatest works of gastronomic literature ever produced:

It should be opened at street temperature in a cool month, never iced, and plucked from its rough irregular shell at once, so that its black gills still vibrate and cringe with the shock of the air upon them. It should be swallowed, not too fast, and then its fine salt juices, more like the smell of rock pools at low tide than any other food in the world, should be drunk in one gulp from the shell. Then, of course, a bite or two of buttered brown bread must follow, better to stimulate the *papilles* [taste buds]... And then, of course, of course, a fine mouthful of white wine.

The Gillardeau oysters at Wepler were served already open on a bed of crushed ice, but everything else was in place.

I therefore forewent the shallot-infused red wine vinegar and even the lemon wedges, because the best way to enjoy an oyster is how God made them. Carefully, I spooned one after another of the engorged creatures into my mouth, enjoying their unique, rock pool taste just as Fisher said I would, just as human beings had done for millennia. I ate the prescribed buttered brown bread and sipped at a glass of chilled Chablis.

It was an appetiser to ready the body for further pleasure. In this instance, it had readied mine for my next course, which was onion soup.

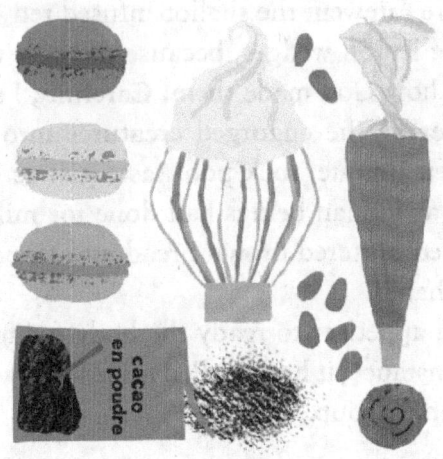

8ème arrondissement

Onion soup is one of the three main savoury dishes that tourists who visit Paris are looking to try. That's not an official statistic; I learned it anecdotally on the Champs-Élysées. As one does.

Onion soup, *boeuf bourguignon* and escargots, I was told over and over by honeymooners, college students and families promenading beside global fashion flagships and Lamborghinis for rent. The modern-day Champs-Élysées is more like a nouveau-riche oil state than it is the rest of Paris. It still has Second Empire window dressing, but much has been obscured by Balmain and bling. Nevertheless, it remains a place where people who want to 'see the city' come in their millions.

Exactly why this gastronomic trinity should have risen so dominantly to the top is hard to say. But these were the responses I received from easily three-quarters of people I talked to, and I talked to a lot of people. Not steak tartare, not *oeuf mayonnaise*, nor *blanquette de veau, coq au vin, steak au poivre* or *magret de canard*, or even ratatouille or frogs' legs.

Onion soup, *boeuf bourguignon*, escargots.

I mean, I get snails, but the other two? Maybe they'd been written about somewhere, by Rick Steves or Anthony Bourdain, or appeared in some top ten article of Parisian cuisine by *The New York Times* or CNN, and most tourists hadn't made it past the first three entries.

One guy I asked, he was German, had even gone so far as to question whether France *had* any other cuisine.

'There's escargots, onion soup and *boeuf bourguignon*,' he said, predictably, 'but apart from that, I think the French eat the same things as we do, right?'

If I really had to guess, I'd say it's because these dishes are exotic enough to be different, but not so strange that they haven't been heard of or appear too dangerous to try. And because the great majority of people don't care enough to find out more. French isn't the only cuisine in the world, and as Geoff Dyer once wrote, 'that's one of the things about travelling, one of the things you learn: many people in the world, even educated ones, don't know much, and it doesn't actually matter at all.'

I was in the Café George V – also on the Champs-Élysées, about a hundred metres down from the Arc de Triomphe – when I decided that Paris's tourist food should be what I tried to discover more about for the 8th.

Yes, this was an arrondissement of great wealth and political importance, home of some of the world's finest dining, of the legendary Maxim's, and of many of the city's secretive supper clubs, which still (or so I've heard) take cooking to levels of peerless indulgence. But nothing could have been as astounding as this: here, in a restaurant located at the heart of world gastronomy, they were offering food so bad that I'd have pushed it away if I'd been served it in prison.

Emerging from the kitchen were pasty, undercooked pizzas and black, overcooked steaks; insipid white fries and soggy cowpats of bolognaise. The *boeufs bourguignons* looked like they'd been tipped from ready-meal packaging, the escargots like they'd been microwaved direct from the deep freeze. Most tables boasted ketchup and hot sauce, and salt and pepper clumped solid in their shakers. Oh, and there were no mains on the menu for less than €20. Most were pushing 30. OK, so maybe not prison, but no exaggeration, the soup kitchen I'd visited in the 12th served dishes much better, fresher and healthier than these.

Yet the George V *looked* like a proper French café. It was deep and long, with a sizeable terrace, a pretty tiled pattern on its floor, some hints towards art deco stylings, long mirrors on the walls, and all the rest. It was the kind of place that people came to Paris to see, to have their dreams confirmed. There were dinner-jacketed waiters, too, though here, despite their uniforms, they looked more like a grizzled squad of ageing criminals, clubbed together for one last heist.

I observed one customer in particular, a middle-aged woman on her own wearing bright-red lipstick and a beret to match. She had ordered – what else? – onion soup and *boeuf bourguignon*, and the two dishes had arrived at the same time, along with a large sun-coloured cocktail (nearly every table in the George V was drinking sun-coloured cocktails).

With a face of what looked to be sad obligation, she tucked a paper napkin over her designer jacket and attacked the soup. She started to awkwardly spoon up strands of jaundiced cheese, pulling them into long gelatinous ribbons, which stretched all the way from the bowl to her mouth. She used her index finger to sever these strands, which then pinged greasily to her lips. She ate agonisingly slowly, paused for long moments between mouthfuls to break from the chore and stare mournfully into the middle distance. And all the time her *bourguignon*, which had started off looking like a reheated corpse, cooled and congealed beside her.

Before I left, I crossed over to her and asked, 'Sorry, I was just wondering, but did you enjoy your meal?'

At once her face bloomed into animated, happy life: 'Oh sure, honey, it was wonderful!'

Tourism, it will come as a surprise to no one, is big business in Paris. In fact, it is mega business. Bringing in $36 billion in 2023, Paris's tourist sector was valued as the largest of any city in the world. And yet I'd always had a suspicion that a lot of visitors don't have the best time; that they leave feeling the city doesn't measure up to its myth.

For a start, many just don't visit the most interesting parts, shuttling instead between Paris's archipelago of museums and monuments, and their surrounding cynical eateries, not experiencing enough of the real city in between. I can't say I blame them. You wouldn't catch me coming to Paris for the first or second time in my life and not checking out the Louvre, the Eiffel Tower, the Musée d'Orsay, Notre-Dame, the Sacré Coeur ... How would I fit anything else in?

Or maybe I was being a typical jaded Parisian (don't think I didn't take some pride in that). The city's monuments to me had long ago lost their mythic sheen, but they were still, were they not, wonders of the world.

And on this subject, there was one other theme that kept coming up in my Champs-Élysées vox pops: a whole genre of Paris food that was mentioned, not by three-quarters, but by almost every person I spoke to, and which was indicative of how these visitors knew something about the culinary scene here that I had too long overlooked or forgotten. Patisserie.

It's not only that I'm diabetic, or that I don't have much of a sweet tooth, for all my friends in Paris are the same. We don't go in for the wonderful glut of tarts, cakes and other pastries that teem from this city's bakeries – not as often as we should. I don't mean croissants, of which I probably eat more than is healthy, but all the rest.

It's like the monuments. After a while you can't help but get a bit blasé in the face of so much beauty. Besides, patisseries are a treat. You can't be eating *mille-feuille* or Paris–Brest or *tarte au citron* every day; they're for special occasions. Like a holiday. Though now I stopped to think about it, I remembered that Paris patisserie remains one of the miracles of human civilisation.

There's a lot been said in recent years – ever since I was born, I think – about the decline of French cooking. That it's not what it was, that the French have lost a ground-up connection with their food, that abominations like the Café George V are more common than anyone would like to admit. This can be debated. As I'd been discovering, in many places the flame still burns. What is undisputable, however, is the continued pre-eminence of the country's cakes. In close to every other street in Paris – in arrondissements high and low – you can still find a cornucopia of sweet confections worthy of any top-end restaurant on earth. That's extraordinary. Flabbergasting, even. But for me, it had become so commonplace that most days – like life itself – I didn't consider it at all.

Over the next week, my eyes and senses reopened by the tourists, I set to discovering just how this marvel had come to pass.

It began, like many of the best things do, in Italy. During the Renaissance, for the first time in modern European history, money found its way into the hands of merchants rather than the nobility. These were not people who could boast divine right to their positions, so they turned to other means to impress. The best-known result of this was the explosion of commissions for artists, but Italy was a marketplace for all artisans, and just as the rulers of Italian city states wanted a da Vinci or Botticelli for their walls, they also wanted the most show-stopping foods. At the time, this meant sugar sculpture: sweet statues spun from hardened syrup, like so many *Davids* you could eat.

When foreign powers twigged that behind the Italian's pomp there was not so much military might, the country was revealed as a low-hanging fruit, ripe for invasion. And as Italian money was diverted to pay for mercenaries, so the sugar sculptors (along with other artisans) looked elsewhere for patrons. Many found them in France.

Sugar, however, was expensive, and only got pricier the further north it had to travel. In Paris back then, a single pound of the stuff was equal in price to eighty chickens or two whole pigs. Even the wealthiest nobles couldn't afford the kind of pure-sugar creations that had adorned Italian tables. And so, patisseries, which still had some sugar among their ingredients, became popular. Many still had Italian origins, but the prevalence of milk and butter in the northern diet soon led the French to an artistry of their own.

By the mid-seventeenth century when Louis XIV came to power, pastry-making had become an art to rival sugar sculpture. This era also saw a divide start to open between sweet and savoury dishes. Since sugar had become available in Europe, there had been no conception that it should be confined to any specific course of a meal. Rather, the sweet crystal was used to flavour everything, including fish and red meat.

But in the new French court at Versailles, banquets were becoming close-to-everyday affairs, with cooks under constant pressure to try new things. All the nobles of France were gathered by the king under one roof, all had their retinues of cooks, and all were out to impress. Entertaining became a competitive sport. Imagine a single continuous episode of *Come Dine with Me* played out over more than fifty years. At a certain point, some food radical in this culinary hothouse came up with the idea of segregating sweet things to the climax of the feast, and lo! Man had created dessert. And he saw that it was good.

The next step in confectionary evolution happened as money seeped down through the social echelons. With bourgeois consumers aspiring to aristocratic delicacies, the focus shifted away from excess and into the realms of intelligence and refinement, and French patisserie began to take the shape that we know today. As the concept of the individual artist genius appeared in the nineteenth century, so the city's confectioners began to identify as such, and their cakes became aesthetically linked to fashion and trends.

This remains true in the Paris of the present day and it brought me back to the luxury boutiques of the Champs-Élysées, where the patisserie shops follow the fashion seasons, work in collabs and, like jewellers, dedicate obnoxiously large amounts of floor space to a relative scarcity of products. For my dish of the 8th arrondissement, the ultimate *quartier* of luxury shopping, I settled on the expression of the baking craft that exemplifies its transition into high-end consumer product better than any other. That edible jewel: the macaron.

There were ten of us in the class, perched on high stools around a forensically clean horseshoe-shaped countertop in polite, attentive silence as our teacher fluttered into the room. She looked like an AI rendering of a Parisian. A petite brunette in ballet pumps, bright-red lipstick and a Breton top. She introduced herself in English with a French accent so singsong that it could almost have been an impression.

'*Bonjour*,' she beamed. 'I pree-zent my-zelf. Marie. I am *enchantée* to meet you all.'

Even after more than ten years in the country, I was charmed. I can only imagine her effect on the rest of the class.

It had not escaped my attention that what I had been doing for my project was already a service that the city offered its tourists for a price. Here was just one of dozens of possible lessons I might have signed up for at the very start, from thirty-minute pastry chef demonstrations to two-day courses that promised to teach the finer points of the perfect *jus*. Of course, for the most part, I'd been glad to go my own way, but macarons were different. They had become Paris's most popular edible souvenir, and here were tourists who'd discovered a hack. Bring back macarons from Paris, you can show off to your family about your holiday for a week; learn to make macarons, you can show off for a lifetime.

'If we are all 'ere zen, we can begin,' Marie said. 'And I am zorry for my Engleesh. You will pleaze forgive me if I make miztakes.' She giggled nervously, and we giggled with her; we'd have forgiven her anything.

We were an international crowd, majority American but also including Germans, a Ukrainian and Israelis; politics, though, were left at the door. We were here to learn how to bake.

'If you would all like to join me at ze front of ze class.'

Dutifully, everyone shuffled over to gather around another table and a free-standing electric mixer. I'd expected a little history: about how the recipe for these dainty meringue sandwiches probably dated back to Middle or even Dark Ages Italy, for instance; about how it was introduced to France by the chefs of Catherine de' Medici, then brought to the French people by two sisters in Nancy during the Revolution; how it was finally refined into its current form by the Parisian patissier Pierre Desfontaines working for the famous Ladurée bakery in the early 1900s. But no, we went straight into the practical. Handily, the separate ingredients of a macaron mix had been pre-prepared in individual bowls set out on the table. Everything was so neat, so precise, seemed so easy; you'd never believe that making macarons was in fact incredibly hard.

'It iz very zimple,' the teacher lied (I'll drop the accent signifiers now; you get the idea). 'As long as you remember to keep all the ratios the same, it is impossible to go wrong.'

She poured the egg white into the KitchenAid so that it foamed magically into meringue.

'Oh my God,' I heard someone mutter. 'I didn't know it did that.'

Marie giggled again.

'Yes, it is quite incredible, *non*? But if you don't have an electric mix at home this will take some strength,' she cautioned, then changed the whisk on the mixer to a flat blade. There was a subtle dexterity in all her actions, and always she held her elbows in tight to her chest. She moved like a ballet dancer performing as a chef.

Now she was pouring in butter and sugar and cocoa powder, explaining how the next stage had to be done very gently, how you had to 'encourage' the mixture into becoming macaron, how it needed only ten seconds in the mixer at a medium speed, and was ready when it began to 'fall like ribbons' from the blade. I could feel the collective fear in the room that we were going to be expected to do all of this ourselves soon, that no matter how easy she was making it look, we were all going to fail.

'Unfortunately, you will have no time for this today. Because afterwards the mix has to rest for five hours.'

Relief.

Still, there was a moment of interaction, as we were called up one by one to squeeze macaron-sized discs of finished mixture onto a tray with a piping bag. We did this with little success – of the people present, only one aside from myself professed *ever* to have baked anything before. Nevertheless, whatever we managed, Marie encouraged us as expertly as she'd encouraged the macaron mix.

'Why does mine look like a poop?' one girl asked.

'No! It is great,' Marie exclaimed. 'It will be the perfect macaron in the end.'

It did look like a poop.

Then it was back off to the horseshoe counter, to mix up our own ganache – the macaron's sweet, creamy filling. All the ingredients for this had been already weighed for us and were waiting in our own individual bowls. All we had to do was stir them together. Then we had to pipe the resulting paste inside a couple of discs of pre-cooked macaron.

'Fantastic! That looks just like macaron,' Marie said to me. And despite the fact I'd actually messed it up slightly by piping too much ganache, I flushed with pride.

Didn't it frustrate her? I asked afterwards. She'd clearly had years of training, dedicated herself to the single-minded perfection of a historic art, and here we were, planeloads of tourists showing up day after day, some of whom didn't even know that egg white fluffed into meringue, massacring her craft?

'No, people are good,' she said without a trace of insincerity. 'You were all great. And I love meeting people from all over the world.'

By then, I had started talking to the rest of the class. Their responses to my questions about Parisian food were much the same as I'd heard already on the Champs. Onion soup, *boeuf bourguignon* and escargots came up a lot, as did a few fabulous restaurants I could never afford – one woman, a retiree from Boston, described her meal at a place called L'Ami Jean as like 'an orgasm in my mouth'.

'Sounds interesting,' I said.

Many classmates spoke about loving patisserie and, naturally, macarons.

'So what about Paris,' I asked, 'has it been everything you thought it might be?'

'Excuse me,' said the girl whose macaron base had looked like a poop. 'But did you say you were a writer?'

'Well, I mean,' I stammered. 'Like a freelance writer, it's not all—'

'I've never met a real-life writer before!' she exclaimed. 'And being one in Paris. That's like a dream!'

'I ...' What could I say? That living here was just like anywhere else? That there were difficulties and headaches and all the problems of any big city? That I had to do a bunch of other things to make money, and don't get me started on the bureaucracy ... But also, I'd spent the last few months talking to fascinating people, many of whom cared deeply not just about food but about the perfection of its creation. How just last week I'd gone to a sex club and called it research? How I regularly got to eat some fantastic things, and how after this I'd go to a café to write up some notes and then spend the evening chatting with friends who'd probably get into an argument about Dostoevsky.

'Like a dream? I guess sometimes,' I said.

Macarons
For 18 macarons
Ingredients:
For the shells:
100g ground almonds
100g icing sugar
20g cocoa powder
100g white sugar
100g egg whites

For the ganache:
100g dark chocolate
60g single cream
40g salted butter

Where could be better to make the macaron recipe I had learned in Paris than rural England? I don't mean practically – practically it was a nightmare – but in terms of replicating what was intended for the people who had attended the class it was perfect. We were meant to bring our new knowledge home with us, to mix up the flavour of the French capital in our respective foreign lands. Now, on a trip to visit my mother-in-law in the quaint Sussex village of Steyning, I had a chance to do just that. Possibly.

My first problem was the lack of a free-standing mixer, but with a handheld electric whisk purchased from a local charity shop this was more or less solved.

My second problem was the ingredients. I had no access to a car and was limited to what the village's two small food shops could provide. Eggs, fine. Sugar, fine. Icing sugar, cocoa, dark chocolate, salted butter, single cream, all fine. Ground almonds, not fine.

To begin with, I was irrationally annoyed. What self-respecting village shop didn't sell ground almonds in post-*Bake Off* Britain? Whither the home bakers of England? But then, I decided, it was OK; this was part of the challenge, and there were two tea rooms on Steyning high street – surely I could blag some ground almonds from one of them. Except neither made their own cakes on-site.

I returned to one of the village stores, trying to convince myself I had just missed the ingredient on the shelves, though I had not. What I had missed, however, in a health food section separate to the baking supplies, was a pack of whole blanched almonds.

Result!

I took these back to my mother-in-law's apartment, where there was no food processor, and went to work on them with a plastic bag and a rolling pin. I bashed at those almonds like my life depended on it. For thirty minutes. Forty. By the end I was sweating, exhausted, half broken, and with about 60g of beautiful smooth almond powder and 40g of almond rocks. Aware of the delicate chemistry of macarons, I knew that anything larger than dust wouldn't do, but that was OK, for as Marie had said, as long as the ratios were equal, the mix would come out fine.

So, I combined the powder with 60g of white sugar, 60g of icing sugar and about 12g of cocoa, and fuck! The white sugar was meant to combine with egg white first, wasn't it?

I could have cried.

'Hey, mum, there's a strange man in the pub who wants me to grind his nuts!'

Yes, I had returned to the village store and bought more

whole almonds. This time, though, I was outsourcing my labour.

'He wants you to do what?' The landlady appeared from the kitchens to join her daughter at the bar, and I explained the situation.

'So, if you've got a food processor, or ...'

'I don't know, love. We've got people's allergies to consider.'

'I can give you some of the macarons when I'm done.'

'Tch, fine then. Give 'em here ...'

Starting again, with my second batch of freshly ground nuts, I combined the dry ingredients in the recommended 100g ratios, this time leaving the white sugar aside. Putting the sugar together with the 100g of egg white, I stirred it all together at a medium speed with the charity shop electric whisk. The meringue was made.

Now, Marie had counselled, I had to change to a flat blade on my mixer and combine the other ingredients at a medium speed to 'encourage' them. This was not an option open to me, though I figured that stirring the mixture as hard as I could with a spoon was probably equivalent.

Until it 'fell in ribbons' from the spoon, I'd been told. But what was a ribbon? I could only think of that woman in the beret spooning up cheese from her onion soup in the George V. But that was a metaphor, this was technical.

Macaron-making, like the rest of baking, is full-on science; and here was the most important step. Well, along with all the other steps. If I did something just a little wrong in any of them, then nothing would work. But at least everything else could be measured. Here, I had to precisely decide what a ribbon was. And if I got it wrong – I remembered Frances talking about croissants – the macarons would taste fine, they just wouldn't be macarons.

The mixture dripped teardrop-like from my spoon. Was this a ribbon? It would have to do.

Now, the piping. My search for a piping bag in Steyning had failed at every turn, so I had to make do with the cut-off end of a plastic Coke bottle and a sandwich bag. These worked passably well – once I'd remembered Marie's tip that it was easier to fill the bag if you placed it in a mug and wrapped its edges over the rim first. Soon enough, I had thirty evenly spaced, 50p-sized poops of my own spread across a couple of paper-lined baking trays. I let them, and myself, rest.

I baked my macarons for fifteen minutes at 145 degrees in a fan-assisted oven. Well, that's not quite true. What I actually had was a non-fan-assisted oven with all the temperatures rubbed off its dial. So I estimated where 145 degrees might be, and I kept an eye on them through the glass. And they came out ...

One second: while they were baking, I also made the ganache. This was easy-peasy. I melted 100g of dark chocolate in warm cream and stirred in the salted butter. Guess what? It tasted fantastic.

My macaron shells, however ... well, they looked like macaron shells. Except about half of them had cracks on the surface – a sign that my mix had not been combined precisely enough. And none had formed the famous '*pied*', the textured edge which comes from correct stirring, precise piping and sufficient resting time (I'd actually only let my macarons rest for two rather than the suggested five hours). The *pied*, Marie had told us, was the hallmark of a true macaron, even while it added nothing to the flavour. Oh well.

I set about assembling them even so, dolloping ganache with a spoon rather than my piping bag on the underside of one small disc, then pressing a second down over it so that it resembled a miniature burger.

The taste was, of course, fine. Sugary, almondy, chocolatey – all things I'd be better off avoiding, but whatever. They even had a decent chewy resistance to my bite, just as they were supposed to. I experienced the familiar flush of triumph associated with most baking endeavours.

What my macarons were not, though, was a luxury product. As well as the cracks and their absence of *pieds*, they were of uneven sizes; some had too much ganache spilling from their edges, some had too little. These were small problems, really, but the skill I would need to acquire to rectify them was immense.

Ultimately, all this only reinforced what I already knew. There was a city out there, over the green horizon of the South Downs, where they made these things every day by the tens of thousands. Perfectly, in a whole rainbow of flavours. And they made other things too that were just as impressive. Only the people who lived in that city didn't always notice – because for them these feats had become normal. It took outsiders to remind them how wonderful they were.

7ème arrondissement

La Fontaine de Mars is the most authentic restaurant in Paris. That's what's written on their website, at least. Looking at the place, I was almost prepared to go along with the in-house copy. Here were red and white chequered tablecloths, scarred wood cupboards, marble countertops; a mix of old posters and forgotten artwork on the walls, and from the kitchen came the scent of weighty erudition, of complex sauces being prepared.

If pushed, though, I'd say that La Fontaine de Mars is a restaurant where the *theme* is authenticity. For while it technically dated back to 1908, the place's current iteration was the result of a 1990s refurb, in the course of which the new owners had meticulously identified all the markers of a traditional Parisian restaurant, recreated them and waited for the patina of the decades to do the rest. But that was OK. For this was in the 7th, an arrondissement of politicians, tourists and money, where even neighbourhood bistros need a USP. What even is authenticity, anyway?

The kitchen of La Fontaine de Mars is headed by a French chef called Pierre Saugrain, bearded and shaped like a watermelon, as clichéd as a Disney cartoon. He commands a staff that hails from around the world, including three Sri Lankans – the country whose nationals over the last twenty years have become as authentic to Paris restaurants as bread baskets and red wine. I had come here to talk to them.

Sri Lankan restaurant staff had been a constant from the very start of my journey. Most notably in Le Mistral in the 20th, where the chef had explained the secrets of *aligot*, but they had been there in the kebab shops too, and in the crêperies. Even the Congolese kitchen of Mbuta Lombi, I'd spied through the pass, was headed by a Sri Lankan chef. My introduction to the phenomenon, however, had come earlier, on a summer night train from Paris to the Pyrenees.

That sounds romantic, but French sleepers are not what they were, packing their passengers tight as a budget airline, and no longer sparing room for that most pleasurable luxury of train travel, the dining car. Still, I've taken enough night trains in my time to have developed a few tricks for wresting back something of the golden age of travel.

That night, I had bought some beers and a small selection of *apéro* snacks before boarding, made sure to bag a bottom bunk, then established myself on the floor at the end of my carriage, away from the dingy, horizontal crush of my six-bed compartment, where despite the fact that it was only 8 p.m., the lights were already off and sleeping encouraged. I sat cross-legged on the scuffed linoleum, sipping beer, nibbling *saucisson*, dreaming of adventure and gazing out of the window at the sunset suburbs of Paris as they clanked by.

'Excuse me, sir,' I was asked in English, 'is this the way to the bar carriage?'

I looked up to see two South Asian men in cheap jeans and sports tops. The one who'd spoken to me was impeccably neat, the other a little worse for wear.

'There isn't one,' I said – a little self-evidently, I thought. 'But I have food, beer. Would you like to share?'

'Oh no,' the man bobbed his head, 'that will not be necessary. We have our own. But perhaps it will be a pleasure to join you?'

'Absolutely,' I said, always glad of company, and gestured to the floor in front of me. The men bustled back to their own compartment and returned with eight extra-strength Kronenbourgs. They meant business.

We started to speak in a fractured *mélange* of French and English, overlaid by Tamil spoken at pace between the two men. They were Sri Lankan, and as I soon discovered, both worked in the restaurant trade.

'Me,' the neater one, who had introduced himself to me as Kuna, said – he was small, and as well-groomed as a photo in a barber's shop – 'I am a cook at the Criée [a seafood chain] in Rosny-sous-Bois. And this is my friend Tejas. He is a diver.'

'A diver?' I repeated. Then, I realised, 'Oh, a *plongeur*.'

'*Oui!*' cried Tejas with a grin. He was as dishevelled as Kuna was tidy, with stained teeth, unruly hair and several days' worth of stubble. He made to flex his bicep. '*Plongeur!*'

It was a term I knew well. Like many people, I first encountered it in George Orwell's *Down and Out in Paris and London*, when the author described working as a *plongeur* in the infamous Hotel X. It meant dishwasher and general restaurant dogsbody, the bottom rung of the restaurant chain, in Orwell's words too low to be able to afford morality, 'too low to be prosecuted'. In the gentlest of senses, it was a role I had once worked myself – or so my dad joked – back in my early teens, on Saturdays and school holidays at my family's bakery. Unqualified for any higher responsibility, I had scrubbed my way through hundreds of pots and pans, cleaned toilets, taken out bins. But that had only been for one day a week, for a shift of six hours, and many years ago; I decided it was better not to bring it up. Instead, I asked the men where they were headed.

'To Lourdes,' Kuna said. 'We're on pilgrimage.'

'You're Christians?'

'No, sir,' Kuna said. 'Hindu. But Our Lady of Lourdes, she is the most powerful god in Western Europe, I think. So we make pilgrimage to her. It is the only time we take off work all year,' he said. 'For three days in a summer we travel south to be baptised.'

I knew a little about this tradition, having visited Lourdes once to write about it for a guidebook. Ailing pilgrims come from all corners of the world to bathe in austere concrete tubs in the supposedly healing waters, while prayers are recited over them to wash away their ills. I also remembered what my old religious studies teacher used to say about Lourdes, that the only miracle was to leave without catching anything.

'I step into the water, I am one person,' Kuna continued, 'when I come out, I am someone else. My entire perspective on the year is changed. I do not have time to go anywhere else, to be away for longer, but just that one minute in the waters, it is like a long holiday for me.'

'Wow,' I said, feeling something close to vertigo at the gulf between mine and Kuna's existence. I turned to Tejas, 'And do you feel the same?'

'Oh yes,' he said. Only I was not sure he had really understood me over the rattle of the train, for he added, 'I am a diver. Life is very hard.'

We cracked more beers and shared our snacks. Kuna and Tejas had brought a kind of Bombay spice mix, which they coated in chilli powder.

'Very spicy,' cautioned Kuna, impressed when I scooped a large handful without flinching. Perhaps he was used to native Parisians, whom I have known to find ginger ale a struggle.

I learned of their gruelling days, relentless morning-to-night shifts, Sisyphean piles of dishes, a million fish gutted and prepped. I asked how they had found work in restaurants, if they had ever cooked back home.

'Many Tamils in Paris are working in restaurants, sir,' Kuna said. 'It is almost everyone I know, they are in restaurants. I think if it were not for Tamil workers now, people would come to restaurants in Paris and they would ask, where is the food on my plate?'

Certainly, I was well aware that a significant portion of all kitchens were staffed by migrant workers – among them, Bangladeshis, sub-Saharan Africans and Eastern Europeans – but I had not previously considered the precise demographics or imagined that one nationality might be as dominant as Kuna was suggesting. Facts and figures were hard to come by, for many such workers are undocumented. Even reliable estimates of the number of Sri Lankans living in France are hard to obtain. Fifty thousand? A hundred thousand? The statistics varied widely. They were, at the very least, the most populous of the country's South Asian communities.

Eventually, I took to gathering my own statistics, seldom missing an opportunity at any restaurant I entered to ask if there were Sri Lankans on the staff. There almost always were. Certainly, in well over half of the fifty or so places I enquired: pizza restaurants, bistros, kebab shops, cafés, bouillons, hotels, right the way across the city.

I decided on the 7th as the place to understand their story precisely because it is the wealthiest of all the arrondissements, the most apparently refined. I wanted to meet the people who made it shine.

'Beginning at the beginning, there is no need to speak French to be a *plongeur*,' Ramesh told me with a friendly intensity. He was stocky and entirely bald, with a neatly trimmed goatee and seldom blinking eyes. Now a waiter at La Fontaine de Mars, that was not how he had started. 'When I came to this country, I am telling you, I knew nothing about France. We know about England because of the colonial history in Sri Lanka, but here not at all. Except it was only here that offered me a visa.'

'It was the same with me,' said Suresh, another waiter who had worked his way up through the ranks – he was nerdy looking, with puffy cheeks and bloodshot eyes. 'And I am educated. I have a master's degree in Sri Lanka. So first when I came to France, I hoped to study. Except they told me I had to do a six-month course in the language first. But I had no money, I had to work as well. So I found a job in a kitchen. Not here. Somewhere else. Washing dishes. But after just a few weeks, it was too much to study. I only had time for the kitchen work.'

'Very few Tamil men have done any cooking back home,' Ramesh put in. 'But here restaurant work is very easy to find.'

We were talking in English, installed on one of La Fontaine's pristine red banquettes at four o'clock in the afternoon – deep between services, the quietest moment of the restaurant day. I'd been surprised by how easy it was to arrange to talk. I'd chosen La Fontaine de Mars almost at random. It was simply a restaurant that I'd cycled past a few times and liked the look of, and I considered this a good excuse to eat there, for it was otherwise way beyond my usual budget. I had simply assumed that there would be Sri Lankans working there. Luckily, I had been right. I'd explained my interest to the on-site manager – bald, officious – and he had led me to Ramesh and Suresh without a sniff of hesitation. The two men, meanwhile, seemed delighted to talk; to tell their stories.

'At the beginning in Paris, for me, life was very hard,' Suresh related. 'I cannot even say how hard.'

'It's true,' Ramesh said. 'I want to say I am very grateful for all the things this country has offered me, but there are also some bad people in the *banlieue*. I was lucky, I found work as a *plongeur* at La Fontaine de Mars very early on, and this is a good place. But I would be coming home late at night after work and people would attack me. Many times, I did not know what was happening. I'd think, am I doing something wrong? I would try to apologise, try to smile. I didn't know the language. I am sure they thought I was an idiot. Many times, I had my wages taken. Many times.'

When he did make it home, unscathed or not, it was to a 15-square-metre apartment in Aubervilliers, one of the poorer northern suburbs, which he shared with three other Tamil men. Life carried on like that for six years. Six years to move from *plongeur* to waiter, six years scrubbing dishes at this high-end restaurant, the dishes of people who could count their salaries in the hundreds of thousands. Once maybe even the dishes of President Barack Obama, who I learned ate at La Fontaine in 2009, just after Ramesh starting working here. Six years of fingers pruned by sweat inside rubber gloves and of aching muscles and early starts and late nights, of living four to a room and negotiating his pay packet through the suburbs at night. His first six years at the most authentic restaurant in Paris.

'We came here because we had to,' Suresh picked up the thread. 'I know there are some who come to this country just because they think they can make more money here than they can at home. But for us, we were running from Sri Lanka, running from the war.'

How strange and often tragic the unexpected consequences of history. During the British Empire, the colonisers came up with a policy to ship Tamil men from Southern India to bolster the Sri Lankan labour force, and in doing so unnerved the island's more populous Sinhalese community and sowed the seeds for thirty years of civil war. This began in 1983 with the torching of Jaffna Library, one of the largest repositories of Tamil literature on earth. Many Tamils took up arms, the desire for an independent homeland on the island metastasising into a struggle of near-religious fervour and brutality.

'I try to explain it to my children,' Suresh said. 'But they have no idea. They cannot understand. I lost many relations, killed by the Sri Lankan army. I myself was arrested three times.' He was going into himself now, his already blood-shot eyes moistening around their edges. 'The third time I spent three months in prison. It was horrible. You would not believe what I went through. When I shared my experience with the woman I went to for asylum, she cried.'

Suresh did not then want to go into further details. I understood. But searching online later, I gained some inkling of what it must have been like. He had been taken to Welikada Prison in Colombo, the country's largest pen-itentiary, a colonial relic overcrowded to almost double its capacity. I read stories of maggots in the food, of stifling heat, of open drains and infestations of rats, and who knows what interpersonal violence besides. And now Suresh had learned how to speak French and was serving millionaires in the most authentic restaurant in Paris.

I don't wish to talk down La Fontaine de Mars. Quite the opposite. They had been more than willing to let me talk to their staff, one of whom had started as a *plongeur*, suggesting to me that they were doing things right, that they had little to hide. Moreover, it was clear that Ramesh and Suresh adored the place. They had progressed to the role of waiters, which meant far more than just an improved salary: it also brought them out of the back kitchen and into the visible, social world, the world of wealthy Paris. This was something that other restaurants could easily have denied them, preferring an all-white or at least native Francophone floor staff. My point is, though, that their story was frighteningly typical. Restaurants across the city were staffed by Tamil men, and many of those men must have biographies to make you cry.

Ramesh and Suresh were both married now, living with their families in the suburbs. Suresh had been granted French citizenship and was now free to return to Sri Lanka should he choose. They were proud, both of what they achieved and where they worked.

'I will tell you honestly, when I first came to this country, I did not like the food,' Ramesh said. 'Everyone talks about this great thing, French food, but I found it very strange. So, yes, to begin with I would eat only Sri Lankan. But then, bit by bit, I started to experiment, started to try the French way of eating. And of course the food in this restaurant – have you eaten here?'

'No, but I'm going to.'

'Oh, the food here is really top notch.'

I asked him if there was any one moment, any meal where his mind and palate had started to change. He thought for a second.

'You know, sir, yes there was. In Sri Lanka, for example, we always cook our meat for a long time, always all the way through. But then one day, the chef here, he was insisting on making steak for me, but he said he would only cook it a little, as you are supposed to, and he offered me a bit, and it was ... I mean, it was wow!'

He offered then a great wide toothy grin that seemed to banish the bags from his tired eyes.

'So, do you eat French food at home now, then?' I asked.

'Me? No, not most days,' said Ramesh. 'I have a wife now, and she is mainly cooking Sri Lankan dishes. Chicken curry with rice, *parippu*, that kind of thing. But sometimes on my days off, yes, I will cook. I cook French food, Italian food, though always with my own Sri Lankan additions. I put spice mix on the food, I serve often with rice instead of potatoes. My kids in particular, they love this.'

'Really?' I brightened at this possibility of a recipe. 'So could you tell me more exactly, the kind of recipes you make ...?'

No. We had run out of time. I had been talking to Ramesh and Suresh for a good half-hour while the small tasks of between-service restauration continued seamlessly around us. Now their boss had started circling too, reminding them that it was time to go back to work.

'You'll come back here soon to eat, though,' Suresh insisted as I left. 'It would be a pleasure to serve you our food.'

I know this has been said before, but it bears repeating as often as possible: it is through the calloused hands and burnt forearms of people like Ramesh and Suresh – people who work hard, turn up on time, have no safety net and a long way to fall – that Paris's service industry, and the service industry across the Western world, is sustained. They are the ones who scrub the pans and swab the floors, work the pass, clean other people's piss from the toilet rim, get paid the least, live in the worst conditions and travel the furthest to work. And they are everywhere – Sri Lankans are simply the most numerous of them in Paris because they are the city's largest underprivileged, non-Francophone group. They are stewing broths in tiny cellars, microwaving meals beyond the Périphérique, peeling potatoes in the 7th. They are people for whom cuisine is neither glory nor art, but a labour through which to get by. Some can get lucky, break the cycle, discover passions they never knew they had, find in their daily dive into greasy dishwater that it has indeed transmogrified into a kind of baptismal font. That is one of hospitality's great justifications as a supposed meritocracy, after all. But for those who are still waiting until that day, it's imperative to remember how important they are to the whole restaurant ecosystem. In 2010 UNESCO granted French cuisine World Heritage status. These men are its foundation.

I went back to eat at La Fontaine de Mars; pinched my nose at how much it was going to cost and ordered one of their 'specials', a cassoulet inspired by the French south.

It was great. The whole experience, not just the cassoulet, was a vacation in the world of wealth. There were complimentary slices of *saucisson* served the instant I arrived, an elegant family discussing politics at the table next to mine, and everything on my table was both clean and sharp, from the fold of my napkin to the shine on my knife – the fingerprints of work that left no fingerprints behind.

Truth be told, I'm not usually a huge fan of cassoulet. For something so calorific and indulgent, I've often found the slow-cooked Occitan stew of white beans and meat lacks variety and crunch. Nevertheless, this was an excellent version of the dish: its usual weightiness had been balanced by the addition of fresh tomatoes, the sausage had a granular smokiness, and the sauce was lifted by a faint sour spice of mustard stirred all the way through. Also, it came in such a huge portion that it was actually quite good value. I ended up taking almost half of it home in a doggy bag to have for lunch the next day. This did not feel very authentic, but I didn't mind.

La Fontaine de Mars was a fine eating establishment, and if dropping €70 on lunch doesn't break you out in a cold sweat, I imagine it would feel finer still. More than anything, they treated their staff well. Ramesh, who was on shift, moved from his section of the restaurant in order to spoon out my cassoulet with that same slightly goofy smile he'd worn when he talked about the steak a few days before.

He reiterated how much he loved this place and its food, how he had found it by chance and how the management had looked after him, showed faith in him, let him hold his head up in this world. I'm not sure if that's authentic to Paris restaurants, but in my dream of the city it ought to be.

There are few places in central Paris further from the calm, manicured boulevards of the 7th, at least in spirit, than the grimy buzz that surrounds La Chapelle metro, the place where the city's Sri Lankan Tamil community has made its commercial hub. Over three or four blocks, in an area dubbed Little Jaffna after the largest city of Tamil Sri Lanka, are scattered curry houses and cash and carries, textile shops and temples, accented by the smell of spice and the flash of saris. It was here that Ramesh and Suresh came on their days off to connect with home and shop for their meals. If I wanted to know what the Tamil population who cooked for the rest of Paris ate in their domestic lives, it was here I would find out.

I had been to this *quartier* before, many times. As an

English person living in Paris, the South Asian flavours of the neighbourhood are also a reminder of home, not to mention that it's practically the only place in the city you can get a curry that hasn't been diluted so much to meet French tastes that it might as well be a stew. Today, though, it felt different.

For the past couple of weeks I had immersed myself in the history of the Sri Lankan civil war and the stories of its Tamil diaspora. Now, the images of military leaders and Tamil Tiger martyrs that grinned from posters in so many of the shops had new meaning. The Tamils had lost the war over a decade ago, but here were the battle wounds and heroes of a struggle not forgotten, of a people still resisting in a foreign land. Moreover, I had read in the media of this neighbourhood's often ignored internal violence: from the early 1980s, local Tamil gangs had begun to form, initially to help protect new arrivals against precisely the kind of abuse that Ramesh had described. But then, these gangs had come into conflict with one another, sometimes based on political disputes back home, sometimes on local power struggles. There was a degree of sensationalism to the articles, no doubt, as, like everywhere, most people seemed to be simply getting on with their lives. Nevertheless, nowhere in Paris had I encountered as much suspicion while simply trying to talk to people in the street.

My question, I thought, was innocent: What do you eat at home? But time after time, I was frozen out, fobbed off or ignored. Perhaps they were simply too tired and busy. Perhaps it was a natural suspicion born of the prejudice they'd encountered in this country, or indicative of individual worries about precarious legal status. I couldn't know for sure.

Still, there were some who were happy to talk. A stooped, older man buying aubergines from the cash and carry, a wiry twenty-year-old with stylishly mussed hair, a round-faced mother leading teenage kids. About half of the time they ate Tamil food, they said: curries, dahl, rice. But for the rest, they ate French and Italian dishes too, always with added spice, just as Ramesh had described. There was little extravagance to these fusion recipes. Most were no more complex than adding chilli to a pasta sauce, or roasting chicken in curry mix. Fish, however, *had* to be eaten with cumin at the very least, one woman told me – otherwise it was bad for your digestion.

Finally, it was a woman who, though born in Sri Lanka, had grown up in the old French colony of Pondicherry, and who suggested a recipe I might want to try.

Meen puyabaisse was a Franco-Tamil version of the Marseilles dish bouillabaisse, she said, and had been being cooked on the Coromandel coast for years. It was as sophisticated and elaborate as anything you might find in a high-end French restaurant, though I'd never encountered it on a public-facing menu. This was another reason why I wanted to cook up Franco-Tamil flavours: despite the huge preponderance of Sri Lankan chefs in this city, I'd not found a single restaurant in Paris where you can find their domestic fusion cuisine. So, while it is tasted in apartments and houses across the French capital every day, it remains even less acknowledged on the city's streets than the Tamil workers themselves.

In any case, this woman directed me to the *meen puyabaisse* recipe in a book called *The Pondicherry Kitchen*, and that is what I followed.

Meen Puyabaisse
Serves 4–6
Ingredients:
Ghee
2 onions, diced
2cm ginger, peeled and chopped
2 garlic cloves, chopped
3 green chillies, chopped
1 bay leaf
1 cinnamon stick
1 tbsp turmeric powder
2 crab claws
8 prawns
Hot water
2 carrots
1 turnip
2 potatoes
1 aubergine
2 fillets of firm-fleshed fish, cubed
1 lemon, for serving

Back in my own kitchen, I scooped out a generous spoonful of the ghee that I had bought in Little Jaffna, watched it slide about my pan and melt into hot oil. Then, it was in with the diced onion, to dance and bubble under the fat's yellow sheen. Next, the ginger, the garlic, and the fresh green chilli, an Asian *mirepoix* that sent the smells rising from my stove lurching east. Now the bay leaf, before I added the cinnamon stick and the turmeric to the pan. I stirred, watched the mixture sweat and crackle, before adding the crab claws and a couple of the prawns.

This was a long way from a Marseillaise bouillabaisse, which must contain calanque rockfish plus a far greater number of sea creatures, but then, the Coromandel was a long way from Marseilles. And I was a fair distance from them both. I added a little water, let the sauce reduce to a spiced fishy paste.

I threw in the vegetables, all peeled and carréd. It seemed to me a peculiar *mélange*: carrot and turnip, potato and aubergine. I drew them about in the paste, coated their porous sides in flavour, let them sizzle for a time, before adding the rest of the water and waiting for the vegetables to soften. In went the cubed fish and the rest of the prawns; every ingredient was bubbling away now, getting to know each other, working their flavours into each other as best they could.

I worried that this dish might not pull far enough one way or the other: too light for a bouillabaisse, not pungent enough for a curry. If this had been my recipe, I might have nixed the vegetables and simply tried to infuse my spice mix with a *soupe de poisson* before adding the fish, or added coconut milk and coriander leaves. But it was not my recipe. I just had to trust that it would find its way.

Soon enough, I was scooping it into a bowl: a sauce of turmeric yellow binding the meats and carapaces of a European sea.

The taste was good. Filling and robust, full of rich sourness, though little like food from either of its parent countries. It was a taste of Paris, I suppose, though one few people would currently recognise as such. Maybe one day that will change.

The Pondicherry Kitchen, by the way, was written

by a woman with an obviously Franco-Tamil surname, Tirouvanziam-Louis. This, however, caught my attention far less than her first name, which was Lourdes.

6ème arrondissement

The first meal I ever ate on my own in Paris took place long before I lived here.

It was August 2003, I was seventeen, on my way to the Dordogne to stay with Antoine for the first time: a journey dizzy with all the unjaded anticipation of youth. And it was taking me through Paris! So what that I would have less than five hours in the city? They were to be five hours of the purest independence I'd ever known, and promised a taste (granted I had no idea how much) of the adult life I was then so impatient to usher in.

What was more, I was a recent convert to literature and like so many young men before me, Ernest Hemingway had been my gateway drug. Paris at that point in my life might as well have been Middle Earth. As I walked out of the Gare du Nord that midsummer morning, there was only one place I could think of to go.

I don't know where I first read about Les Deux Magots, or how this 6th arrondissement café was associated with my idol. Nor can I recall why it was this café I settled on and not its equally iconic neighbour, Café de Flore. I certainly didn't know that this corner of Paris was more famous for its link with the philosophers Jean-Paul Sartre and Simone de Beauvoir. (That obsession was, blessedly, to come; peaking exactly when it should, during my first year of university, when an unread copy of *Being and Nothingness* sat performatively splayed on my desk for months – but I digress.) Yet this was not a literary pilgrimage to Hemingway per se, so much as an attempt to place myself, however briefly, inside one of his novels.

I was enraptured by the idea of café culture, of life lived in public; of these places of rendezvous and writing, of people-watching and intellectual debate. I knew nothing then of how this culture had come about, how cafés had evolved from the craze for coffee in the seventeenth century, as well as a need for warm, comfortable social spaces in a city of cramped, dingy domestic living arrangements. I did not know that they were once centres of political rumour and gossip, considered more reliable than the printed news; I did not know that the French Revolution had begun when Camille Desmoulins had brandished a brace of pistols and summoned a mob from atop one of the tables in the Café de Foy over at the Palais Royal. I just knew what I thought I liked. And that was to sit on a storied Paris terrace and drink a half-litre of red wine and observe the world and eat something that was simple and true and good.

I went to Les Deux Magots, convinced – with the blindness of any recently discovered passion – that I must be the only person in Paris who still cared about it, ignorant of how deeply entrenched in the tourist matrix of the city it had become.

As it happened, I don't remember crowds, I only remember sitting at one of its terrace tables and being a little shocked by the prices, but figuring that probably the whole city was just as expensive these days. I lit one of the cigarettes that I was also starting to experiment with. Then, because reading Hemingway was not something a character in Hemingway would do, I pulled out a notebook. I know I did this because I still have it, and this is what I wrote:

> Notes from the terrace of Les Deux Magots ... Sunshine and people, the sensation of a city rushing through me, and of hunger and excitement and anticipation. This table is scratched with the use of plates and glasses of people gone before me. Who? I wonder. What did they discuss? There is cigarette smoke in the hot, bright air. There are French voices. There is a lady walking a dog.

A waiter interrupted this nascent work of genius by asking what I wanted to eat. Though Hemingway would have ordered the oysters, I was not as brave as Hemingway and I did not know how to say oysters in French. So I asked for an omelette.

I'd be lying if I said that I remember exactly what this tasted like. Presumably it tasted like a pretty good omelette. What I can be certain of is that it was one of the best things I have ever eaten. Because it was a taste of the adult world, or at least the adult world as I wished it to be.

Here I was in a foreign café that had been frequented by legends, and I was *allowed* to be there. Not just that, I had been welcomed; someone had made *me* an omelette. I had rented a space on the Paris kerb and in Paris history.

'Yah, yah mate, I'm in, like, a literary café?' the young Englishman with floppy hair a couple of seats down from me on the terrace was shouting into his mobile. 'No, um, *Less Duzz* something. Flic's off shopping with the gals, but I said, no thanks. Just give me a bloody table and a glass of plonk, that's how I see a city. One sec ...' He raised his free hand into the air and beckoned for one of the passing waiters. 'Uh, can I see the wine menu, mate? Cheers.' The waiter gave the subtlest nod and disappeared. The Englishman continued speaking into his phone: 'Ah, gotcha ... But I'll call you back later, then, right? Once I've got a couple of *verre*'s down me. Ha ha.'

Here I was, back in Les Deux Magots for the first time in twenty years, and already having the qualms that had made me avoid it for so long confirmed.

When I actually did come back to Paris to live, the group of friends I fell into declared you were as likely to see a real artist in the café these days as you were Arnold Schwarzenegger in Planet Hollywood; that you'd get a more authentic Paris experience in Disneyland. I had bitten my tongue about the omelette and my experience there on the threshold of adulthood and agreed with them. 'Disneyland, huh, yeah ...'

Now, though, at last searching to replicate that first-ever meal Paris, to search for romance in the heart of Paris's 6th arrondissement, I had the sinking suspicion they'd been right.

I tried to tot up the better points I'd spotted since I'd arrived. The pristine, green-and-white rattan chairs and the smattering of French being spoken in the queue for a table. That it was spring. Sure, Les Deux Magots couldn't claim credit for the season, but what the hell. The dappled freshness of Paris that day was so beautiful it made the clichés true. Except I was not the only one to have noticed.

'Yah, I don't know,' the Englishman said to the waiter the moment he returned with the wine list. 'Just give me one that tastes like spring.'

'*Pardon, monsieur?*'

'Yah, you know, it's springtime in Paris. So I'd like a wine to match it.'

'*Alors,*' he thought for a few seconds. 'So something with a fresh, mineral taste. A Riesling, perhaps?'

'Um,' I could hear a frown in the Englishman's tone. 'Yeah, but I really wanted a French wine.'

'Of course, monsieur,' the waiter's voice did not falter. 'Maybe then you would prefer a Sauvignon?'

'Yah, perfect. I love Sauvignon. A glass of that. Uh, mercy.'

The waiter disappeared.

I tuned my attention to another table. There, another waiter was leaning over the menu, speaking English with a mother and daughter who'd told him they were from Poland, patiently talking them through the various dishes in English.

'Might I recommend the cod with the herring caviar? It is, in my opinion, more interesting than the monkfish.'

'OK, then we shall have that,' said the mother, 'and some snails. I have never had snails. And an Americano.'

'All served at the same time?' said the waiter.

The Polish mother looked confused, 'When else would they be served?' she said.

'At the same time, then.'

If there was any pain in either of the waiters' voices in their responses to these requests, I did not register it. Nor was there a trace of obsequious superiority. No such thing as French Riesling? An Americano with fish? These were remarks that could get you laughed or shouted at from even the least caring of French dinner tables. And these waiters were anything but uncaring when it came to cuisine. You don't come up with a wine that 'tastes like spring' in seconds, or suggest cod and roe as more interesting than monkfish if you don't care about cuisine. Moreover, you'd never learn to be a waiter of the patent quality of the men bussing the tables in front of me.

Les Deux Magots sits at a spectacular Paris crossroads, with tourists and tramps, shoppers and chic Parisiennes bustling in from every direction along those wide Haussmann canyons, but the waiters were by far the better show. First, they were all, to a man (they were all men), impeccably dressed and very handsome. You know the uniform, but here it was pressed five or six times in a faultless ideal. Their dinner jackets were all a deep, lintless black, their bow ties fixed in rigid perfection, and best of all were their starched white aprons, which hung stiff from their waists, making them into so many classical busts gliding frictionlessly between tables and tasks. I watched them performing as showmen and stagehands both, conjuring plates to and from the tables, slipping between registers of focused professionalism and easy flirting, to serious teaching about the menu and back again in the space of seconds. It did not matter if they were speaking French or English, talking to obvious tourists or to people who perhaps came from the *quartier* – their performance and poise was the same.

They were giving the bad reputation of French waiters a bad name.

For my part, I had been allowed to settle for about a minute when I arrived, to feel at home behind my table before a waiter arrived in front of me, menu proffered. The moment I'd gathered my thoughts and folded it back in two, a waiter materialised to take my order.

'An omelette, very good. And with that, maybe a red wine?'

'A red wine, yes!' How had he known?

'A Brouilly perhaps?'

I allowed myself to be guided. 'Yes, a Brouilly.'

'*C'est fait.*' He snapped up my menu and glided away, while I pulled out my notebook and started to write in it, much as I had done twenty years before.

'Hmm, left-handed,' a woman sitting to the other side of me observed in French. I glanced over. To be fair, a quiet running commentary on the world is a surprisingly common habit among a certain class of French person. Often, they have the excuse of talking to their dogs, but not always. This was perhaps the third such comment I'd heard the woman sitting next to me mumble since I'd sat down, though it was the first one directed at me.

'That's right,' I smiled, and she jumped.

'Sorry, I wasn't looking at what you were writing. But I noticed you were left-handed. I am left-handed as well.'

She was wearing a spotless black-and-white striped rain-coat and had gunmetal hair that was pulled back as tightly as her tastefully Botoxed cheeks; I'd have bet the price of a Deux Magots omelette (€23!) that this woman was not a tourist.

'Are you a local,' I said, 'to Les Deux Magots?'

'A regular,' she replied. 'I live in Neuilly [a bourgeois Paris suburb] these days, but I come here whenever I'm in town.'

'Right, so, sorry if this seems rude, but then Les Deux Magots isn't only for tourists?'

'It's not rude at all,' the woman smiled. She had bright-blue eyes and wonderfully straight teeth. 'There are a lot of tourists here, of course, but I think quite a few regulars as well.'

She pointed some out to me. Men and women in their autumn years clad in conservative, well-tailored clothes, adorned with expensive, eccentric accessories: a pair of bright-red spectacles, a linen keffiyeh, a Basque beret.

'And do you know if any of them are writers or artists?' I asked. 'Like they used to be.'

'Not so many these days,' the woman conceded. 'At least no more than any other bar in the *quartier*. Gallimard still have their offices nearby, which is really how Les Deux Magots and Café de Flore started attracting writers in the first place. The big difference today is that there are no international writers any more.'

'How do you mean?'

'French publishing has become so nationalist,' she sighed. 'Before yes, yes, there was Sartre and de Beauvoir, but also there were many translators, and they would invite the writers whose books they were working on. Chinese, American, African, it was a real community.'

The way she was talking suggested to me that perhaps she had been a part of this world – I later discovered she had worked in film – though she stressed that she did not come to the bar for its literary connotations.

'I'm here because they do the food exactly how I like it, and because the waiters are so nice.'

At this point, my Brouilly arrived, the whole bottle of it, which the waiter presented grandly, alongside an empty glass, on a silver tray.

'It's a new bottle, monsieur,' he told me, setting the glass down in front of me and pulling the cork from the bottle all with one hand, 'so perhaps you'd like to taste it first.'

A soupçon was poured into my glass, and I sniffed at it, playing my own role. It smelled of smoke and cherry.

'*Oui, c'est bon*,' I said, marvelling at how once again, even at the age of thirty-seven, Les Deux Magots had managed to make me feel like an adult. I received a generous (though admittedly €10) glass.

The regular from Neuilly and I talked a little longer, which was when I found out she had worked in film and had, improbably, been involved in making the video game tie-in *Assassin's Creed*. She left just as my omelette arrived.

It was a beautiful thing, though almost confrontationally austere. Here was an elegantly folded cheroot of glossy egg, flecked with just the tiniest hints of caramelised brown, and a single head of gem lettuce sliced in two and dressed in an imperceptibly delicate vinaigrette suffused with a fine *brunoise* of shallot and chive. And that was it.

The omelette had been cooked to perfection, its interior walking a tightrope line between liquid and solid states, and with next to no salt. It was asking for concentration from its eater.

I ate that simple dish with more concentration than I

253

had in a long while. Every bite was seasoned by the storied history of the place, by the smoky flavour of the wine, by the money I knew it was costing me. I knew too that, through the waiters, any passing whim I might have could be catered for, and nothing was being expected of me but to sit and enjoy what I had just been given. But please do enjoy it.

Then, because I wanted the experience to continue, I ordered a €5 espresso.

Now, I recognise that in some places – London sometimes, New York certainly – €5 for an espresso might be close to expectations. But in Paris, it is an outrage. City-wide, espressos seldom push the €2.50 mark, and there are plenty of bars where you can still get *un p'tit café* for closer to €1. And let me say now that Les Deux Magots' espresso, when it came, was hardly better than any average Parisian cup. Which is to say bad. Yet I paid the price gladly.

I got chatting to my waiter, whose name was Camille. I complimented the service, then asked if they received any special training, wondering if Les Deux Magots ran a staff boot camp, had flowchart expectations for how its waiters should behave, as many franchised restaurant firms do.

'Not at all,' said Camille. 'It is simply the case that no waiter here will have been working in the industry for less than ten years. And by that time, most will already be known to us in any case. The world of professional waiters in Paris is quite small, so it is rare that we are surprised.'

He continued: 'We learn the specifics of Les Deux Magots quickly. On the job. Often a senior waiter will take a new one under his wing. I was taught by an old guy here when I arrived. That was in 2016. I hope to be here for another ten, fifteen years, at least.'

We were now at the far end of the lunch service, just before the *apéro* shift began. For a brief moment, Camille had not so much to do, and he had read the kind of customer I was, understood what I was after; I did not have to prompt him much to say more.

'This place could very easily become a tourist trap,' he said. 'It's Les Deux Magots: Sartre, the surrealists, all of that. People would keep on coming whatever we did. But that wouldn't be right because also this place is a representation of Paris, it's like a beacon. We're ambassadors for our city. We have to create something worthy of that. We have to be polite, attentive ...'

He paused for a second; I caught his eyes flash left and right, scanning that he was not currently needed elsewhere before he went on.

'Because when you step into a café, you're in a world that is different from the street.'

'How do you mean?' I asked, taking a 50-cent sip of espresso.

'On the streets of Paris, you know, it's still Paris, but people can be rude. They have other things that they are doing, going this way and that. But here, on our terrace, things must be better than that. It is a place where we extend a hand, where we make you feel welcome.'

Finally leaving the curated bubble of the Deux Magots terrace, I must admit to a passing flicker of cynicism at Camille's high-spoken words. Sure, it was easy to talk of welcome at a place where people were routinely spending more than €50 on a light lunch, and no doubt there was a degree to which the waiter was trawling for tips. I was probably the third earnest bloke with a notebook he'd fed the same spiel to that day. There was also every chance that all the suggestions I'd heard proffered – the Riesling, the cod over the monkfish, the Brouilly – were in fact upsells or based on the demands of the kitchen; I know how restaurants work. But did any of that really matter?

The point was that the illusion had succeeded – and it had succeeded because it was based on something real. Camille's professionalism, and that of his colleagues, was undeniable. If he was deceiving me, he was also in some way deceiving himself. The waiters had sold the wines and the fish so that they really did seem special. I *had* felt welcomed, like I belonged in this place at the heart of Paris, and so it seemed had the regular who once worked in film, the Polish woman and her daughter, the Englishman who wanted his wine to taste like spring; or even me, all those years ago: a far younger Englishman, who knew nothing about Paris apart from what he'd read in the pages of an American writer's novels.

Moreover, wasn't this sense of welcome and belonging offered in a small way, or at the very least aspired to, by all Paris cafés? Wasn't this what made them special? The fact that, on their terraces, for the price of a coffee, you will be looked after or left alone by true Parisians as you wish; and you can simply read, or people-watch, or write an undiscovered masterpiece; be not just in the city, but of it.

The omelette is the tangible corollary of all this theatre of welcome. A deceptively simple dish requiring great skill, the omelette also represents a direct communication between diner and kitchen staff. Nothing in an omelette can be prepared ahead of time; it comes into existence only at the point of being ordered: just for you.

To prove my theory that it was not only the highest, best-known of Paris cafés that offered this kind of welcome, I decided to seek out my omelette recipe not in Les Deux Magots, but rather in the lesser-known backstreets of the 6th – and here I encountered a conundrum.

Here was Paris as it exists in dreams, or at the very least guidebook photographs. Narrow, winding streets, shadowed by elegant pre-Haussmann blocks, skirted by ancient pavements, and flush with luxe independent art galleries. There were also cafés. My problem, however: none were cheap and most had their own historic renown. Many would have their own Wikipedia page, if not a handful of academic works published about their histories. I was in the streets of Paris where Paris had happened.

At last, though, I found somewhere promising. Le Balto, on the corner of rue Mazarine, which runs south from near the quay at the tip of the Île de la Cité towards the boulevard Saint-Germain. There was no establishment date above its door, it had road workers crowding its *comptoir*, and a glance at its menu showed that the prices were nearly half those of Les Deux Magots. And it served omelette. This, I decided, was my place. Except I was wrong.

The staff at Le Balto were interested in my request, said they'd be happy to introduce me to their chef, to show me how their omelette was made. Only, they said, what they made there, well, it was not a real omelette.

'*Pas une omelette vraie?*' I repeated, nonplussed; even on the 6th's backstreets it seemed they took an interest in phenomenology.

'For that, you will need a café,' Le Balto's barman explained. 'Here we are only a bar.'

I'd had my suspicions about this already. The difference between Parisian bars and cafés is a subtle one, further complicated when you include brasseries and bistros. I can't say I've ever fully understood all this. I know their technical definitions: bistros tend to be smaller and concentrate on food; brasseries are large Alsatian-inspired places, which historically brewed their own beer (*brasser* is the French verb for 'brew'); bars are obviously more dedicated to drinking and focused around the counter; while cafés can be pretty much any size and are primarily dedicated to serving coffee, though offer meals and drinks as well.

As far as I see it, mind, I would argue that 'café' is just an umbrella term that includes these other categories. Le Balto, after all, had rattan chairs on its terrace and served alcohol, coffee and food. But then, I never did get round to grasping French philosophy's take on the world of forms.

Still, Le Balto's barman was now offering his own kind of welcome – in the sense of very considerately leading me somewhere else. He emerged from behind his counter to walk me down the street to a café (this one I could be certain of because it had the word 'café' on its awning) where he said they not only made a real omelette – in point of fact they made 'the best omelette in all of Paris'. It was called La Palette.

I would not be surprised to learn that La Palette – founded in 1902 – had not had a refit in a hundred years. Best of all – along with the faded red leather of its tabletops, its chip marble floor, its grand mirror spotted with age – was the copper bar, polished bright as the sun but beaten and dented down its whole length by the hammering of a billion drinks orders past.

The waiters were neither as chic nor as efficient as they were in Les Deux Magots – some had even completed their penguin suits with black jeans – but they greeted my request to see an omelette made with enthusiasm and with pride. I was taken to the kitchen.

I say kitchen; there are submarines with larger galleys. It was a cupboard with a stove, and there was barely room inside for the two chefs to stand shoulder to shoulder. Surely this wasn't it? I'd seen La Palette's menu: there were proper meals on it, most costing north of €30. And the café's maximum capacity couldn't have been under sixty people.

'How do you do it?' I asked the chef – a young, very petite woman called Marjorie.

'*On bosse*,' she explained. We graft.

Fortunately, lunch service was long over at that point, so she had the time, if barely the space, to demonstrate how La Palette's omelettes are made.

Omelette
Welcomes 1
Ingredients:
3 eggs
A gas stove

I tried to recreate what I describe here half a dozen times. I could probably try another hundred and not get it looking or tasting as good as Marjorie's did. Omelettes, despite their apparent simplicity, are not for nothing known as one of the highest tests of a chef's ability. Making that omelette took just a few minutes, but it was the product of half a lifetime's learning with food and heat. That is the level of welcome an omelette represents: they are a work of art for one.

Marjorie began by lighting the stove and turning it to a high flame, then she squirted the thinnest film of vegetable oil into an ordinary Teflon pan and left it to heat.

'No butter?' I asked.

'No butter,' said the chef.

She cracked eggs; three in total, opening them up by breaking the weaker part of one shell on the stronger part of another. Their contents slid into a small stainless-steel bowl. With a fork Marjorie began to beat, harder and faster than I could possibly achieve, whisking the raw whites and yolks together in seconds into a single creamy emulsion.

'You have to stir hard,' the chef explained. 'It must look more white than yellow. Then, a little salt ...' She took the smallest pinch between finger and thumb and dropped it into the mix. 'Now, we cook.'

I cannot write 'she moved over to the stove', for in fact she was already at the stove, had been beating those eggs with her torso pivoted away from the heat. She pivoted back, turned the flame even higher and tipped the egg mix into the pan. Now, suddenly, she was cooking in the most active sense of the verb. Fighting with the egg mixture, tossing it, stirring it, not allowing even the tiniest hint of it to caramelise or catch. A French omelette – *une omelette vraie* – should be as pale as the dawn.

Even so, I thought, surely this won't be an omelette, this will be scrambled eggs.

Only then, for a few perfectly judged, impossible to teach

moments, she let the whole thing settle, let it develop a base structure. Then she flipped one third of its circular form over into its centre, and at last, in a single action magicked a plate from a hitherto invisible shelf, and tipped the cooking egg onto it, turning it over itself again as she did, so that when it landed, steaming on the porcelain, it found instantly its perfect, final form.

'*Voilà*,' Marjorie said, trying to affect nonchalance but unable to keep a grin of pride from her face. '*Une omelette.*'

5ème arrondissement

My first spring in Paris, I spent mostly in and around the famed Shakespeare & Company bookshop, when blurry nights out in bars of the 5th often stretched into blurrier dawns. Back then, the bookshop still functioned as a de facto hostel to an unlikely international crowd of artistic waifs and strays, offering a free bed among the stacks in exchange for a couple of hours' work and the proviso that you read a book a day. The blow-ins who took advantage of this were my first social circle in the city. They were a rogues' gallery of bed-hopping, *Ulysses*-quoting youths from Buenos Aires, Brisbane and everywhere in between. Kids who mainlined rot-gut wine, stole for sport, and maintained they'd grow up to be recognised as geniuses who'd change the world. A lot of them were awful, clearly, though at the same time in their anachronistic pursuit of the bohemian dream, they felt exactly what I had come to the city to find. And I still have brilliant, unrepentant memories of those mornings when, full of alcohol and adventure, we would stumble from wherever it was we'd been setting the world to rights, to discover the city resetting itself under the full, crisp glory of sunrise, ready to let us do it all again.

Just as in those days, there was the orange blush of first light hitting mansard roofs, the scent of boulangeries as their ovens warmed, and the sound of birdsong. And just as in those days, I felt dreadful. You don't stay up all night drinking without suffering a few body blows, even in your early twenties. Today, it wasn't booze that had wrecked me – I'd simply gone to sleep after 1 a.m. and my alarm had sounded at 4, and these days, that was enough. But what I wanted to witness – as with so much of what makes Paris function – I had to be up early to catch.

I heard it before I saw it. The low thrum of truck engines, the hollow clatter of metal hitting metal, shouts that seemed too bright and sober for the hour. I remembered all this from the old days too. It was the sound of the market at place Maubert beginning.

Paris is a city of markets. The first was established in the fifth century AD on the Île de la Cité, and even today, there are eighty taking place every week within the bounds of the Périphérique. I might have gone to any of them: pushed my way around the stalls under the overhead metro tracks in the crush of Barbès in the 18th, salivated over the mouth-watering produce at the 'chefs' market', at Alma in the 16th, or played the *flâneur* beneath the nineteenth-century pavilions of Aligre in the 12th. But I had come to place Maubert in the 5th because it was the first Paris market I felt close to, often pitching up here after those fantastic nights out to sit on the newly laid terrace of a café called Le Village Ronsard and drink coffee and think brilliant, bleary thoughts about love, art and my future while I watched the market assemble. When I was young.

In need of a coffee this morning too, I made a beeline into the Village Ronsard, still reliably there, a clean, well-lighted sanctuary in the blueish gloom. It could have been ten years ago in that empty café, it could have been a hundred.

A lone barman was going through his morning routines: stacking cups, wiping the zinc, polishing spoons. He welcomed me with a timeless *bonjour* and set to making my espresso with zoetrope motions he must have spun through a million times. I sat on a bar stool sipping at the coffee, which hit my gut like a claw. I was entirely loving every second of this and entirely hating it at the same time.

'*Salut, Pascal!*' an overalled market worker strode in. '*Un p'tit jus de pomme, s'il te plaît.*' A little apple juice, if you please.

With a half-smile and a nod, Pascal, the barman, turned wordlessly to his spirits to take down a bottle of Calvados and free-poured a generous double measure.

The two men saw me looking, and the market worker raised the glass in my direction. 'Apple juice to help wake me up,' he grinned. 'But this is why I only ask for a little. Too much would put me to sleep.'

My younger self would have been tempted to join him, but not these days; a Calvados right then would have seen me off. In any case, fortified by my coffee, it was time to hit the square.

Daylight had almost arrived by now and the place Maubert, ringed by elegant apartment blocks and bordered by the still-empty boulevard Saint-Germain, greeted me with crisp perfection. Everywhere there was unhurried movement: the assembling of stalls, the wheeling about of produce-teetering pallets, the arrangements of displays. To my right, along the square's northern edge, a boulangerie had rolled up its shutters, was breathing out its buttery croissant waft.

I watched the worker who'd just had his 'little cup of apple juice' return to his stall. It was a *poissonnerie*, a fish-monger's, and unlike much of the rest of the market, it had already been almost fully prepared: the slither-shiny fresh-ness of its wares gleamed under a string of electric lights.

I observed as he hauled a bucket of chipped ice from the back of a nearby van and started to shovel it like snow onto the stall's last empty table. Then, he fetched a box of soggy brown skate and began to fan the fish out onto the ice bed he had just made. Transforming, in a gesture, dead fish into living art.

'It looks beautiful,' I observed, admiring the red mullet face-down in the ice of a large silver chalice, the squid Dal-matian-spotted by their own ink, the two dozen langoustines fanned like an opening flower.

'*Bah, merci,*' the worker shrugged and stopped what he was doing to light a cigarette.

'Do you have a system?' I asked. 'I mean, do you know how you're going to display everything before you begin?'

He eyed me, smiling, and rolled the cigarette to the corner of his mouth; was perhaps a little buzzed from his Calva. He was about my age, with large features and olive skin that looked ashen in the morning light.

'Not at all,' he said at last. 'Every day it's different because every day we have different produce. So I put down the ice, then,' he pointed into the blue sky with a rubber-gloved hand, 'I search for inspiration. Some days it's easier than others.'

We continued chatting as he got on with his work; he was already halfway through his working day.

'I wake up at midnight,' he said, 'to go to Rungis market to select the fish. The most important thing is that it's fresh,' he said, and reached for a bream to expose to me its still-violet gills, 'so we never know exactly what we'll be getting.'

The butchers at a nearby stall, whose glass cabinets were plump with sausage strings and rosy pink chops, had a similar routine. They were young, two of them barely out of their teens; the boss, though only around thirty himself, had a substantial, well-groomed beard. He'd woken at 3 a.m.

'We're based right next to Rungis,' he told me. 'So it's quite convenient.'

'So how many other markets do you work in a week?'

'Fifteen.'

Testament to the brain-fogging early hour, I frowned at this, trying to remember how many days there were in a week.

'Huh?' I said.

'I mean that's how many the business does,' he explained. 'It was founded by my grandfather in the 1960s. There are several teams. I only work here and in Bastille. I like Maubert, though. It's got good footfall and there are a lot of locals.'

I could imagine this last point coming as a surprise to some. Here was very much central Paris, less than five minutes from Notre Dame. But of course there were locals. People live everywhere in Paris.

A couple of cheese counters had now been completely stocked with gooey sophistication; there were more fish and meat stalls, and lagging a little behind in their set-up, the fruit and veg stalls, the *primeurs*, which had only just got their trestles ready, were trolleying cling-film-wrapped crates from nearby vans.

The workers were mostly, but not all, men. They were of all ages and wearing what seemed a near-uniform of faded T-shirts and ripped jeans. A lot were smoking *as* they worked, fags chugging expertly from their lips as they arranged their produce into beautiful organic collages of colour and taste. Occasionally they stopped to talk to one another, try each other's produce, comment on its quality. It was like witnessing the function of a single organism: everything connecting with, relying on, everything else; using the city as fuel to the business of fuelling the city.

Émile, one of the *primeurs* I got talking to, had been working the markets since he was ten years old. 'And now I'm nearly eighty,' he said. 'I deserve a chest full of medals.'

Low on his chair behind the trestles, sporting a black beanie perched high above his ears, he looked a little like a garden gnome. His skin was bleached the colour of weak tea, and his eyes were a silvery damp blue, the whites tinged with pink in the corners.

'It's changed a lot,' he said. 'A lot, a lot. Once, we'd have had ten, fifteen pallets of produce. Today, it's just two. People don't want to go to markets any more.'

They still seemed popular to me, I said, in the north of the city certainly. The markets I was most familiar with

– Barbès, Joinville, Belleville – on their weekend dates, you couldn't move for shoppers.

'No, the young don't care about good food any more,' Émile continued as if he hadn't heard me. 'Around here you have, how many – three, four supermarkets? Two Franprixs, a Carrefour, I don't know what else. People want convenience. They go there day or night. The markets are dying.'

I remembered a quote from Paul Theroux about how old men can sometimes confuse the end of their lives with the end of all things, but who was I to tell this veteran market seller he was wrong? Paris markets still seemed healthy to me, but thirty or forty years ago, perhaps things were on another scale.

While we were talking, a seller from a neighbouring stall arrived proffering a bowl of apricots like so many dawning suns.

'My apricots are good today,' he said, handing them around for members of Émile's stall to try. I got one too. It was as sweet as hope.

'Yes, they're not bad,' Émile conceded, then yelled to no one in particular, 'Where are our apricots?'

'So do you go to Rungis every morning too?' I asked.

'*Mais naturellement*,' Émile said. 'You have to. I go, I taste everything. Everything on my stall. Here, we only sell the best.'

At the Rungis wholesale market, fruit and veg is sold in two categories: 'extra' and '2'. The *primeurs* who sell the best only buy from the 'extra' category, and they get there as early as they can to get a chance to taste the produce and have their pick. Other fruit and veg stalls content themselves with second-tier produce, though they can sell a little cheaper. For the sellers from the mostly northern markets I frequent, quality takes a back seat to quantity. They are almost like wholesalers themselves, sometimes teaming up with fellow stallholders to buy massive amounts of cheaper, older leftovers, and relying on bulk sales to turn a profit.

Émile was warming to my presence now, telling me how he'd worked in markets all over the city. In the famous covered Aligre market near Bastille, and in Belleville, where he was born.

'It's much more chaotic there,' he said. 'I worked in Belleville with my sister for years.'

His parents had been market traders too, he said, and the woman standing next to him, who was patiently working her way through punnets of strawberries, discarding any that were not up to standard, was his daughter. She looked up and grinned at me.

'It's true, and that's his wife,' she said, indicating a vampish older woman (who was still a good twenty years younger than Émile) at the other end of the stall.

'I am not his wife,' the woman snapped at once. 'I am still only his girlfriend.'

'Ah, and how many years has it been now?' Émile laughed.

'Too many years,' she said.

There had already been much laughter across the market, in which I was now finding myself included. It served as a reminder that stallholders lived or died not only on their produce, but on the relationships they could cultivate with their customers, though I didn't sense anything artificial or forced about the banter.

'So, what is it, then,' Émile's girlfriend asked me, 'do you want a job?'

'I don't know,' I said, 'it seems like it might be fun.'

'No, you could never handle it,' she grinned. 'What time did you get up this morning?'

I told her.

'For us it was 3 a.m. Every morning of the week. And yes, it is nice right now, but many mornings it will be raining, freezing cold. Even today, it will be hot later – very tiring.'

'So why do you do it?' I asked. 'What keeps you coming back?'

'This guy!' she pointed at Émile. 'We're all his slaves.'

Émile scowled at this, and muttered a string of curses under his breath. His daughter screeched with laughter: '*Ah, c'est ça l'amour.*'

'Truly,' Émile's girlfriend resumed, 'I like the chance to be mean to as many people as I can throughout the day. If you're just nice to all your customers, they'll forget you. You have to have fun with them so they come back.'

'Ah, so you do think I could work here, then, really?' I said.

She looked at me properly then: at my flushed morning skin, at the bags under my eyes.

'No chance,' she cackled.

The day was fully upon us now. The city's taxonomies were changing. When I'd arrived, it had still been the Paris of drunken youths. Then, there were me and Pascal, the *boulangers* and the market workers. Now, tourists were starting to spill from the metro. Foreigners who hadn't got the memo that Christophe the libertine had shared with me in Moon City that Paris was (mostly) late to bed, late to rise; who again seemed to have guessed something that most of us who lived here forgot: the city is at its best at dawn. They would be followed by street cleaners and joggers, and then gradually, the full machinery of the modern city would start to turn again.

Maubert market put me in mind of the final prep for an event. Its workers were putting the last touches to the city before one of the greatest shows on earth: Paris, on a perfect day in the spring.

It was happening inside restaurants too; and in the waiters lining chairs and tables on the empty terraces; and with the hydrants opened in the gutters, like urban brooks babbling forth to clear away the detritus of the night. But here it was at its most visible, most profound, where stall after stall was sorting through its strawberries, or starting to roast its chickens, or carefully setting its live lobsters in a row; arranging food bought in the darkness in ways that it would illuminate the City of Light.

Which all sounds very romantic; and it was. Though it was also physically demanding, backed by tired hands and slowly waking eyes. Romance doesn't come from nowhere. Even drinking through the night to see the dawn takes a certain dedication, one that no matter how great the memories, I hadn't been able to summon for years. And even this, now, simply waking to come witness it: I was glad I didn't have to stay for the whole shift, glad I didn't have to wake at four to come again tomorrow. And in this I marvelled at how it was sustained.

The market at place Monge was, if anything, even more beautiful, more romantic than the one on place Maubert. I'd arrived a little later, to be fair, at around half-past eight this time, so I was in far better physical shape to appreciate the magic. Still, it was another crystalline morning, the teetering quaintness of the rue Mouffetard along which I approached splendidly empty. There were pollen motes on the air, plane trees in full neon leaf, and the limestone of the buildings shone as bright as butter. Here was the Paris of *Emily in Paris*. And another taste of Hemingway's Paris. He'd lived just off Mouffetard, and described the days when goatherds still drove their flocks along its cobbles. There were no goats now, but still plenty of other life brought in from the fields of France.

The people who came to buy were mostly women, some men, mostly well north of middle age, dressed in impeccably restrained clothing and dragging two-wheeled shopping carts at their backs. They were the good people of the 5th arrondissement – no one I spoke to had come from further afield. This was their twice- or thrice-weekly ritual. No, they did not use supermarkets, not unless absolutely necessary. Their motives for coming to place Monge instead were almost all identical.

The quality of produce, I was told again and again, its seasonality and flavour. Only one woman, younger than most, suggested she also came to the market because it was quite simply a pleasant thing to do. The only real variation was in peoples' choice of stalls. Some shoppers were willing to compromise a little on taste for a slightly lower cost, while others gravitated strictly to the best of the best. I learned that their relationship with individual sellers was important too. Vital, in fact. I witnessed countless acts of ritualised banter: comments on the weather, the news; on apricots and artichokes. It was not only that the same families of vendors had been at the market for generations; in many cases they had been serving to generations of the same clients too.

'My father used to buy at *his* father's stall,' the younger woman told me of a particular *primeur*. 'So it's just where I have always come. Oh, and he is the best, of course.'

So it was not only the vendors who made the Paris markets what they were. It was also the local shoppers and their Parisian tastes. For all the sellers' hard work in selecting produce every pre-dawn, in setting up come rain or shine, in presenting their wares beautifully, the whole ecosystem could not continue without an appetite for and an appreciation of that beauty, or a dedication to turning up, two or three times a week to buy.

I love the Paris markets. I love all food markets. I would go so far as to say there is something hardwired that makes all human beings love food markets. They are places of socialising and sustenance, necessity and fantasy – what will I eat today? And yet, like many Parisians, I don't go to them as often as I should. They take a degree of forward planning – of weekly meal plans, of setting time aside to cook – which sits at odds with the pace and spontaneity of modern Paris life.

So it's worth pointing out that these 'Paris tastes' I was getting misty-eyed over are not shared by all of the city's population – and, as I said, the majority of the shoppers I spoke to on the place Monge were growing old.

Even more of a reason, perhaps, to celebrate what they do for the rest of us, these people who resisted the quick fixes that are one of the main seductions of life in a major city; who came here twice a week almost as if it was their job too, and in doing so helped maintain something beautiful for everyone.

Salade au Chèvre Chaud
Serves 3–4
Ingredients:
  For the salad:
  1 head of red leaf lettuce
  ½ bunch of fresh parsley leaves
  ½ bunch of fresh tarragon leaves
  3 spring onions
  1 fresh goat's cheese
  1 baguette

  For the vinaigrette:
  Juice of 2 lemons
  1 tsp honey
  1 tsp mustard
  Olive oil (1:1 ratio with rest)

There was one stall at the place Monge that everyone I spoke to would visit regardless of other loyalties. A whispered legend of a seller, not only famous among the locals of the 5th, but across the whole city. He was, according to almost every source I later consulted, the best fruit and veg vendor in all of Paris. His name was Marc Mascetti, though he went by Marco, and I stumbled upon him by chance.

There was a category difference in the produce at Marco's stall compared to nearly all the others at place Monge, and it was visible at a glance. For while all the rest resembled collages of glossy colour, his looked more like an unkempt field, all shaggy green leaf, dun dirt and tangled roots. Marco himself was unassuming, with short white hair, a leather tan and large, thick-fingered hands, and when I approached, he was in the midst of a conversation about how the people in Brussels were idiots and didn't know anything about the land. He looked and sounded, in fact, like a farmer – and this impression was more accurate than at first I realised.

Bypassing the wholesale market at Rungis, Marco belonged to another, rarer breed of vendor who also frequent the markets of the capital. In fact, according to many I spoke to, he wasn't really a vendor at all, but rather a producer who just incidentally came into town to sell his wares.

Marco's farm, about an hour from central Paris in Essonne, Île-de-France, was legendary. Not only did he avoid all pesticides, neither did he use irrigation systems. Whatever it was that made his crops grow, they took entirely naturally from the soil. When I passed on the many compliments I had heard about him, Marco merely shrugged.

'If I am the best market stall in Paris, it is not because of me,' he said. 'It is because of the work done by my produce. It has done the hardest work.'

I asked him what was best on his stall today, and what he would recommend I make with it. Another shrug.

'Honestly, you've come at probably the worst time of year. I'm at the mercy of the weather, the seasons. Any other month, I could have offered you far more.'

It was an interesting contrast to the apparently glorious spring day. This romantic weather, Paris's most mythic season, apparently did not translate into the best food. Nevertheless, Marco talked me through what he did have. There was rhubarb, he said, which I could make into a crumble. That sounded a bit British, though.

'Or there are my carrots, my potatoes.' These looked like so many clumps of fresh earth, so encrusted with soil you could hardly see the vegetable underneath. 'But that's not so interesting. No, what are really good now are my herbs and my lettuce. So ... an aromatic salad for spring? You can have it with goat's cheese, which you can buy at the stall behind.'

'Perfect.'

I bought two heads of muddied red lettuce, a bushel of racing-green tarragon and some rigid fresh parsley, plus a bunch of spring onions with stalks so brawny they were almost leeks. All that earthy, organic texture and colour; it was a market haul that looked not only tasty, but tasteful as well.

'Just make sure to serve it with a good vinaigrette,' Marco was saying as one of his customers butted in – a small, elderly man in a trilby hat.

'It should have a base of lemon,' this man instructed me. 'For a goat's cheese salad, it should have a base of lemon. You stir into that a spoon of honey and a spoon of mustard, and some salt. Stir it all together until the acid has dissolved them. Only then should you add the oil. No more oil than lemon, though. It is a vinaigrette.'

Marco looked at his customer, looked at me, and once again he shrugged.

'Anything else?'

I went to buy my goat's cheese from a great counter bursting with more culture than the Louvre. For a spring salad, the *fromager* told me, and with Marco's vegetables, the cheese should be light and fresh. He even counselled me how to slice it, into centimetre-thick discs.

'You see, my cheese is already the perfect size to fit on a slice of baguette.'

Toast the rounds of bread for five minutes first, he said,

then layer on the cheese, and put it back into the oven to melt.

Cleaning Marco's salad leaves in my sink, the dirt came off it in rivulets, a positive mudslide into the white enamel. I dropped the leaves into the bowl with the chopped parsley and tarragon, their pepper and aniseed perfumes newly released by the rocking of a sharpened blade. Then, the spring onion, which I sliced into thin washers of pungent crunch.

The hot goat's cheese tartines I placed on top of the leaves like so many boats on a sea of green, and finally I drizzled over the sweet, lemony, mustard punch of vinaigrette, giving those deep matt colours a popping sheen.

It was a dish of wonderful simplicity, which let the produce shout for itself. Each bite was an insistent celebration of the ongoing now, a reminder of how Paris markets are a cure for nostalgia. For they remain all that I had feared was fading into the past of this city – into my past – renewed with the dawn.

4ème arrondissement

'I've been going for the past thirty years. There's
a line out the door, but it's worth the wait.'

Lenny, fifty-nine, musician (interview with the *Financial Times*)

Most of us refer to it simply as 'the falafel place'. Or we say,
'Shall we grab a falafel?', and no matter where we are in the
city, we know the place we mean. At a push, we might want a
'Lenny Kravitz falafel', but that's a nickname, telling of the
familiarity the place has for us all.

We go here on nights out and in the middle of the day,
between meals and for meals, in groups and alone. I don't
just mean my friends and I. I mean nearly everyone in central
Paris; I mean a lot of people from the *banlieue*; I mean

tourists. In fact, if you had any knowledge about Paris's food scene before buying this book, I probably mean you as well.

You know? The falafel place! The one in the Marais. The name above the door is L'As du Fallafel – the Ace of Falafel – and it is quite possibly the most successful single restaurant for its size in the entire city.

Midday, midweek: L'As du Fallafel already had queues spilling from both doors. One queue consisted of ten or so people waiting for a table in its packed 110-seater dining room, the other a constant dozen or so – continually being added to and whittled down – in line for takeaway treats.

Things were poised to get busier; the atmosphere that bright noon was of gathering carnival. There were new customers arriving all the time from all directions along the narrow cobbled streets of rue des Rosiers and rue des Écouffes – the shop sits at an ancient T-junction in the midst of what remains of medieval Paris – and staff were directing them into the right lines, switching between French, English and Hebrew to take orders and payment so that the instant the customers reached the service counter they'd find their food waiting and be on their way. Meanwhile, on a trestle across the street sat a boom box, blasting klezmer pop, surrounded by bottles of water and soft drinks for the waiters and friends of the shop, which had been run by the same family for the past forty-five years.

Watching all this, dazzled by the movement and the obvious joy, by the tumbling cacophony of languages and the sunlight that bounced from the medieval walls of the nearby buildings, the question I had come here to answer asserted itself with a new force.

How?

In Paris, the home of rarefied tastes, of a comparatively nationalistic palate and deep-seated deference for ritual and tradition, a city of more than 44,000 restaurants – how had this straight-up falafel shop risen to the top?

L'As du Fallafel stands in the Marais, to the north of the 4th arrondissement, right in the centre of the city. Founded on land reclaimed from the Seine in the Middle Ages – *le marais* means marsh – as Paris got bigger, so this area, just across the river from the Île Saint Louis and the Île de la Cité, grew in popularity. By the seventeenth century it was one of the most fashionable neighbourhoods in all of Paris. A cluster of spectacular urban mansions, known as *hôtels particuliers*, were built there by noble families, as well as the oldest planned square in the city, the place des Vosges. However, as the French court moved out to Versailles under Louis XIV, the Marais gradually lost its sheen. Eventually, it was abandoned by the chattering classes, on account of most of them being indisposed, that is to say decapitated in the French Revolution/Terror. The area fell into decay and became a stronghold of the working class. It was only saved from destruction during the mid-nineteenth century renovations of Paris thanks to the campaigning of the writer Victor Hugo, who recognised the value of this medieval enclave's architecture and sought to preserve it as representative of the older glories of the city. Indeed, it's one of the few parts of Paris that is still truly old, harking back to the city's appearance in a much earlier age.

Nevertheless, it remained a poor neighbourhood, becoming a centre for Jewish émigrés fleeing persecution from, mostly, Eastern Europe. France, incidentally, was the first country in Europe to grant emancipation for its Jews, which it did after the Revolution (they got some things right), and it remains home to the largest Jewish population in the world after Israel and the US.

By the late nineteenth century, the Jewish area of the Marais became known locally as the Pletzl ('Little Place' in Yiddish), and thanks to the presence of a couple of synagogues was centred on the rue des Rosiers – the same street on which L'As du Fallafel stands today.

After the Second World War – a period which spelled untold hardships for the Marais' Jewish heart – real urban regeneration began. The French government had finally woken up to the treasure that their capital city represented. *Hôtels particuliers* were restored and transformed into museums, while, on the Marais' western edge, the Centre Georges Pompidou was built – still one of the largest and most important modern and contemporary art galleries in the world.

And so the Marais started to regain its lost reputation, becoming a hub for tourists, fashionistas and for Paris's LGBTQ+ community.

Founded in 1979, a decade or so before the effects of this regeneration really began to be felt, L'As du Fallafel was there to serve them all. But it was not alone.

'We've bought out Mi-Va-Mi,' the guy taking orders from the takeaway line told me when I pointed to the shuttered shop the other side of the road that had for a long time been L'As du Fallafel's most proximate rival. Though there are several other falafel restaurants on this winding street,

Mi-Va-Mi was the one I always went to when I couldn't face the queue at L'As.

'Why do you think your place was so much more successful?'

'You've eaten at both?' He had a distracted energy, and clearly little time to chat. The queue was still growing, after all.

'Yes,' I said.

'*Et donc?*'

'L'As du Fallafel is better,' I admitted – though in truth my memories of eating at the other place were hazy. If I was being completely candid, I'd say what really set the two apart was that Mi-Va-Mi used a more pungent, garlicky tahini, which was more in-your-face tasty than the one at L'As, but would also leave you stinking – and I do mean stinking – for hours after consumption. Perhaps the sauce was a handy cover-up for lower-quality ingredients. But side-by-side comparison was no longer possible – and when there is a clear winner, they write the history.

Only later did I discover what a battle there had been between the two establishments. True, the warring restaurants trope is a favourite among journalists, but it really did seem there'd been little love lost. Mi-Va-Mi was established in 1999 by a Russian Jew from the same Tel Aviv neighbourhood as the founder of L'As, and offered a menu that was identical down to the last chickpea. Cue a war of words, then actions, which L'As du Fallafel won by buying Mi-Va-Mi's building and campaigning to get their kosher licence revoked. Through all this time, however, the original had always been by far the more popular establishment.

'I'm sorry, I don't have time to talk.' The server extracted himself from our conversation. 'You're better off speaking to one of my managers.'

'Perhaps I could come back when it's quiet?'

'It's never quiet.'

I was kicked genially up L'As du Fallafel's chain of command. The queue manager passed me to the restaurant floor manager, who knocked me to the general manager, who delivered me at last to the boss. The staff put me in mind of professional football players. They all wore expensive, athleisure clothes over bodies kept match-fit by their frenetic workload, and bounced between languages with polite, media-trained ease. Unlike with many other restaurateurs I had approached, there was no suspicion of my motives. The team at L'As du Fallafel was used to journalists; I was just another kind of customer to be triaged with everyone else.

'It's all about the quality,' the boss, Yomi, told me simply. 'We only use the best products. The other falafel places around here ... don't.'

Yomi also looked like a football player. Or rather, one who had recently graduated into a managerial role, which I suppose was not so far from the truth. The son of the founder, he was tall, with an obsessively neat beard, a shaved head and tinted spectacles. Wearing a thin puffa and skinny jeans, he was friendly and generous with his time, though he had the brusque, insistent manner of a man who always had more things to do than time to do them in.

'Seriously, go to any of the other places on this street,' he said. 'Try their tomatoes, try their whatever, then try ours. It's completely different. Everything we use is fresh.

Anything left over at the close of business, we throw it out. And we change our oil twice a day.'

We stood on the street in the boarded-up shadow of Mi-Va-Mi, watching the two queues contract and expand as we talked. In the twenty or so minutes that our conversation lasted, the takeaway queue alone must have accounted for at least forty people. With every order costing a minimum of €10, that was easily €400 that had changed hands. And the day had barely begun.

'My parents came here from Israel in the 1970s,' Yomi told me. 'That made them quite recent arrivals in the Marais. A lot of the other Jews in the area have been here much longer.'

'So here wasn't the first falafel shop to open, then?'

'No, it was. All the others are copies. Well, apart from Chez Marianne. That's older, I think. But that was always more of a sit-down restaurant.'

He gestured down the road towards the grand establishment on the next corner, at the bottom of rue des Hospitalières Saint-Gervais. I knew it well by sight – a large maroon building festooned in ivy – but couldn't remember ever having eaten there. It looked a lot more formal than L'As de Falafel, though it also offered takeaway now, and its prices were much the same. Right now, the tables of its terrace were filling, but there was not a single person in its takeaway queue.

'So you've always worked to the same recipe?'

'That's right,' said Yomi. 'That's another reason why people come here. They have always known exactly what to expect. We make falafels our own way. Because all falafel recipes are different depending on region. It's like with couscous, you know couscous?'

'I ... yes, I know couscous.'

'So, it's the same. There's Lebanese falafel, Syrian falafel, and so on. Our recipe, it's Israeli, but it's also got some Yemeni flavours because it was my grandmother's originally and she was born in Yemen.'

While L'As du Fallafel had been popular right away, the business really began to take off in the early 2000s – around the time that the Marais, too, was resurging. This was also when Lenny Kravitz first came to the store.

When asked to explain L'As du Fallafel's rampant success, many people will point to the rock star's endorsement – probably because there are pictures and newspaper clippings of Kravitz throughout the restaurant. Personally, I never really bought it. What, suddenly everyone in Paris had been desperate to follow the gastronomic lead of a guy who had a couple of top 10 singles in the late 1990s? Besides, bigger stars had since visited.

'Many stars,' Yomi confirmed. 'Leonardo DiCaprio, Vanessa Paradis, Natalie Portman ...' he thought for a moment, '... the King of Morocco.'

They have also served Benjamin Netanyahu.

'He loves my parents,' Yomi said; it took me a moment to realise he had returned to Lenny Kravitz. 'And he still comes here every time he's in town. Even if he can't make it in person, he'll send someone to pick up a falafel to take to him at his hotel.'

Maybe there was something to it, some strange tessellation of product and star – a kind of George Clooney Nespresso phenomenon. There's no doubt that Kravitz adores the place: he mentions it in interviews all the time.

'You have to understand, though, we've never done any

285

advertising,' Yomi continued. 'We got popular way before social media. It was just word of mouth, and a few newspapers that wanted to write about us. And slowly we grew. Now we employ forty people. And you see, it's still only quite a small store.'

Asking questions will only take you so far. To really comprehend L'As du Fallafel's success, I was going to have to eat there. Again. As I've already made clear, I'd tried these falafels more times than I could count, and with a fair amount of respect for their flavour – a long queue has a way of concentrating the taste buds. But I had never sat in the restaurant. Moreover, I had never required these falafels to justify themselves as one of the most popular recipes in Paris. Which is to say, I took my place at the table both with high expectations and a determination to try to forget whatever opinions I already thought I held about the food.

L'As du Fallafel's interior was a whirl of movement and branding. To the left, as I walked in, was a long corridor of a kitchen, hosting the various stages of falafel prep, and staffed by about ten men of Sri Lankan origin, as I later learned. Everything was out in the open. If I wanted, I could stand and watch each ingredient being prepared. Not that I had to, for there was also a handy TV screen in the corner of the tight-packed room broadcasting a high-production video of their falafels being made in ever-closer detail: the grinding of chickpeas, the baking of aubergine, the rolling froth of hot oil into which the raw falafels were plunged. But it was time to eat.

I opted not for a falafel sandwich, but rather its

deconstructed cousin: the *assiette falafel complète* – I should mention that they do serve other dishes, many of which looked excellent, but I was here for the star attraction.

The *assiette* arrived at my table within minutes. This was not a restaurant committed to the dining rituals of France, it was fast food. Very fast.

Similarly, the view I had of the dining room offered nothing of Paris, nothing of the historic Marais that surrounded me. I could have been in a mall. It was all artificial foliage and images of L'As du Fallafel's logo – an image of the globe which I suppose is also meant to resemble a falafel – and a slogan written in neon that read in English 'Think good and it will be good'. This is attributed to Rabbi Menachem Mendel, one of the most influential Jewish thinkers of the twentieth century. It's a bit like Martin Luther King being co-opted into selling hamburgers. Which he probably has been. Somewhere.

I looked at the plate in front of me: at the glossy purple and white chopped cabbage, the cucumber and tomato salad, the charred aubergine, the dips and the crinkly deep-fried falafels, and I thought good. And good it was. But not amazing.

Don't get me wrong, this dish was essentially the best version of itself it could be. The vegetables were indeed fresh and doused with a subtle citrus dressing, the aubergine was full of bitter, gooey warmth; the hummus and tahini were as smooth as cream. There was maybe not quite enough of the jammy harissa, which was the only sweetening element, but the falafels themselves were as perfect as I could imagine falafels being: with a biscuit-crunch surface and fluffy interiors like lightly spiced clouds.

At the end of the day, though, it was still fried chickpeas and a salad. Excellent for what it was, but hardly grab you by the tzitzit, slap you round the cheeks fantastic. Which, given the restaurant's enormous popularity, I had almost fooled myself into thinking it might be.

The nagging question returned: why this place in particular?

Reflecting on how it also served street food, I asked myself: what if the Khai Tri banh mi shop from the 13th had been located here in the heart of the Marais instead? Now *that* was a sandwich – a zigzag of different flavours and sensations of such stay-in-your-mind brilliance that I'd already gone back three times, all the way to Les Olympiades, for another hit. If *that* business had been located here for forty-five years, would *it* be the most successful restaurant in Paris?

I doubted it.

Fundamentally, I realised, what L'As du Fallafel offered was a total antidote to conventional Paris cuisine. Their food was unfussy, portable, healthy and vegan. It was kosher, which also meant it passed as halal. Without the bap, it was gluten-free. Added to that, it still had the hit of junk food, had crunch and salt and grease, but not so much that it could not represent light relief from a tour of buttery croissants and patisseries, heavy onion soup and *boeuf bourguignon*, or from a lifetime of living in Paris. The falafel may not be the most mindblowingly delicious thing in the world, but there is only a small fraction of people who could not eat it, and a barely larger fraction of people who would not like it, or want more if they tried it.

What was more, L'As du Fallafel was still family run. I knew from my own upbringing that this continuous, dedicated involvement was significant in the world of food service. Yomi was there every day, his brother too, and their father still called in often, making sure that even if there was an unlikely lull, standards did not slip – in the quality of their product, the élan of their staff or the efficiency of their crowd management. You work harder, pay closer attention when it's your family's name on the lease. You have skin in the game. L'As du Fallafel offered all this from a cobbled crossroads right in the heart of old Paris.

Finally, I couldn't entirely discount the other thing, which always lies somewhere behind any form of success in this life. Luck.

Falafel
Serves 3–4
Ingredients:
For the falafels (makes around 9):
400g dried chickpeas, boiled for an hour
2 tsp ground coriander
1 tsp ground cumin
1 bunch of fresh coriander
1 bunch of fresh parsley
A pinch of baking powder
1 egg white
Oil for frying

For the rest:
¼ red cabbage
¼ white cabbage
1 cucumber
5 plum tomatoes

200g hummus
200g tahini
3–4 pittas
Harissa (to taste)
1:1 ratio of lemon juice and olive oil for dressing

I know a thing or two about 'secret recipes', for my family bakery had one of its own. For a kind of custard tart, since you ask, called a maid of honour. What I discovered when I came to learn it myself, was that the 'secret' usually lies less in a list of ingredients, and far more in apprenticeship and practice. You can be given exact instructions on what to do, but without making a thing again and again alongside the recipe's guardians, your creation is only ever going to be a shadow on the wall of the cave of the original.

So when Yomi said that L'As du Fallafel's recipe was as 'secret as Coca-Cola' I was no more daunted than I would have been if he'd told me how to make them in detail, recognising in his words a kind of company branding.

I could literally watch the process of the falafels being made on the TV screens of his restaurant, and the other ingredients that joined them in the pitta were as plain as day. Lacking weeks of personal tutelage and practice however, I knew I would only ever be able to create something that came close.

Perhaps that's why after his Coca-Cola comment, Yomi nevertheless went on to offer a handful of tips. Don't use tinned chickpeas, he said, and heat your oil to 180 degrees. The falafels had to cook fast. Everything else, though, he cautioned, took a long time. It's one of the paradoxes of fast food – it can only be served quickly thanks to hours of prep.

Of course, the other thing I knew was to only 'use the best ingredients', and for these, I knew exactly where to go.

'Red cabbage, white cabbage, cucumber, aubergine and tomatoes?' Émile repeated. 'You're in luck, they're all coming into season. We have them all. Apart from aubergine. I won't be selling aubergines until the summer. Go ask someone who doesn't care about their produce.'

I arrived back in my apartment with a bag of resplendent market bounty from the Marché Maubert – plus some supposedly subpar aubergines. I drained my chickpeas from the water they'd been floating in overnight, their pebble hides now digestibly soft. I poured as many as I could into my blender and added a generous tablespoon of coriander spice and a slightly less generous one of cumin. Then, the leaves of two great bunches of green herbs: coriander and parsley. It was all just as I'd seen in the video, nothing secret here. Or maybe there was. The falafels had been so fluffy that while I hadn't *seen* any baking powder added I felt it must have been involved. So I added a pinch of baking powder, plus the raw white of one egg, not wanting to run the risk of my creations falling apart. Pulsing it all together, a reassuring scent of uncooked falafel was released into the air.

I set to chopping: shredding cabbage, julienning cucumber, dicing tomatoes, copying the geometries from a picture I'd snapped of L'As du Fallafel's counter. A bit of industrial espionage, sure, but then I don't see Coca-Cola leaving its recipe out in the sun.

I moulded the falafels by hand. I knew L'As has a machine, I'd seen it in action. They could do dozens in seconds. The twenty or so that I made took me the better part of half an hour.

Now, I began heating my oil. I had no deep-fat fryer, however, and so soon had a great terrifying pot of boiling fire hazard in my kitchen. Not wanting to deep-fry my thermometer, I couldn't be sure it had reached the 180 degrees centigrade that Yomi had counselled, but it sure looked hot. I dropped my raw falafels in one by one, watched them fidget and pucker, being seared to a golden carapace. There was no timing to go on here; I had to do it all by eye. At last, I fished them free with a slotted spoon, and dropped them onto kitchen paper to dry.

I can't lie. I imagine that L'As du Fallafel bake their own pitta; they certainly make their own hummus and tahini and harissa. They were not an establishment for cutting corners. I, however … Well, it was *meant* to be fast food. I just didn't have the patience or the time. So I had bought these essential elements from the shops – though I had bought high-end.

I dressed my chopped salads in a simple mixture of oil and lemon juice, and then I— Shit. I'd forgotten the aubergines. Aubergines that I'd meant to bake incredibly slowly until they formed a charred black crust and a molten interior of bitter goo. Ah well, they were off season, after all.

I served up the falafels as a meze platter to friends who had gathered in my apartment, waiting patiently for nearly an hour for their so-called fast food, and as it turned out, the falafels tasted good! Full of aerated, herby bounce, locked in by their salty crackling skins, and perfectly balanced by the lemony salads.

I was delighted. Even if it lacked aubergine, even if my pitta wasn't home-made, even if most of my condiments had been bought from the shops. And I started to wonder, had the speed I'd been served at, the conveyor belt of its queues and the fast-food stylings of its interior caused me to judge the quality of L'As's falafels too harshly?

Because slowed down, shared as a dinner between friends, this was an excellent meal, even though objectively it wasn't anywhere near as accomplished as the meal served by L'As du Fallafel. Maybe I was just unduly thrilled about having made it myself, but I would prefer to consider it a small victory for the French way of doing things, after all – for the reminder that food tastes better when you take your time.

3ème arrondissement

Consider the Bouillon République in the dead of night. The largest restaurant in Paris: two floors, 480 seats, 1,800 square metres – entirely empty. The only motion the occasional drift of headlights across its ceiling from the boulevard outside. Their searchlight swing flashing quietly off ready-laid glassware, clawing shadows from the wood carvings that line the restaurant walls: the bas reliefs of Alsatian peasants with their blank eyes wondering where all the life that was here just hours before can possibly have gone, whether it will return.

This restaurant in the 3rd arrondissement is so big it is practically a town in itself. Since its founding in just 2021 it has become as ingrained in the fabric of Paris as a rattan chair, and dominates this small district's culinary scene like a colossus.

The Bouillon République is both modern and traditional; it serves to tourists and to true Parisians, to the well-off and to the struggling-to-get-by. It is staffed by college graduates and immigrants, by cooking professionals and part-timers. It bakes its own patisserie, boasts a workflow structured on old-fashioned catering lore, and has its own buyers sourcing fresh produce direct from Rungis before the dawn. It is Paris dining in microcosm, and was even founded by people from the Auvergne, the neighbouring region to the Aveyron in France's south.

I wanted to know how it all functioned, to talk to the people who guided that space from out of its night-time emptiness, then through a whole day of cacophonous, controlled chaos and back again. I wanted to learn the recipes of its success.

The Bouillon République was the brainchild of two brothers, Pierre and Guillaume Moussié, who back in 2017 saw the Paris dining scene as primed for the reinvention of an old restaurant form.

Bouillons were everywhere in Paris once. A precursor to fast food, they were invented in 1854, by a butcher called Adolphe-Baptiste Duval who had the idea of a restaurant that served simple meat broths, 'bouillons', for very cheap and on an enormous scale. The idea caught on; bouillons soon started opening across the city, their menus quickly expanding beyond the broths to include all manner of classic French bistro dishes (arguably the bouillons helped make these classics): *steak frites*, *cuisse de canard*, *oeuf mayonnaise* and more.

A victim of their own success, however, by the early twentieth century, the bouillons had started to attract a more middle-class clientele and made the fatal mistake of straying from their roots. They upped their prices and the complexity of their cooking, gloried in ever-more beautiful décor. They lost the customer base that had sustained them. Hundreds closed, and of those that survived few could really be called bouillons in the original sense.

When I first came to Paris, only one remained, the Bouillon Chartier on the rue du Faubourg Montmartre. It's still there today. Still has a beautiful, enormous belle-époque-style dining room, still boasts extraordinarily low prices, and still gets by serving food just as vile as the year I arrived.

Enter, though, the brothers Moussié. Sizing up the post-2008 crash dining scene, they recognised a growing customer base who still wanted the formal pleasures of dining out, but lacked the finances to pay for it. They established the Bouillon Pigalle on the boulevard de Clichy – just a few doors down from Moon City – dedicated to the same low prices on which the bouillon phenomenon had originally been based. The difference between here and Chartier, though: the Moussiés would not compromise on quality. It was to be a real restaurant, everything made fresh on the day.

Bouillon Pigalle was a massive success. I remember the first time I went myself. The jubilant atmosphere, the low cost, how the taste of the dishes seemed to have been extracted direct from the folk memory of France. For the first time since living in Paris, here were inexpensive classics as they were *supposed* to taste. It was a confirmation of something so many of us longed to believe about this city's food, but had secretly begun to doubt; tantamount to an affirmation of the existence of God.

Bouillon Pigalle forced restaurants across the capital to up their game, to reclaim the city's reputation as a place where eating cheaply could also mean eating well. Then, four years later, post-pandemic, riding on this success, the Moussié brothers launched an even more ambitious operation, the Bouillon République. Employing a staff of 140, it took over the old premises of a huge, handsome Alsatian brasserie, Chez Jenny, which overlooked the boulevard du Temple in the 3rd arrondissement. Almost immediately, it became an institution.

I met up with Clément, the Bouillon République's *chef de cuisine*, and Paul, its on-site manager, in one of the restaurant's enormous second-floor dining rooms during the relative quiet of a Wednesday late afternoon. It had taken some time to arrange this interview. Everything at the Bouillon is – by necessity – so tightly controlled that it was not the kind of place I could employ my usual wander-in-off-the-street-and-start-chatting technique. Instead, I'd had to go through the Bouillon's PR department, and so arrived acutely aware of my presence here as a unit of time on a workflow, rather than an incidental moment of human generosity. Clément and Paul soon caused me to forget this, in much the same way their restaurant did for its customers as well.

'It's true, it's a factory here,' Paul said shortly after I'd sat down. 'Except that's not quite right. Because it's a factory that makes the food of a small kitchen, a grandmother's kitchen.'

Paul was a fair-complexioned man in his mid-thirties, originally from the Auvergne, like the Moussiés themselves. He had started out at the Bouillon Pigalle more than a decade ago as a waiter, then worked his way up steadily through the ranks, so that now the responsibility of this whole teeming organisation lay squarely on his shoulders. I'd say he wore it lightly, though he had a pronounced stutter, which at least gave the impression of nerves.

'You want to know how the Bouillon République works?' he said. 'It's because it's so well organised. Everyone here knows their particular role, their function in the machine, and we practise it day after day until we can virtually do it in our sleep.'

I pressed for more details. If the restaurant was a machine, I asked, then at what time each morning was it turned on?

'Well, you have to understand, the Bouillon is almost never really turned off,' Clément picked up – stocky, also in his mid-thirties, the Bouillon's *chef de cuisine* was a veteran of kitchens high and low, and carried himself with an approachable ease that belied his role as general to a whole army of cooks.

'Even at night, when there's no one in the kitchens, there's the next day's ham shanks and *bourguignon* sauce being cooked,' he continued. 'But if you really want to know the first people who start working for the Bouillon on any given day, that would be our buyers. The ones who head to Rungis wholesale market for about three in the morning.'

'It's part of the restaurant's mission statement,' Paul put in. 'When the Moussiés came up with the idea of the Bouillons, they made a commitment to preparing all dishes fresh on the day, using seasonal ingredients, and where possible the produce of France. That's about quality, of course, but it's also practical. When things are in season, and when they come from close by, it's cheaper.'

The Bouillon buyer's job at Rungis is not straightforward, however. Because unlike a *primeur* or a butcher or a *poissonnier*, they can't get all their wares from a single section. There is the whole menu to fill. And so the buyers must walk every main pavilion of the massive wholesale market. It takes time for all the fish, the meat and the huge quantity of vegetables to be loaded onto palettes – usually eight in total – and trollied into the back of the van.

'That's all taking place around the same time as I wake up,' grinned Clément.

'What time's that?'

'Around six. Not so bad, eh? I live in Belleville, so it's only a couple of stops on the metro.'

'So Clément's first to arrive?' I asked both men.

'That's right,' said Paul. 'I usually get here for the second half of the day. Sometimes I'll help lock up.'

At around 7 a.m., then, Clément would arrive at the Bouillon, walk up past its gilded frontage, past the big, street-facing windows, the glass awning supported by wrought-iron filigree, the name repeated three times in italicised lights across its front, and let himself in through the side door.

'On a good day, that's when the market produce arrives, too,' he said. 'Along with the dawn shift members of the kitchen staff.'

The running of the Bouillon is not based only on the Moussié brothers' own formulas, but on an ingenious template for managing a restaurant of this scale that has been passed down for more than a century. The most famous breakthrough in this field was made by Auguste Escoffier, one of the greatest chefs of all time, who pioneered the idea of the *brigade de cuisine*, a military-like system in which cooks are ranked into specific, specialised roles, maximising efficiency by working on different elements of dishes, rather than having to cook each from scratch by themselves. It is now how nearly every big kitchen in the world is run.

Clément told me how the Bouillon employed a full 'brigade'. There were line-cook *commis*, sauce-making *sauciers* and higher ranking *sous-chefs*. Particularly important here, he said, was the *légumier*, whose main job was to prepare vegetables.

'Every morning,' Clément said, 'there are hundreds of leeks, carrots, onions that need to be chopped, and nearly a metric tonne of potatoes.'

I thought of Gabriel, whom I had met at the Cordon Bleu school, still chopping away alone in his room every night; what he wouldn't give for six months in this role!

'So most of the food preparation is done in the morning, then?' I asked.

'The majority,' Clément said. 'But some of it will carry on well into the afternoon.'

The job of this brigade, he explained, was to make ready the many hundreds of meals that would be ordered later, so that when service came no dish would take more than three gestures to plate.

'We have it so that an order for a table of ten people all asking for different things can be prepared and brought out in no more than ninety seconds,' Clément said. 'We've timed it.'

'So what are you doing while all these things are being chopped and prepared?' I asked him.

'Me? A lot of things. Mainly, I have to keep an eye on the produce. How much was used yesterday, how much is left for today. I have to place tomorrow's order with the market team by 11 o'clock.'

He's aided in the task, he said, by fastidiously crunched statistics. Consumption at the Bouillon may seem random, but customers are all but guaranteed, and certain dishes are proven to sell more night after night. The ham shanks, for example, and the steaks, for which there is seldom more than a 6 per cent variation in sales regardless of the shift.

'On a business of this scale, nothing can be left to chance,' Paul explained. Portion sizes are not eyeballed, I learned, but weighed. Even the prices are set by computer. 'If any calculation is off, even by a fraction, we could start losing money very quickly.'

So our conversation went on, about the other cogs and gears that started up at various different times as the day continued, and the engine of the Bouillon started to turn over in its full glory.

'But maybe it is wrong to keep talking about it all as a machine like this,' Paul concluded. 'Really, to fully understand, you should meet some of our staff. Now is perfect, in fact, for many will be coming off shift.'

After our conversation was over, then, Paul led me back through the downstairs dining hall, its rows and rows of tables, its yell of conversation, its ballet of waiters and clatter of plates. It was only about half full, but already showing signs of getting busier as the early-evening service began.

We headed outside, to stand by the Bouillon's side entrance where weary men, recently out of their whites and back in civvies were exiting unseen into the Paris streets. Paul stopped and introduced some to me.

Men like Kabaille, forty-six, from Kinshasa in the Congo, who was one of the Bouillon's several *plongeurs*, part of the morning shift who arrived around the same time as Clément to help with deliveries, to wash the *bourguignon* pots and make sure the kitchens were ready for the cooks. Men like Stéphane, a Paris-born pastry chef in his fifties, who'd spent the day whipping up tonight's desserts. Built like a journeyman boxer, though, with tattoos the full length of his shovel-head forearms, Stéphane was keener to talk about his passion for Harley-Davidsons and heavy metal than chou pastry. Men like Yaya, late thirties, born in Algeria, now living with his wife and kids in Vincennes. He was just off from working the pass – the place where plates are sorted from the kitchen so they can be taken out onto the restaurant floor. Had a great chef's burn on the inside of his wrist. I knew these, used to get them all the time myself. The fault of a single clumsy moment, or of moving too fast as you pull a hot tray from an oven and its scalding corner catching three inches or so below your palm. I'd never had one as bad as Yaya's, though, which was a good two fingers wide and starting to blister over – liquid white across raw pink flesh. But the man was cheerfully phlegmatic. 'It happens sometimes,' he grinned.

'You see, we are far more than just a machine,' Paul said. 'And these are just the kitchen staff – I have to go now, but you should really also talk to some of our waiters as well …'

*

The first waiters would have arrived at the Bouillon at 9.30 a.m., I'd been told. More than just servers, they also cleaned the main dining rooms and toilets, polished glasses and tonnes of silverware, made sure the condiments tables were well stocked, the dozens of salt and pepper shakers filled.

Like the kitchen staff, the Bouillon waiters are also split into different ranks. There are the *chefs de rang* who are in charge of different sections, or *rangs*, of the restaurant floor. Helping them, are the *commis de salle*, who help clear tables and bus food, and the *préparateurs de commande* who help keep on top of orders.

Kicking around a little longer outside the Bouillon's front, I soon encountered one of these waiters. A *chef de rang* called Ibrahim, grabbing an insouciant cigarette before his service began – and if anyone in the world can smoke more insouciantly than a Paris waiter, I haven't met them.

'It's tiring work in the Bouillon, yes,' he shrugged, all sunken-cheeked indifference, 'but once you get used to it, it's not so hard. The most difficult thing is the weight of the trays. Have you seen them?'

I had – great broad platters that could carry more than a dozen plates at a time.

'And if you get a *rang* far from the kitchen you can easily walk twenty kilometres in a single shift.'

Ibrahim was not Parisian, he told me, but a '*banlieusard*'. He may have been born only a few blocks outside of the Périphérique, he said, but the city had no claims on his identity.

'I never expected to become a waiter,' he said, 'but have been doing it for many years. I am thirty-one now. I don't imagine I will ever do anything else. And it can be fun. At the height of service, moving between all the tables, keeping so many things in your head. The smoke breaks are good too.'

Bouillon République is so popular that at peak times, despite its near 500-seat interior, there is almost always a queue. Actually, as at L'As du Fallafel, there are two queues: one for walk-ups, the other for reservations. The waiting time in the first can easily push an hour. Even joining the reservation queue – the queue the restaurant knows is coming – it can take you as much as twenty minutes to get inside. And bookings fill up fast.

Managing these two queues takes yet another category of Bouillon staff, the *hôtes d'accueil*. There are never fewer than two on shift, and on evenings and weekends, it's four. Queuing myself to get back inside now, I spoke to one of them.

Diane was a twenty-one-year-old mathematics student with an explosion of ringleted hair and a smiling, welcoming face: the embodiment of her role. She only worked part-time, she said, helping fund her studies. In France, maths is the king of subjects, which suggested Diane would not be working the Bouillon queues for long. Rather, she was doing this while waiting in an entirely other kind of line: one leading to the nation's cultural elite.

Now, though, she explained how she saw her job as a kind of game. People arrived randomly in groups of all sizes – couples, families of five, gatherings of eight, parties of twelve or more, that kind of thing, Diane was constantly calculating the fastest way to fit them all inside.

There aren't a designated number of four-person,

two-person or eight-person tables in the restaurant, she said. Instead, it was entirely modular, with spaces coming available at different rates.

'It can feel almost like playing Candy Crush,' she said. 'I love it when it's busy. I'll be working everything out, getting people inside as fast as I can, and making jokes with them too. It's important.'

I was already familiar with the kind of clientele who made up the queue. The Bouillon's customers are varied but tend towards being young and middle class. They are a post-credit crunch demographic – consumers with upwardly mobile tastes and limited wallets. People who cannot afford the historic brasseries (or not on a regular basis), but still see good food served to them in a beautiful place as a God-given right – and don't mind standing for an hour to get it.

Besides, it's all part of the experience. Here they were, me among them, smoking and chattering, and indulging in that most Parisian of pastimes: looking at other people.

True, there were also a handful of older customers in the line, plus no small number of tourists, but the queue's overall spirit was, as it always is, one of vitality and youth. It was Paris's future embodied by people who wanted their own way of tasting the flavours and experiences of the city's past.

By the time I made it back inside, the dining room had begun to roar. It was the beautiful communal sound of hundreds of people feasting at the same time, the kind of feasting that was in ancient memory associated with festivals and harvests and royal banqueting halls. And that here had been whipped into existence simply because it could be, on an ordinary Wednesday night.

Before heading to my table, I paused at the final node that I'd been told about that allowed the Bouillon to function, the staff member in a wooden booth at the top of the stairs to the kitchen: the *caisse*. Historically, a *caisse* would have been a common feature in restaurants, centralising the cash. In our largely cashless, more computerised world, they've fallen out of use. It's only the biggest places that need them now, to keep the waiters honest and the restaurant's massive quantity of incomings and outgoings strictly measured, with a second set of eyes confirming every order that makes its way onto the dining room floor, every bill that is paid.

Despite *caisse* work having mostly become an anachronism, the woman working it that evening told me it was her métier. Her name was Katie, she said, and she had been working what remained of Paris's *caisses* for years. In her fifties, effortlessly chic in a black lace top with toned, tanned arms and a sleek brown bob, she looked ready for a night at the opera. And in fact, what her job put me most in mind of was that of an orchestra conductor – she even used the end of a pen to catalogue dishes onto her touch-screen computer, wielding it like a baton, both to follow the rhythm of the restaurant and to keep it in line.

At last, it was my time to eat. I was guided to a table at the very back of the downstairs hall, where I had a perfect view of the massed lines of other tables already filled for the evening service, though it was hardly much past seven. Despite my interactions with Paul and Clément, there was no question of special treatment; I had at once become just another customer, another unit to be processed.

A waiter (not Ibrahim) thrust a menu at me – a single

paper sheet, printed in the last week, almost as fresh as the food it promised. I was familiar with most of the dishes on offer, having eaten here many times, and though I knew there were choices that better proved the quality of the kitchens – the artichoke salad, say, or the sea bass fillet – I ordered two of the most basic and classic dishes, of the kind on which the Bouillon's reputation is maintained: *oeuf mayonnaise* and *steak au poivre*. To accompany them, a 25-centilitre carafe of Côtes du Rhone.

While I waited for my food to arrive, I watched the waiters pacing up and down their individual *rangs*, those great trays hoisted above their heads. It was hypnotic. A great dance of balance and lifting, of abundance being waltzed between tables, of customers narrowly avoided as they were shown to their seats. Stick it on stage, people would pay to watch.

'*Votre oeuf mayonnaise, monsieur.*' A plate was glided onto my table, along with a basket of bread and the red wine. The *commis de salle* who had brought it disappeared as swiftly as he'd appeared.

Here it was, then, the product of this whole massive enterprise. I was, in that moment, the end of the chain.

It was an excellent *oeuf mayonnaise*, the Platonic ideal of *oeuf mayonnaise*. Though, admittedly, this is a simple enough dish that, so long as it's fresh and hasn't been messed around too much and has been made from scratch with half-decent eggs, it is almost impossible to get it wrong. Egg in egg sauce: a cool blast of unctuous protein that went excellently with the cutting tang of the wine.

I luxuriated in the small privacy of eating, my slow concentration on every bite all the more heightened by the contrast to the tightly controlled chaos still booming about me, as well as on the floor above, and in the basement kitchens under my feet.

The steak in *sauce au poivre*, when it came, was excellent – if conventional, too: a fresh-cooked plate of simple, brawny, peppery, creamy goodness. The taste, for me, of nostalgia, of childhood holidays. It is perhaps the most accessible dish in the whole French larder, and it came in a portion small enough that I had room, as I was meant to, for dessert.

While my plate was being tidied, ready for whichever *plongeur* had replaced Kabaille on shift, I cast my eyes the fifty or so metres across all the room, out to the Bouillon windows, where I could just about make out Diane, and the queue, which was still growing.

My profiterole dessert was a wonderful choux bap, filled with a helter-skelter of whipped ice cream and lavishly dressed in chocolate sauce. It was a long way from the technical masterpieces of the sweet arts that otherwise grace the patisserie counters of this city, but Jesus was it tasty! As I ate it, I thought of Stéphane whose tattooed hands had almost certainly brought it into being earlier that day.

The bill was, of course, wonderfully reasonable. Three courses, plus wine, in this beautiful room with its throbbing atmosphere, and it barely crested €20. It represented the Bouillon's ultimate achievement. All this floor space, all that organisation and work. Only on a scale this enormous could food this good cost so little.

I paid gladly. Left a decent tip, then walked anonymously out the door. A face lost in the crowd. More diners still pouring in around me.

Before I went to bed that night, I thought of the Bouillon
again. It was gone midnight now, the very last of the customers would be finishing their plates. The queue outside
would be gone, the kitchens dark; tomorrow's braising ham
shanks and bubbling *bourguignon* the only smell, the only
sound.

And upstairs the waiters who had finished with their
rangs would be redressing tables, vacuuming floors, putting
the whole enterprise neatly to bed.

Now, the final bills would be being paid, Katie tapping
out the numbers on her screen. Workers would be sloughing
out of sweaty uniforms, back into civvies. The final customers would be gone.

I thought of Paul giving the place a final pass, the day's
energy dissipating on the air. If he was closing, he usually
made it out around 1 a.m., he'd said, pulled down the shutters, which I thought of clattering loudly against the quieting
Paris night. Then, he'd head home.

And I considered the Bouillon République in the dead of
night: still, apart from the doppler swing of headlights across
its ceiling and walls, illuminating those wooden carvings,
their blank, frozen faces, their blank eyes waiting, wondering at those silent hours before the show began again.

Oeuf Mayonnaise (as part of a feast à la Bouillon)
Serves 5
Ingredients:
  For the eggs:
  15 large eggs
  A handful of coarse salt, to season a pan of boiling water
  A bucket of iced water

For 375g of mayonnaise:
1 egg yolk
1 tsp Dijon mustard
1 tbsp old sherry vinegar
31 cl peanut oil
1 pinch of salt
1 turn of the pepper mill

For the feast à la Bouillon:
1 copy of the Bouillon cookbook
At least 5 willing friends

Pretty much as soon as the Moussié brothers launched the new bouillon project, they also published a cookbook detailing most of the recipes that their kitchens produce. I bought it right after the first time I ate at Bouillon Pigalle, and have tried my hand at a good third or so of its dishes.

It was of particular comfort during the pandemic, when we all reached for anything we could to remind us of the social world. More than anything, I cooked up the restaurant's *oeuf mayonnaise*, precisely because it felt the kind of dish that – though I love it – I would usually *only* eat in restaurants. Also, the Bouillons' oeuf mayonnaise is famous, award-winningly so – according to *Le Bonbon* magazine it is the single most ordered restaurant dish in all of France.

I remembered on those long slow days how fastidiously I'd follow its recipe on my own. Or almost fastidiously, for the recipe in the book is actually for truffle egg mayonnaise, which only appears on the bouillon's tables in summer. I, however, was after simpler, more traditional flavours, not to mention was saving the pennies in that precarious time.

(Should you not be feeling so frugal, simply substitute 6cl of the peanut oil for truffle oil, and add 4 grams of truffle crumbs to the mix.) Heating the eggs for exactly nine minutes and thirty seconds in cold, salty water brought to a boil; then plunging them immediately into ice to halt the cooking process, before the tricky peeling of their shells, the slicing in two. And I recalled that time I almost broke curfew in my search for peanut oil for the mayonnaise. Sunflower, rapeseed, olive: these would literally not cut the mustard I'd already whisked into the yolk. No, it had to be peanut oil, just as it had to be old sherry vinegar that I added gradually to that yellow mixture, beating desperately until it began to thicken into the restaurant flavours I knew. And because of my fastidiousness, because of the precision of the recipe, I *did* manage to get it all to taste the part. I remembered scooping that glossy emulsion onto those two hard-boiled half-moons, and taking a few brief bites of normality again.

Which is all to say that I knew the recipes in the Bouillon's cookbook were honest; that when followed precisely, they could offer an almost exact reproduction of the dishes served up by their thousand every day in the Bouillons République and Pigalle themselves. I did not need Clément to explain to me further how they made their dishes. They were all there already in stylishly arranged, sans serif font.

Instead, the real 'recipe' I took from my time at the Bouillon République was that of delegation. I had seen over and over that the way the whole enormous place could function was through many individuals grouping together to perform many small tasks. Just like the spirit of Paris itself, the Bouillon was not the accomplishment of any single person, but of many.

And so, I conceived of a dinner for far more people than I could possibly cater for by myself. I'd send friends pictures of recipes from the Bouillon cookbook, and get them to make ready the dishes in their own homes, then bring them all to mine for a final celebration, further stretching the definition of a moveable feast. It felt a straightforward way of capturing the place's spirit, and had the added advantage that I would barely have to do anything at all. Well, all right, maybe I'd make a few *oeufs mayonnaise*; see if I still had the knack.

In the end, however, I did not get round to doing any of this. I took only the idea. For I was getting close to the end of my journey through Paris's arrondissements now. And I did not want to squander my friends' goodwill on making a meal of only the Bouillon's dishes when I had gathered so many recipes of my own. If I was going to play the *chef de cuisine* to my own feast at this point, it would have to be more personal in its scope.

First, though, I still had some questions left to answer.

2ème arrondissement

'It's that people do things here purely for the sake of their being done.'

It was late in the evening. I was sitting with Albert, half drunk on the terrace of a bar just back from the Seine, looking out at the illuminated dream of the Île de la Cité, and musing on my journeys through the food of Paris and what I thought I'd learned.

'I mean doing things well, doing things correctly ...' I stopped, sipped my beer, tried to concentrate my thoughts. 'Like with croissants,' I said, 'there's no reason for them to be as good as they are, no reason for people to work as hard as they do to make them on-site in so many boulangeries every single morning. Or that guy, Gabriel, he's putting so much effort, so much focus into perfecting his craft, and sure, he wants to make something at the end, but I really got the feeling that just perfecting it was his actual goal.'

Albert nodded, thoughtfully. Albert has a way of nodding thoughtfully that seems very much like he is really shaking his head.

I ploughed on, evoking Khai Tri in Les Olympiades, where the family have recreated the same laborious banh mi recipe for four decades; Camille, the waiter at Les Deux Magots, whose calling was simply to be the best waiter he could be; the delight that the market workers at place Maubert and place Monge took in their produce – Émile who could still get excited by a punnet of apricots after more than sixty years.

'And it's inspiring, right?' I said. 'Because there are a lot of bad things happening in the world right now. And a lot of cynicism, and people only doing things because they think it's going to make them rich or famous or a viral sensation or something. But here are all these people trying to enjoy and make good things because Paris is a place that knows what good things are, and believes they should and can be made.'

I took a triumphant glug of beer, waiting for Albert to tell me how right I was, how I'd made him feel better about Paris and the world. Instead, he had stopped thoughtfully nodding and was now doing something even worse: stroking his chin.

'I'm not saying I don't think that's true,' he said at last. 'It's just, well, it's not true everywhere, is it?'

'Huh?'

'Well, there are obviously some good formal restaurants

here still, and I completely agree with you on the bakeries. But a lot of places *don't* enforce the *entrée, plat, dessert* thing any more. I could find you plenty of people who don't shop at the markets. You and I, for example, we go to Carrefour.'

'We go to the markets,' I said. 'Sometimes.'

'And what about all these Parisian *bobos* you had such a problem with. The ones who are having brunch to rebel against the ritual? And you can't tell me that somewhere like the Bouillon isn't a business concern before it's anything else.'

I was momentarily struck dumb. Had I been being too idealistic? Concentrating only on the more romantic things I had encountered. Wilfully forgetting what I had been told about all the bakeries that did not make their own croissants, the market stall owners who bought wholesale, the rampant success of L'As du Fallafel and the kebab shops with their fast food. I remembered, from the bois de Vincennes, Bolec's disgust over the primness of Paris terraces; and thought how there were many people here who long for the exact opposite of what I'd been praising: *liberté* from ritual.

'OK, let's try this,' Albert continued. 'If what you're saying *is* true – about ritual, about craft – and speaking from my great authority as a Frenchman, I know that in a lot of places it still is, how did it get that way? How long can it last? Where's it going in the future?'

'Ah,' I brightened, 'I don't know.'

'You seem quite happy about that.'

'Because those are exactly the questions I want to answer next.'

The next day, hung-over, I dragged myself down to the 2nd

arrondissement. And immediately started having a terrible time.

It was hot. Well, warm, actually. In fact, it was beautiful. If I'd been feeling my normal self, or even just been somewhere with fewer petrol fumes and more sky, it could have felt such a day as dreams are made on. As it was, the crush of Paris's central organs in this district of narrow roads and gorgeous palaces exerted horrible pressure on my temples. There were just so many people! Tourists and office workers, students and locals revelling along the old streets. A whole pageant of them braying from restaurant terraces: starting on their lunchtime cocktails and *demis*, poring over menus, picking at *entrées*, devouring *steak frites* and *poké* bowls and Thai green curries and pizzas and *salades niçoises*. I felt suddenly overwhelmed, and couldn't help gawping in dismayed wonder at the scale and variety and cost of all that consumption, even here in the smallest arrondissement of them all.

Albert had been right to call me out, I thought. For all the high-minded things I'd said last night about Paris food culture, I needed to remember that food in this city was still, primarily, a business. More to the point, the restaurant specifically was a French business idea that had conquered the world.

I had come to the 2nd to look on the very oldest of them – the eateries whose history or spirit stretched back to the earliest days of Paris dining, when service in this city was not about perfecting tradition so much as the creation of something entirely new. However, given the state I was in, first I needed sustenance. What I needed was a restorative broth – which, in a way, could not have been more fitting.

There had been inns and taverns and mess halls and cooks with roadside cauldrons who had offered food outside of a domestic setting since pre-Roman times. But seldom did they offer much variety in their dishes. Dining in such places took place at communal tables, there were no menus, no fixed prices. Food was either an afterthought for drinkers or a practical necessity for people travelling through. As William Sitwell put it in his book *The Restaurant*, these proto-eateries were less 'eating out', more 'eating away'.

Moreover, in Paris itself, for much of the city's history making food for public consumption was tightly controlled by a caste-like system of laws and privileges. Only those in the guild of *'traiteurs'* had the right to sell cooked meat.

By the 1760s, however, as the city fattened and stewed with thoughts of the Enlightenment, so a change could be sniffed on the wind. Inn and cabaret and café owners started to look for workarounds to the old monopolies, appealing to the courts for exemptions to let them cook and serve their own food. And as with so much in the tale of human endeavour, these gradual, half-conclusive rulings have come down to us as a single decisive myth.

The story goes that in 1765 a man known now only as Boulanger set up a Paris-based establishment serving, in its own words, 'restoratives fit for the gods'. His trick for getting around guild law was to offer hot broths made from boiling down meat and bones rather than the cuts of meat themselves. One of these broths got him into trouble: sheep's foot in white sauce. The *traiteurs* seized their chance to take Boulanger to court. In what has been described as a landmark ruling of food history (notwithstanding that there's no trace of it in the official record) they lost. The people would have their restoratives; the age of the *restaurant* – from *restaurer*, to restore – was born.

Thank God, I thought, for that. For the cloudy miso ramen I was served in the cool, pine-clad interior of Hokkaido restaurant on rue Chabanais seemed in that moment like an IV of nutrients or a plunge into a hot spring on a forest floor. Both it and I grew better with each sup, with each free-floating treasure I chopsticked from its depths: the salt-rich mangetout, the smoked rubber of mushrooms, the gleaming hunks of pork. It was the kind of dish that makes you glad you were hung-over in the first place. The hang-over was the seasoning! Restaurants may be a business idea, I thought, but what a terrific business idea they were.

The concept did not hit an instant boil, however, so much as a slow simmer. Twenty-five years after Boulanger's (supposed) victory against the guilds, there were still fewer than fifty restaurants across Paris, with the most famous – now spoken of as the first luxury restaurant in France – to be found on the rue de Richelieu, just one street away from where I was now, slurping my way back to health.

Feeling restored, I tottered towards its old address, back down those thronging summer streets, to take a look. And I found ... nothing. Just a blank nineteenth-century facade. There wasn't even a plaque. Could this be on account of the restaurant's name? For it had been called La Grande Taverne de Londres – The Great Tavern of London. Imagine, the first luxury restaurant in France was English-themed. *Quel blasphème!*

Truth be told, the English stylings of La Grande Taverne de Londres probably did not run deep. (A dart board? A few commemorative plates of George III above the bar?) It was more like a miniature Versailles, with fine linen tablecloths, gilded mirrors and heaving crystal chandeliers, presided over by larger-than-life chef Antoine Beauvilliers – who suffered the indignity of being described in every source I read as 'triple-chinned'.

Finding no inspiration in this gloomy bank building, my hangover and I continued our wanderings. Le Grand Véfour, just a few streets further on, is the oldest restaurant left in Paris. Founded in 1784 and along the same kind of style guidelines as La Grande Taverne de Londres, it could barely have changed its décor in over two hundred years.

I stood outside feeling unworthy of stepping in. It was more than the prices, which though substantial (€92 for a ravioli starter) I knew were par for the course with fine dining. What intimidated me more was the place's fortress-like air. The windows were high and part-frosted, so I could only glimpse the rarefied interior of red velvet banquettes, rococo patterns painted on glass, vast mirrors, tassels, gilding. An impeccably dressed waiter stood scowling at me from the centre of the room. I offered him an apologetic grimace and withdrew.

It was instructive of what restaurants used to be. Today, openness is the more usual approach: the typical large street-facing windows that as well as letting customers look out are a kind of advertising; an egalitarian illusion that means even if you don't have the cash or confidence or desire to step in, you can still imagine yourself as one of the diners inside. Le Grand Véfour and other places like it were clearly still wrestling with the idea of being truly public spaces. Le Grand Véfour seemed to me more like a private members club.

It was true that Le Grand Véfour came into being in a different, more stratified age. At the date of its founding, the true catalyst to the new eating out phenomenon was yet to come. By 1800, the number of restaurants in Paris multiplied ten-fold in what surely was among the great food revolutions of modern times. It also happened to be *the* French Revolution.

'On the day of the storming of the Bastille, there were some estimated 2 million servants in France,' writes William Sitwell. 'With a total population of 28 million, that meant one in every twelve men or women were in service.'

As well as severing the heads of nobles, then, the guillotine also cut free a staggering number of staff from their employ. Many of these were highly trained chefs and butlers, who descended on Paris in their thousands searching for new opportunities to ply their trade. Restaurants were the obvious fit.

Moreover, the revolution was a time of indulgence, of hedonism and extremes, not least among the condemned aristocrats themselves. The guillotines could only work so fast, and thus, while awaiting their fates in squalid state prisons, many of the fallen nobles would order out to these new restaurants for gargantuan feasts. No price was too high for this Death Row Deliveroo. These were last meals, after all. Almost right from the start, Paris restaurants were in the business of the fullest possible celebration of corporeal life.

It was against this background that one of the most influential chefs of all time was born, and in this small area north of the Palais-Royal he later received his training. Renowned as the 'king of chefs and the chef of kings', his name was Marie-Antoine Carême.

*

The son of an impoverished, alcoholic labourer who abandoned his fourteen children, Carême found work as a *plongeur* in exchange for shelter, and, like many who came after him, this kick-started his ascent up the ladder of culinary success.

At fourteen, he secured an apprenticeship with a famous *pâtissier* called Sylvain Bailly on the rue Vivienne. This was where I was headed now, just a short walk from the colonnades that house Le Grand Véfour and past another ancient restaurant called Le Grand Colbert – why did all these places have names like Victorian conjurers? – to visit not a patisserie but the Bibliothèque Nationale de France, the place where Carême had perfected his trade. Because while most of his days were spent endlessly turning dough, folding and rolling and folding and rolling it by hand to make peerless puff pastry constructions, Bailly awarded him two afternoons off a week to cross the road to the library for literary study and improvement. Amid the stacks, newly plumped by books that, like domestic servants, had been requisitioned from nobles by the Revolution, Carême read up on different cooking techniques from around the world, on the history of French cuisine and on architecture.

The library reading room was another kind of palace. Its great curving oval ceiling rose as high as a church's, and around its curved walls ran three levels of stacks, packed top to bottom, almost as though the books themselves were holding the building aloft. Doubtless it had changed to some degree since Carême's day, but not in its essentials. How easy to imagine the labourer's boy coming in here, still dusted by the flour of his trade, to sit among students and scholars and find inspiration to push at the very boundaries of food-making.

Carême became famous for his teetering sugar and pastry sculptures based on the great works of architecture about which he'd read. And as the 2nd arrondissement was then a meeting place for the great and the good, his talents soon caught the attention of the grand men of state. After opening his own patisserie on the nearby rue de la Paix, Carême embarked on an illustrious career as a *chef de cuisine* at some of most spectacular social occasions and banquets that had ever been held.

He cooked for Napoleon, for Talleyrand, for Tsar Alexander II of Russia. In that time, he codified the mother sauces, invented the chef's hat, and was a pioneer in France of *service à la russe* (the *entrée, plat, dessert* model for dining, which replaced *service à la française,* where all the dishes were served at the same time). He died at only fifty years of age from lung disease, the result of working in poorly ventilated kitchens all his life. 'Burnt out by the flame of genius,' wrote one French poet, 'and the charcoal of the roasting spit.'

Leaving the library and stepping back out into that bright day, I reflected on how Carême's story and that of the chefs and culinary revolution among which he moved and which he in turn inspired, all revealed a fundamental truth about Paris food that I had ignored until now. That for all the city's regard for ritual, for repetition, for the perfection of craft for craft's sake, this city had also been a place of radical innovation – of throwing out the old rules, creating the new.

With this in mind, I turned east, away from these temples of dining past, in search of the places where the future was being cooked.

*

Chef Greg Marchand also had a tough and lonely start in life – by the time he was twelve years old, both his parents had tragically died, and he had been sent to an orphanage in his home town of Nantes. The year was 1990.

There were no kitchen staff in the orphanage at weekends and so the kids were left to cook for themselves. This was Marchand's origin story: while still in his early teens, he prepared his friends an *escalope Normande* (tenderised chicken breast cooked in a sauce of mushrooms, cider and cream) and saw the delight in their faces brought about by something he had made. Chef's biographies are full of these moments – remember Gabriel and his banana bread? The delight in the power of creation; the discovery of what that creation can do for others. These are the central enchantments of cooking: the unchanging certainty that ingredients will always respond to touch and heat, and that people will need to be fed. Turning these enchantments into genuine sorcery, though, is the destiny of the few.

Marchand entered cookery school in Nantes at sixteen, where he learned the founding principles of the French kitchen: how to a *brunoise* a carrot in seconds, how to whisk a *velouté*. Then – when he left at twenty – in his own words, he followed his suitcase: departed France to work the kitchens of the world.

In Britain, Hong Kong and New York, Marchand picked up new flavours and techniques that he might never have learned in his home country, even in its libraries. He worked his way up through the culinary world until, still not yet thirty, he was made head chef at Jamie Oliver's Fifteen. Oliver gave him the nickname 'Frenchie'. This was something else he would bring with him, when at last he returned to the country of his birth, to establish a new kind of food empire.

Frenchie, Marchand's flagship restaurant, sits on the rue du Nil, a short, narrow street in the Sentier neighbourhood of the 2nd. Serving a seasonal, always changing menu, it soon became identified as a leader of the so-called '*bistronomie*' movement, which reimagines French classics with global flavours for the modern age. This was closely linked with the advent of *Le Fooding*, a new French restaurant guide launched in Paris in 2000, which sought to offer an alternative to the famed Michelin guide, promising listings that 'reflect the taste of the times'. Neither bistronomie nor *Le Fooding* were expected to hang around for long, were thought of by most as a brief fashion moment rather than a cultural shift. But two decades later, *Le Fooding* has become the second most popular restaurant guide in France after Michelin, and Frenchie had won one of the latter's prestigious stars. More than that, it was no longer just a restaurant, it was an industry.

Rue du Nil was a kind of surprising gap in the ordinary fabric of the city, a Diagon Alley of food – it was lined by a complete larder of *épiceries*, their produce so fresh it almost looked artificial.

Here was a *primeur* spilling forth purple-green artichokes, a sweet massacre of strawberry punnets, and curling aubergines with black-mirror skin. Next, a *poissonnerie*, with fish bright as the family silver and a spacious tank of muscular lobsters and crabs whose claws tapped quizzically against the glass. A butcher's ceiling was hung with a bunting of smoked sausage, its shelves stacked with the marbled cross-sections of prime cuts. There was a coffee dealer, a chocolatier, a *cave aux vins*; even the bakery, in this city of fine bakeries, was stocked with unusual abundance. Right at the centre of it all, was Frenchie: the reason for the existence of all these other shops. For while they were open to the public, their highest purpose was to furnish this sought-after restaurant with their wares, not unlike the *traiteurs* of old.

It was four in the afternoon; Frenchie was closed for business but its door was open. How different to the fortress of Le Grand Véfour. Even if the prices were the same, I felt no hesitation in stepping over the threshold, and sure enough was welcomed warmly by the staff within.

They were an international crowd – majority French, yes, but mostly anglophone. After a few words of negotiation with the Franco-American *hôtesse*, I was directed straight to the current head chef (Marchand, with other Frenchies in London, Biarritz and Switzerland in his portfolio, is now more of a general manager). His name was Andrés, from Colombia, and with his piercings and tattoos and meticulously maintained facial hair, he was instantly recognisable as part of the international foodie style tribe. He looked, in other words, like a very clean punk. He was busy wrapping spoonfuls of mint-green paste into fronds of chard as we talked.

'There are French techniques here, yes,' he said, 'but the flavours are of the world.'

He told me of his own cooking journey. Culinary school in Colombia, moving up through the kitchens of South and Central America – Peru and Panama – until eventually he made it to the US.

'I learned a lot of French cooking at school,' he told me, 'but the best training is in kitchens.'

'So what made you want to come to Paris?'

He gave a half-grin, 'I was only supposed to come here on holiday for a couple of weeks. I wanted to see what it was all about, but then a friend of mine introduced me to Chef Greg. He thought I might be a good fit for this kitchen, so I came to try out. That was two years ago.'

'I see,' I said, thinking for a moment. 'And so, what was it all about? What makes cooking here, in France, different from anywhere else?'

'The produce,' came Andrés's simple reply.

Tartare de Veau
Serves 1
Ingredients:
300g veal steak
1 tsp XO sauce
3 pickled mussels
1 tsp chive mayonnaise
¼ leek

Frenchie's Michelin-starred cuisine is a little out of my price range – its flagship tasting menu starts at €145 per person – but fortunately for me, further along rue du Nil is an associated wine bar where small house dishes can be sampled individually, for a mere €20 or so a pop.

Albert and I found a table amid a clientele that seemed as international as Frenchie's staff. Chatting with a few, I discovered that even the native Parisians turned out, for the most part, to have lived in other countries at some point in their lives. The menu was similarly hard to pin down. It had the whiff of France, but was also decidedly international in its blending of flavours and ingredients. There was 'spicy margherita oyster', miso-roasted cod, pappardelle with lamb ragout, and so on. I opted for the veal tartare, seeing it as the most classically French dish on offer. (I later discovered that steak tartare probably originated in America, and only became a French bistro standard in the early 1900s, but that's another story.)

The veal arrived in a matte-grey bowl, pink and elegant under a green and yellow garnish of edible flowers and deep-fried leek. Albert, an evangelising vegetarian, did not ask how it tasted, but I'll tell you now. Fucking fantastic! The veal had a more delicate flavour than beef but had been cut thicker than a tartare usually is, and so had a chewiness to every bite that made it unmistakable as flesh. Throughout, a complex hit of spice singed the dish's rawness. There was salty crunch too, in the form of the leeks, and best of all, two chilled mussels on top, dressed in a generous dollop of chive mayonnaise, the sour cut of the condiment helping to scissor through the resistance of the meat. Here was a recipe considered from every angle, a product of centuries of culinary refinement – by France, and by the world.

'So,' said Albert, trying not to look too disgusted, 'have your conclusions changed?'

A pause here to prepare our veal tartare. I returned to the Frenchie wine bar the next day, where a generous young Brazilian chef, Sabine, took me through the recipe in painstaking detail – and there were a lot of details to be painstaking about.

First, I was to freeze the meat, so that it was easier to cut. 'Into a *brunoise*,' I was told – the small, cubed dicing technique I'd learned from Gabriel so many months before. Then, it needed to be mixed with XO sauce – a Cantonese dried shellfish and meat paste, which Frenchie made on-site from scratch, with the addition of chorizo to lend it extra spice. I bought mine from the Chinese supermarket beneath my flat. The mussels were pickled in a home-made vinegar infusion. Ah, just getting pre-pickled ones couldn't hurt. The mayonnaise was made half with normal oil, half with chive oil, which required a day-long infusion process. I split the difference and stirred the chives directly into my egg emulsion from the start. Finally, the leeks, which were julienned, battered in maize flour and deep fried. I forewent the maize flour.

The result was, naturally enough, almost a completely different dish to the one I'd had in Frenchie. All those small, time-saving alterations I'd made had added up to a substantial drop in its quality. I'd argue it was still perfectly tasty, but it cried out far less to be noticed. If a diner were to spend €21 on what I had made, they'd have to justify the price with their own generosity, and a belief not so much in what my tartare was, but in what it was trying to be.

'Paris,' I declaimed grandly to Albert, 'has a traditionally conservative culture, but it's prone to revolutions.'

'Right ...' he said. 'Go on.'

'It has a revolution,' I said, 'it settles down; it has another revolution, it settles down.'

'OK,' he said.

Restaurants, I went on, were a product of one of these

revolutions, and they were a revolution in themselves. Except they inherited the principles and the staff of an earlier, more conservative age. In working for the aristocracy, people were part of a culture that served a higher principle than money or their own desire for personal expression; they were in service to a cultural idea, a version of God. And thus, their perfection of craft. I didn't think it was going too far to call this a kind of worship. And even after the subject of this worship – the aristocracy – was destroyed, the desire to be perfect that had characterised it remained.

Albert had started nodding again, in that way he had; I ignored him.

Meanwhile, I continued, the 'ordinary' people of Paris became the beneficiaries. They learned to receive the ritual, to become discerning about the *pieds* of their macarons, the honeycomb of their croissants, the crease in the trousers of their waiters. Even as the years passed, and old ideas of aristocratic service faded, consumer habits helped keep the makers in line. That's why I had found more pockets of artisanship and passion than I might ever have suspected – particularly in the bakeries, but also in the markets, the historic cafés and in the new Bouillons, which corporate though they are, give even people with relatively shallow pockets the chance to eat like kings.

'So every Parisian thinks of themselves like a mini-Louis XIV?' Albert said. 'Ha! That's an idea I can get behind.'

'Right,' I said, 'but it's only part of the story. Because working against this conservative idea of craft for craft's sake are other factors, like economic need, for example. These days in Paris, there are a lot of places that get by through offering knock-off versions of the old serving rituals and almost completely forgetting about the food itself. You know, not all the waiters are like Camille, and places like the Café Georges V are probably more common than either of us would like to admit.'

'That's true.'

'And then there's the fact that a lot of Parisians are tired of the conservatism. Or they feel trapped by it, that it's making them out of step with the rest of the world. That's where you get this desire for brunch, or for falafel, or kebabs ...'

'I thought you said there was ritual in kebabs.'

'Well, I ... let me think about that later.'

Albert, again, began to stroke his chin.

I pushed on. Places like Frenchie were products of the Revolution too, I said, but they'd been on a different journey. They were the heirs of Carême, of individuals not just repeating craft, but pushing it to ever newer heights.

'Because the idea of allowing ordinary people to dine like royalty was eventually exported,' I said. 'What they used to learn only in French kitchens now gets taught in London, New York, Bogota ...'

In all these places, I continued, chefs begin their culinary training by learning the techniques and dishes that evolved from service to the *ancien régime*. The training is still rigorous, the work is still extraordinarily hard, the standards still almost pointlessly high. Dishes that could be made almost as well in a handful of steps are refined into ones that take dozens.

Only, over the years, far from France lots of new ideas and flavours started to creep in. Chefs and consumers in other countries were less wedded to cosplaying an aristocratic ideal. It mattered less to them that things were done right, and much more how they tasted, how they could make them new. So this became a culture of its own. An international movement built on the old French foundations, but which was not afraid to import ideas, to try things differently. Forget the rules, have fun. And now, because Paris tastes were pushing against the old ways too, they could start coming home.

'Right,' said Albert, 'so what you're saying is, there's also globalisation.'

'Well … I mean. Yes.'

'It's definitely a theory,' Albert conceded.

'It is,' I agreed.

We sat in silence for a moment.

'There is something else,' I said.

'Oh yes?'

Yes, I continued, another older element at play that underpinned everything else, that more than ritual, more than inspiration, explained why food-making should have been elevated to such a height in Paris even before the fall of kings. Something that has made the culture possible to sustain.

Albert stopped stroking his chin.

It was here, I said, in the shops along the length of the rue du Nil, and on almost every plate I'd cooked or tasted. It had been the subject of the most recent attempt at revolution that I'd witnessed, when farmers drove their tractors into the city in protest. Andrés had told me, so had Gabriel, so had Nicolas all those years ago in the Dordogne: '*La terre en France, Christopher, c'est magique.*' I just hadn't been listening properly. What, more than anything, makes Paris food is France's bountiful, beautiful produce.

1er arrondissement

In 1873, Émile Zola, the great novelist of French modernity, published a book called *The Belly of Paris*, set in and around the city's vast central market Les Halles. In the work's famous opening scene, a virtuosic description of the market coming to life, it's clear Zola wants us to see something frightening in its beauty. This is a hard ask for the modern reader. The procession of delivery carts Zola writes about, today, sounds almost bucolic: horse-drawn, teetering with cauliflower and turnip, plodding a regular though lazy pace through the Paris pre-dawn. And as to the market itself, it appears only as a sight of thrilling grace. Gas lights illuminate the luxuriant fullness of artichoke bundles, the delicate green of lettuces, the rosy coral of carrots ... On all sides, there is the coming and going of porters' baskets and the clamour of voices wrangling over price ... Then there are the beautiful pavilions with their forest of pillars and their black lacework of iron overhead: a teeming, flowering vegetation of luxuriant metalwork.

Les Halles was new back then, however, or at least the iteration of it that Zola wrote about was. There's been a market on this site in the centre of Paris, in what is now the ıst arrondissement, since the twelfth century, when the area was just marshland north of the Île de la Cité reclaimed by King Louis the Fat. Over the years, Paris grew out around this market, and it expanded piecemeal, trying to keep pace with the city's growing hunger. By the 1800s it was clear a major redevelopment was needed, and under Napoleon III – as in much of the rest of the city – the old market's crumbling medieval infrastructure was swept away, and in its place ten glass and iron pavilions were erected: the new stomach of an empire. To Zola's eyes, this was the very pinnacle of modernity, dehumanising our relationship with food.

Personally, I'd love to have seen it; would give anything to live in a Paris with such a market at its heart. By the 1970s, the building that spelled modernity to Zola had itself become hopelessly outdated, infested by rats, no longer up to its task. It was pulled down. Today, Les Halles is mostly empty space: a public garden and a largely subterranean shopping mall that looks like an airport departures terminal.

Much as with the old abattoirs in the 19th, however, some traces remain around the edges. The all-night restaurants and cafés that used to serve the workers and feed from the market's cuts, for instance. Places like Au Pied de Cochon and Le Louchebem, versions of which crop up in dozens of novels of Paris ex-pat excess as places to guzzle oysters and pig's foot and drink a final dawn bottle of champagne after truly legendary, ill-advised nights on the town.

I'd often looked at these places with a certain melancholia. In the absence of the market around which their business ought to revolve, I saw them as robbed of their *raison d'être* and their inspiration. On darker days, I wondered how much more authentic these and restaurants in other parts of Paris would be if they still had a proximate connection to their suppliers. Yet the longer my journey through Paris's food scenes continued, the more I realised this connection did still exist. Les Halles market had not simply disappeared, it had moved. In the 1970s, the centre of Paris food – and therefore, for the purposes of my journey, the centre of Paris – was re-established in a south-eastern suburb called Rungis.

The 1st arrondissement today is a place of old palaces, mass tourism and government. It is home to the prow of the island where Paris began, the Île de la Cité, as well as the Pont Neuf and the Louvre. Nevertheless, for over eight hundred years, the area's most fundamental, lived character for most Parisians would have been as the place they came to get their food. That character had been displaced, so I would follow to where it had gone.

Rungis at 4 a.m. was like touching down on the surface of an industrialised moon. I drove through its great wall of toll gates into an ever-growing fractal of neon-lit warehouses, roundabouts and white trucks. So many white trucks. All different shapes and sizes, from articulated lorries to squat delivery vans, most with the distended frontal lobes of refrigeration units over their cabs that made them look like

Star Wars droids. They moved at pace, criss-crossing and weaving on tight lanes, headlights tracing blue on the dark.

Here was what Les Halles had become, an unseen presence that had been orbiting my journey through Paris food from the very start, the place from which almost all of my meals had come. Built with the singular vision of surpassing the original market, and centralising food supply for the entire city and its surrounds, Rungis was and still is the largest fresh produce market in the world.

I'd read the statistics. It employs over 13,000 people, processes close to two million tonnes of food every year, has a surface area bigger than Monaco. Being here, though, was something else – a reminder that what most of us experience of the modern world is just its surface sheen. And I was still only looking at it from the outside.

At last, I found my way through the white truck ballet to the car park of the place des Pêcheurs and the bar where I was meeting my guide. This had not been an easy rendezvous to arrange, the result of weeks of emails and pleading phone calls. Since the pandemic, Rungis has been cut off to the public; the only people normally allowed in are those with professional links to its trade. It's almost as though the French realised there was something shameful about the fact that every quaint corner bistro, every market trestle, every gentle, romantic cliché of Paris traces back to this industrial mega-hub in the dark.

My guide, Francis, was by contrast a small, rather old-fashioned man. With his squarish baseball cap, grey hair and thick scarf under his white coat, I could easily imagine him behind the counter of a provincial butcher's shop. Not racing about the halogen-lit byways of this alien colony as he had done as a buyer for the past seventeen years. Rungis was his village, he boasted: he knew half the people who worked here by name. A reminder that however advanced our systems grow, it's still the same old human beings at their core.

The bar we met in was similarly anachronistic, with its long zinc countertop and suited waiters – a part of the old Paris transplanted. Unlike in the city, however, time here was not a shared concept. Right along the zinc were men at different hours of individualised days. For me, rolled from my bed just an hour before, reaching for a much-needed coffee, it was still early morning. Francis, who'd got here at 1 a.m., was just cresting 'noon'. Further along were a couple of market workers coming off shift, sharing oysters and Muscadet. It was not yet dawn on Friday, but their weekend had already begun.

'There are nineteen restaurants in Rungis,' Francis was telling me as he handed me the white overalls that were obligatory inside the pavilions. 'They were the only ones in the whole country to stay open during Covid.'

'Right,' I said, still feeling a little overwhelmed, mostly able to concentrate only on my coffee.

Francis scowled, seemingly annoyed by my monosyllabic response. Who was this English stranger he'd been asked to show round his home town?

'It was because Rungis could not be shut down during Covid,' he went on. 'And the market director made a deal with President Macron himself that the workers should not starve.'

'I see.'

'It's interesting, no?'

'It is.'

'Hmm,' said Francis. Clearly we needed more time to warm up to one another. 'You've finished your coffee? Come on, then. We will start with the fish pavilion.'

Stepping back out into the night, Francis explained how our tour would follow the rhythms of the market. Such were the quantities dealt with here, Rungis could not function if all the pavilions had their peak hours at the same time; that seamless, steady flow of delivery trucks would soon become a snarl. So the pavilion opening times were staggered. First fish and seafood, then meat, then cheese, then fruit and vegetables.

'What time does the fish pavilion open to customers?' I asked.

'Two a.m.,' said Francis, 'but they will have started work there two hours before that.'

The pavilion was an aircraft hangar of a building with a plate-glass facade giving onto an interior hall so vast that its dark floor, white walls and high, strip-lit ceiling converged to a vanishing point in the distance.

'You are not to touch anything,' Francis cautioned before we went in. 'Or cross the blue lines.'

'Right,' I said. 'Sorry, what blue lines?'

I got no answer. Francis was already leading me in through an electric roll door, which snapped up automatically to greet us.

Inside was a space of chipped-ice snowdrifts and water-slicked concrete; of trolleys and forklifts being operated by men in white. It echoed cold with shouts and pneumatic clatter. Different suppliers were arranged along the entire length of both walls. They had simple frontages that backed directly onto docking bays behind. The whole area was entirely open plan, the divisions between businesses marked by the blue lines Francis had warned me not to cross. These, he said, were treated like solid walls; there were market officials on constant patrol making sure no one's produce strayed even a centimetre from its designated zone.

'All the produce you see has already gone through one level of trade,' Francis said, leading me down the pavilion's central aisle. 'From people who buy directly off the boats, then organise the trucks, which drive through the night from all over Europe. Lorries are arriving here every morning from the Atlantic, from Spain, from Norway. From Scotland, even.' He smiled at me then for the first time, as though I should be pleased at this mention of my almost-homeland. 'They bring salmon from Scotland,' he said. 'Lots and lots of salmon. You know that the French eat more salmon than any other country in Europe?'

'Wow,' I said, making sure, this time, to look enthused.

There was far more than salmon here. The different supplier zones were stacked with pallet after pallet of tuna, hake, ray and countless other species that I could not name, would not even have known existed, let alone thought possible to eat. They grimaced unseeing from their ice-beds at the towering cold ceiling above. Most had been sorted into individual crates labelled for specific restaurants – destined for the day's menus at the Ritz, Les Deux Magots, La Fontaine de Mars and more.

The atmosphere in the pavilion was slipping into day's end relaxation. The motion of the trolleys had started to slow, the shouts become less intense. A snowball fight broke out among the workers, who hurled clods of chipped ice at one another across sections.

'Rungis makes its own ice,' Francis told me as I watched. 'There's a tower behind this pavilion dedicated to doing only that. Twenty to twenty-five tonnes a day.'

'Every day?'

'Yes,' Francis grinned. 'And I know it's quiet now, but in the other pavilions you'll see, Rungis gets much busier than this. And at Christmas time, obviously, it's hell.'

Nearing the end of the hall, there was at least one supplier still operating at full tilt. Possibly because the owner was there in person to oversee the staff.

'Madame Gillardeau!' Francis waved to her – an incongruously glamorous woman in full make-up and a brilliant white puffa. 'We're very honoured,' he muttered to me, before assuming a stance of supplication in front of this Rungis aristocrat, falling into obsequious conversation with her about – what else? – the price of fish. This, I learned, changed every day.

Madame Gillardeau was the scion of the Gillardeau oyster dynasty, whose produce I had tasted in the Brasserie Wepler – the finest oysters in France. A whole orgy of the creatures heaved from the pallets on her stall, their jagged, silvery shells packed tight in dozens of baskets waiting for Paris's libidinous mouths.

'It's not uncommon for the owners to be here,' Francis told me as we walked on. 'They come to make sure their employees are working hard, and to keep an eye on everyone else's workers as well.' He gestured back across the full length of the hall, across its partitioned floor spaces, to the big glass windows at its front where the night was just beginning to purple into dawn. 'That's one of the difficulties when you can see what everyone else is doing. Good workers here are hard to find. The hours are bad, the work is physical, it's cold. You don't know how well someone you bring in from outside will handle it, but in here you can see very clearly if your competitor has someone who's doing everything faster, more efficiently than the people on your team. A lot of poaching goes on.'

Before I could express my genuine interest, however, Francis had spun on his heel and was leading me out of the fish pavilion, to where a private van was waiting to pick us up.

Outside, I noticed the smell. Inside the hall, it had not seemed to smell so much of fish. Everything sold in there was extremely fresh, most flipped in under twenty-four hours, with surfaces constantly being hosed down. But sitting in the van, I caught a horrid sour stink that had sunk into my clothes. We had been in the fish hall for less than thirty minutes. No wonder employees were hard to find.

We drove at speed under the cresting dawn, rejoining the flow of trucks along the arteries of the market. By chance we pulled up alongside a van with the familiar branding of Bay Tat – the kebab manufacturer I had visited some months earlier. I knew exactly where it was heading – over to the nearby suburb of Morangis where its innards would be processed into columns of compressed meat to be delivered back up near where I lived, to the kebab shops of the 19th.

There was something else to remind me of home at the entrance to the meat pavilions: a huge, photographic mural of the Abattoirs de la Villette back in the nineteenth century. There were the stern monochrome faces of its workers, now as long dead as the butchery that surrounded them. Leaning up against this image, a gang of those men's modern-day successors were smoking and chattering in white coats tinted pink by the spatter of their trade.

Inside, the scene was a horror movie chilled to 3°C. Just as in the fish hall, this pavilion had a central corridor, only here each supplier was separated by physical walls and the ceilings were low. From those artificially cooled ceilings hung meat. No, not meat; bodies: whole herds of them, flayed and disembowelled, swung from a hundred bunched hooks.

The hooks were attached to an intricate railing system so that the bodies could be rattled any which way like the merchandise they were – rattled on and off of trucks, making space for more. Many were still dripping blood, which hit the floor beneath and trickled into crimson rivulets running into concrete drains.

I'm not squeamish about such things. It's my view that if you can't look the reality of butchery in its peeled-back face, you've no business eating meat. It certainly did not, though, make me hungry. Francis, however, was getting excited about the breeds, was asking one of the butchers if these really were cattle from the Vendée. 'Oh la la, they would be perfect to braise in a red wine sauce!'

It went on and on. There must have been nearly twenty of these rooms of hanging carcases – some in various states of dismemberment. The cold was starting to get into my bones. I marvelled at how the butchers about me – mostly heavily built, mostly black men – were able to work every day in this man-made winter. When we at last left the pavilion, I felt the gilding morning warm me like an unexpected bath. There was little time to luxuriate in it, however, for Francis was already leading me into the hall of tripe.

At university, I read a book by the anthropologist Marshall Sahlins, in which he explored the relative disgust towards offal in English-speaking countries, arguing that this was down to our disconnection from the realities of farming, our desire to disassociate the meat on our plates from anything that even remotely resembles ourselves. The heart, brain or liver of any mammal could, judged by appearances, just as easily belong to a human, Sahlins wrote, and therefore in America, the UK and Australia, eating these organs has become dusted in taboo. In countries like France, however, there remains at least a perceived closeness to the land, an acknowledgement that meat comes from creatures that share our world. Eating offal is an accepted confrontation with our corporeal existence, with reality and death.

None of this knowledge prepared me on entering the tripe hall for the group of middle-aged French women being taken round on a separate tour who were crowding enthusiastically around a bucket of freshly severed lambs' heads.

'They're so pretty,' I heard one woman coo.

'Look how small they are!'

'C'est mignon.'

The tripe hall had a Roswell quality. It could have been the site of a thousand alien autopsies, assuming aliens have a more than passing resemblance to sheep, pigs and cows. Compounding this impression was the fact that any complete body parts – heads and shins – had been boiled, all vestiges of hair and pigment stripped away so that they sat in resinous whiteness, like the remains of creatures that had never seen the sun.

Hundreds of hearts and livers, mostly shrink-wrapped, had been sorted into piles on silver benches, always with one fully displayed purple-scarlet sample unfurled and hung from a spike above. At one point, Francis walked over to a pallet of flimsy cardboard boxes, dark blue and tightly trussed. He picked one up and handed it to me, enjoying himself now, proud of his market. The box had an uncanny organic weight.

'*Voilà, monsieur*,' Francis said. 'Brains.'

It was time for a drink.

Back in the van, we went speeding down the motherboard of Rungis's streets – back into that automotive buzz of lorries, trucks and forklifts across to the market's wine cellar.

'Monsieur Agostino's place is a Rungis institution,' Francis said as we went. 'He started off at Les Halles, and moved when the market did in the seventies.'

Rungis, in general, did not deal with anything as non-perishable as wine. For the most part, it was about the flows of freshness, of flipping produce at pace. But it made some sense for at least one wine merchant to be at the same site where restaurants were getting a lot of their other supplies too. Which is to say that Agostino's store was big, but not supply-all-of-Paris enormous. It was also a refuge, dry and warm, redolent of wooden crates and cork; a place of gentle sanity after the chilly netherworld of fish and meat.

'All qualities of wine are stocked here,' Francis told me as we stepped inside. 'That's Rungis by design. Every pavilion stocks both ordinary, cheaper produce, and the very best.'

The wine I was offered was somewhere towards the former category. (To be honest, I was delighted by such an act of hospitality in what I'd imagined would be a wholly perfunctory tour.) It was a sweet white of the Domaine Tariquet, which

Francis told me was 'perfect for the morning', though what his definition of morning was, it was hard to say. We were joined for the tipple by the women I had seen cooing over the lambs' heads. Slices of foie gras on toast were served.

Between bites of the salt-fat magnificence of the goose liver pâté and sips of the wine that cut through its richness like a razor made of honey, Francis, the group of women and I got talking. It turned out that their tittering over the lambs' heads had actually been bravado.

'Frankly, the tripe halls were too much for me,' one was saying.

'For me as well,' said another, 'the more I saw, the worse it was.'

'Oh yes, and the smell.'

I had not noticed the smell, being still too distracted by the fish-stink of my clothes.

'I'd have preferred not to see it,' said another, taking a further slice of foie gras from the tray. 'All those poor animals.'

'I am afraid that is reality, *madame*,' said Francis. I nodded along and he winked at me. We were on the same side now.

After wine, it was time for cheese. We joined forces with the women, who I learned were all relations of market workers here, to head to the cheese pavilion, which Francis referred to several times as the 'biggest cheese platter in the world'.

The impact of the cheese pavilion on the French women was striking to behold. Any lingering nausea from the tripe halls disappeared in an instant, replaced by cheek-to-cheek grins. The cheese pavilion was indeed amazing – endless shelves stacked with huge, waxy, pungent wheels, a library of taste. Yet it was clear that whatever pleasure I was taking in it, the women and Francis were taking more. Everyone knows that the French love cheese, but it was only now that I could see quite how deep the passion runs. If Roald Dahl had come from Normandy or the Savoy or the Auvergne, Charlie Bucket would have gone to a whole different kind of factory: a place of fondue rivers and Roquefort so ripe it could say its own name.

'Do you want to know why French people are so in love with cheese?' said Francis, as if reading my thoughts.

'Absolutely!'

'I will explain it to you by showing you the best cheese in the world!'

He stepped over to a nearby pallet and pulled out a tray, on which stood six small, mottled pyramids of cheese.

'This is called Valençay,' Francis said. 'A goat's cheese. Nothing else comes close to its taste.'

Oh no! I'd never heard of it. My relationship with Francis was in jeopardy again.

'Don't worry, I don't expect you to know it,' my guide twinkled. 'It is not famous and they do not make a lot. You want to know why it is the best cheese in the world? Because it is from my home town.'

'So ... the French like cheese because of local pride?'

'*Précisément*,' Francis looked like he was about to hug me. 'Anywhere you go, cheese is the *fabrication* of France itself. Even in the places that do not make cheese, the cities, the people will have their connections to places that do. The cheese they have eaten on holidays since they were children. They will have their local cheese.'

I had never heard this theory before, not from any of my French friends, not anecdotally after all my years living in Paris, but I liked it. How do you govern a country with 246 varieties of cheese, Monsieur de Gaulle? You start with the assumption that at least everyone likes cheese.

The time had come for the grand finale: the fruit and veg pavilions, where Francis had promised the full reality of Rungis. It was gone 7 a.m. now, full daylight on this summer morning, and Rungis was still revving.

Francis pointed over to a café as we drove. 'That's the Saint Hubert. It is famous for serving the most coffee in all of France. Three thousand cups a night.'

This did not surprise me. For all the produce that it handled, it was clear that coffee was the substance on which Rungis was truly run. In each pavilion I had never been more than a few metres from a coffee machine.

'Coffee and weed,' Francis sniggered. 'Truly, smoking weed is endemic to Rungis. You smell it everywhere. You'll be wandering round and suddenly,' he sniffed, 'what is this exultant cloud?'

The smell emanating from one of the seven fruit and veg pavilions of Rungis market was not weed, but it was exultant. It was a scent I knew but had never experienced like this: the high, thin, chlorophyll odour of shoving your nose right up against the stem of a plant. Fresh, grassy, affirming life.

Stepping into the pavilion – which was easily bigger than a football pitch – I suddenly understood the passion of the street market *primeurs* like Émile, still invested after more than fifty years in the trade. In fact, I would defy anyone to walk into that massive, open-plan hall on a bright summer dawn and not be stirred to their core.

There was the movement, of course. The trolleys and the forklifts flew this way and that with an almost clairvoyant intensity and grace: the fruit and veg pavilions were still at peak operating hours. There was bartering: a racket of shouting performed from the wooden lecterns of each supplier, a scene which surely could not have changed since Zola's day.

More than anything, though, it was the produce. The quality, the quantity, the variation – all the riches given to us by the natural world. Life that sustained life. Tonnes and tonnes and tonnes of the stuff: apricots by the thousand, cherries by the tens of thousands. Whole fields of carrots, potatoes, cabbage, tomatoes in all their forms. Everything was neatly stacked, but there was no neatness, no mark of human order that could quash such a stupefying chaos of abundance. And this was only one pavilion of seven.

It was almost impossible to comprehend that the display in front of me was not just a one-off. It hadn't been assembled only for today, or for this week, but rather this copious marvel was always being built and built again afresh. It was a wonder of the world that could only exist through the constant tending of uncountable hands.

There was something frightening about Rungis's beauty, no doubt. Here was modernity to make Zola weep. Whatever the writer had feared about Les Halles, that same thing was here too, only super-charged for the modern age.

In the days that followed, I started to see Rungis's emissaries everywhere in Paris. Those same bulbous, refrigerated white vans bumped up onto kerbs right the way from the 20th arrondissement to the 1st, unloading behind restaurants, at markets, at local *traiteurs*. And I would think about where they'd come from: that alien world that allowed everything around me to function, that had fuelled almost every meal I had cooked over the previous years, every meal I had eaten.

Rungis was not a city; it was the seat of an empire. Paris was just a territory that it happened to possess. If anything, Rungis made the very notion of a city defunct. How easy it was to imagine a future where there was no Paris at all. Only houses, restaurants and roads, and Rungis at their centre. Think about it. Rungis is the biggest wholesale market in the world, whereas Paris is a very long way from being the biggest city. The fact, then, that it should boast the world's largest food hub – instead of, say Tokyo or São Paolo or Chengdu – suggests that Rungis is not really about practicality. It is ideology.

Francis told me as much as we shook hands at the end of our tour. Rungis existed, he said, because of the French government's belief in French food. They had dreamed of a single space where all the restaurants and markets, and by extension the people of the city, could connect directly with the produce of the country as a whole.

Rungis was the ultimate port where this could happen. A monument both to French cuisine and French producers. A place that declared that France was as much a nation of agriculture as it was urbanism – and that all the dedication of its chefs would be nothing without their *terroir*.

France has always been a fertile land, but more than that it is a place where the land speaks. *Terroir* refers to the particular socio-environmental conditions that lend themselves to the cultivation of a particular foodstuff. From the limestone soil of Champagne that both feeds the grapes and allows for the cool caves in which they can be left to develop their sparkle, to the earthworm- and insect-rich hedgerows of Bresse that provide the nutritious diet of the region's famous poultry, to the way salt from the Guérande combines with Breton milk to make butter that keeps, France's great culinary secrets lie in its *terroirs*.

In some respects, the *terroir* is a kind of myth, just as it is a myth that Rungis is a conduit to the bounty of France – at the very end of the tour, Francis confessed that over half of the year as much as 70 per cent of its produce is brought in from abroad. But, by local practice, by government policy, by the collective belief of millions, it is a myth that retains the ring of the real.

Snails

Serves 2

Ingredients:

12 *Escargots de Bourgogne* with parsley butter (to be bought frozen)

It had to be. Here was an emblematic dish of France in the shape of my food journey, its Fibonacci shell spiralling in the same pattern as the layout of Paris's arrondissements. I could even think of its mouth as though stretching east into the suburbs towards Rungis, gathering food far from the centre to sustain the whole. Add to that the fact that snails are Paris's most enduring cuisine, introduced to the city by the Romans more than two millennia ago; it was here that they first began to be flavoured by the northern ingredients of garlic and butter. Finally, it just so happened that Paris's most famous snail restaurant, L'Escargot, stands just a couple of streets back from the old marketplace of Les Halles. It is a venerable, dark-wood institution where Parisians have been slurping gastropods for almost two hundred years.

At L'Escargot, once again my preconceptions of a pure, enduring tradition collided with the realities of the modern world. I learned that these days the snail meat is delivered to Paris separate from the shells. How one creature would then be stuffed inside the former home of another, along with garlic, parsley and butter, then baked for fourteen minutes in an oven, its many parts steeping into the resemblance of a single thing. I also discovered that most snails served in Paris, nominally *escargots de Bourgogne*, are farmed in Hungary or other countries in Eastern Europe.

This devastating knowledge, I felt, at least let me off the hook from preparing my own snails from scratch. For I had come to the end of my journey through the food of Paris's arrondissements and I had something bigger in mind. I went instead to my local Picard – a frozen goods chain that fuels more domestic dining in Paris than the French would ever want the world to know – and I bought some pre-prepared snails. They were to be the appetiser for a banquet.

It was the day of the second round of the French parliamentary elections. Talk was that the far-right National Rally could be headed for a majority, an outcome that for most Parisians would herald the darkest time for the Republic since the Second World War and potentially make precarious my own status as a foreigner in France. It was also a good day for a moveable feast, which is to say a picnic.

I had spent the week haranguing friends, assembling them into a *brigade de cuisine*. My idea was that we would all cook as many recipes as we could from the range I had encountered on my journey, set up a table on the banks of the canal, and eat and drink our way through to the potential collapse of the liberal order, or its defibrillation for another year.

My friends were in search of welcome distraction, and my challenge was accepted. So now, in kitchens across the capital, they were stirring *aligot*, baking malangwa, boiling *sarmale*, frying falafel, fixing goat's cheese salad and *tartiflette*, even folding croissants. OK, that last one was professional 17th arrondissement *boulangère* Frances, who had been folding croissants every day of her career, but it still counts.

I had taken personal responsibility for five dishes – six if I included the concept of getting other people to do most of the work: ratatouille; Nicole's couscous with meatballs; oysters; snails; and a bottle of Saint-Émilion – not from 2008 as that would cost close to €700, but a 2015 bottle I'd found that would have to do.

So here I was, going through the increasingly familiar knife cuts, scything through Rungis produce with a blade I'd kept sharp ever since my conversation with Gabriel all those months before.

One difficulty of the endeavour was timing, especially when trying to organise non-professionals from all points across the Paris map. My wife Alice and I walked our extendable home table the hundred metres or so from our apartment through the disassembling Joinville market – the fishmongers and butchers and cheese sellers and *primeurs* packing up for another day – and placed it in front of a bench on the waterside. We took turns going back to collect the dishes. Then, we waited.

My friends began to arrive with Tupperware and trussed-up pans in backpacks and bicycle panniers. Peter and Lucie, whose Noisy-le-Sec house had been the scene of my kebab experiment, brought a second table, and others arrived with their own chairs. The feast began to take shape.

Still, there was a tacit agreement among all of us that we would not start eating until everyone arrived. We were from England and America, Kenya and Czechia, Poland, Australia and France, but we knew there were rituals to be followed. So we sat, feeling rather like a piece of performance art, around two tables heaving with plenty but not touching any of it. Just waiting, chatting a little about the things I'd learned but mostly about the future of France, drinking our *apéros*. Passers-by eyed what we were doing, smiled and wished us *bon appétit*. And though fewer than a third of us were French it still felt as if we were spreading a particularly French kind of joy.

Finally, the last guest arrived, brandishing a goat's cheese salad in a large plastic tub. Sorry he was late, he said, but he'd felt he had to do things properly and buy his produce from Marco down in the 5th. We uncovered all the dishes. For me, it was a table of memories: the white velvet of the *aligot*, the combined geometries of the ratatouille, the resistant weight of the *tartiflette*, and the rest: an unlikely collage that somehow resembled the city I'd come to call home.

We started, as seemed appropriate, with the snails, which thanks to a well-timed dash back to my apartment to use the oven were mercifully hot. I picked one up between thumb and index, felt its molten warmth radiate through its shell, looked into its aperture, butter-yellow and parsley-green, then with a disposable chopstick I swirled out the delicacy inside.

The flavours were not all quite as I remembered. But then, that's cooking. Even when following a recipe, dishes change every time you make them, and here my friends had found their own way. We had almost reached the end of the meal, and I was pouring the Saint Émilion, alarmed that I had neglected a cheese course. As if by instinct all of us reached towards the remaining slices of goat's cheese to pair with the wine.

The wine, which was celestial. The taste of sophistication and summer fruit, and of a journey's end. I can't say or not if it tasted of my time in the Dordogne, and it certainly did not take me back to the night of the Christmastime party with Antoine. Rather, it was the taste of the here and now, of a moment shared.

We ate croissants for dessert. Or at least most of us did. Two friends, Peter from Australia and Matthieu from Aubrac, declared that they never ate croissant after 11 a.m. – didn't I know that rule? And then we drank some more, and we waited for the election results to come through.

The cheering started, the sound moving up the canal in a wave. An alliance between the left and the centre had held firm, knocked the National Rally all the way into third place. Paris, at least, was ecstatic. And when I looked behind me at the *tricolore* flying from the front of the canal-side fire station, I felt an inexpressible joy that it still could stand for all the things I wanted this country to be.

Paris is one of the great battlegrounds of modernity and tradition anywhere in the world. It is by tradition that its myths are maintained. And throughout the city the tradition has its guardians both large and small: from the bakers who make masterpieces every dawn to the waiters who pull on their penguin suits each day for work; the bourgeois families and the street market vendors; the government officials who insisted on the existence of a place like Rungis and the farmers who sustained it all. Yet there is also another, much larger, more complex Paris. A place of individuals and immigrants and capitalist fancies. I had encountered many of these, too, and understood now that, even after years and years more research, the complete truth of this city would remain eternally out of my grasp.

But it didn't matter too much because tradition, which shores up all the clichés that almost everyone knows about Paris – the surly waiters, the barflies at the zinc, the terraces of small tables and rattan chairs all facing the street; coffee, croissants, *steak frites* – bleeds in a thousand ineffable ways into almost everything it touches. I had seen it in the kebab shops and the soup kitchens, the banh mis and the Sri Lankan kitchen staff, in the humility of a sex club manager and a Tunisian chef. Even now, I had seen it in my friends as they waited for everyone to arrive before we started eating, in the enthusiasm of passers-by, in the unspoken way we had all reached for cheese before dessert.

Some people, many people, actively react against the tradition, but they know of its existence. It is a gate through which everyone here has to pass, just as nearly all the food in this city first goes through Rungis before it finds infinite expression on our plates.

Which is all to say that I had realised it takes very little to belong to Paris, to feel that a part of Paris belongs to you. Certainly, if you are lucky enough to have lived here, even only for a short time, then wherever you go for the rest of your life, it stays with you, for Paris is a moveable feast.

Acknowledgements

Thank you first to my agent Rachel Conway, whose suggestion that I write something about Paris was what encouraged me to start hanging around the Belleville bar tops from where the rest of this book resulted. Your support and counsel, backed by the rest of the Georgina Capel team, were fundamental in this book coming together.

My boundless gratitude too to my wonderful editor, Rowan Cope, whose willingness to take a punt on an unknown writer was something I strove with every word to repay. Thanks to Rowan also for her brilliant edit of the text, streamlining the prose, keeping the chapters on point and even tidying up my French.

Thanks as well to the copyeditor Seán Costello and proofreader Clare Sayer, and to the rest of the team at Profile: Claire Beaumont, Steve Coventry-Panton, Alex Elam, Lisa Finch, Emily Frisella, Louis Gabaldoni, Siân Gibson, Anna Howarth, Robert Loyko-Greer, George Lucas, Rosie Parnham, Leila Sackur, Sarah Ward and Dahmicca Wright.

Thank you to the book's illustrator Lexi Vangsnes. The playfulness and modernity of her work felt the perfect accompaniment to what I was hoping to achieve in the text.

I remain in a state of pinch-myself glee that *Moveable Feasts* won the Jane Grigson Trust Award for New Food

Acknowledgements

and Drink Writers. Thank you so much to the patrons of the fund Paul Bailey, Sophie Grigson, Geraldene Holt and Claudia Roden; the trustees Linda Challis, Felicity Cloake, Henrietta Green, Lucy Hambidge, Diana Henry, Sally Holloway, Clarissa Hyman, Jeremy Lee, Jill Norman and Donald Sloan; and the panel of judges Diana Henry, Jill Norman and Donald Sloan (again), and Georgina Hayden and Sami Tamimi.

I'm hugely grateful for the Trust's continued support, and specifically, again, to Diana Henry, Sami Tamimi and Jeremy Lee, who were kind enough to read the finished book before it went to print and offer such lovely praise. Thanks also to Carolyn Boyd, Ned Palmer and Ferdia Lennon for doing likewise, and their own kind words.

Thank you to Lucie Wright and Alistair Snook for casting their eyes over the draft proposal, and to the members of the Damrémont Writers Group, to whom I am indebted. To Peter-Adrian Altini, Peter Brown, Coralie Colmez, Amanda Dennis, Megan Fernandez, Nina-Marie Gardner, Heather Hartley, Rachel Kapelke-Dale, Will Kitson, Corinne LaBalme, Ferdia Lennon (again), Sam Leader, Alberto Rigettini, Jonathan Schiffman, Nafkote Tamirat and the many others who have dropped in on the group along the way: I couldn't have done this without you. In particular, thank you, Albert Alla, Rafael Herrero and Helen O'Keefe for founding the DWG in the first place, then keeping it running for so many years, fostering exactly the kind of writing community that so many people come to Paris to find.

Thank you also to my friends beyond the group. In particular, Lucie Wright (again), Peter Kowalczyk, Edward Bell,

Leah Soeiro and, last but by no means least, the inimitable Peter Brown.

Then, of course, I must thank all the people whom I met and talked to throughout the course of researching *Moveable Feasts*, who gave me their time, their recipes, their stories, and sometimes even fed me as well. In particular, thanks to Frances Leech, who continued to help my journey far beyond teaching me how to make croissants in her bakery.

Thank you to Amanda Brace for giving over your flat to my macaron experiments and putting me up for several weeks over the book's writing. And thank you to my sister Katie, for being both one of my greatest cheerleaders and inspirations!

Moveable Feasts is dedicated to my parents for all the usual reasons of love and support they have shown me over the years, though most of all because of the things they taught me growing up about the value, dignity and hardships at all stations of the catering trade. For getting me to appreciate the skill and labour it takes to wash a sink of saucepans, to decorate a restaurant or a cake, to work a service or to cook a decent meal. Thank you.

I also need to add thanks to Antoine Blondet, wherever he may be, who was also a kind of parent for a time.

Finally, thank you to Alice, my best friend, life companion and most valuable critic. Thank you for indulging me in everything it's taken to get this book written, for brightening all my days and for sharing the moveable feast together.